THE DEVELOPMENT AND MEANING OF PSYCHOLOGICAL DISTANCE

THE DEVELOPMENT AND MEANING OF PSYCHOLOGICAL DISTANCE

Edited by

Rodney R. Cocking
National Institute of Mental Health
K. Ann Renninger
Swarthmore College

LEA

LAWRENCE ERLBAUM ASSOCIATES, PUBLISHERS
1993   Hillsdale, New Jersey   Hove and London

Lawrence Erlbaum Associates, Inc., Publishers
365 Broadway
Hillsdale, New Jersey 07642

Library of Congress Cataloging-in-Publication Data

The development and meaning of psychological distance / edited by
    Rodney R. Cocking, K. Ann Renninger.
        p.   cm.
    Includes bibliographical references and indexes.
    ISBN 0–8058–0747–0 (alk. paper)
    1. Mental representation.   2. Learning, Psychology of.
3. Cognition.   I. Cocking, Rodney R.   II. Renninger, K. Ann.
III. Title: Psychological distance.
        [DNLM: 1. Cognition.   2. Human Development.   3. Learning.
    4. Psychological Theory.   BF 311 D4885]
    BF365.D47   1993
    153—dc20
    DNLM/DLC
    for Library of Congress   92–49448
                                                                 CIP

Books published by Lawrence Erlbaum Associates are printed on acid-free paper, and their bindings
are chosen for strength and durability.

Printed in the United States of America

10 9 8 7 6 5 4 3 2 1

This volume is dedicated to our friend and colleague,
Irving E. Sigel. His collaborations have guided many scholars
and his ideas continue to inspire basic scientific inquiry.

Contents

Preface

Research on psychological distance dates back at least to Ebbinghaus' (1885/1914) observations that there are notable differences among individuals in the way in which they engage in tasks. His use of the nonsense syllable launched a research tradition focused on eliminating the impact of such differences on whatever aspect of functioning was under study. Eradication of such differences has the advantage of permitting researchers to focus more directly on discrete elements of human functioning. They have little generalizability beyond the laboratory (c.f. Neisser, 1976), however, and as such, are of limited use to those whose focus is the developing individual, a person undergoing change.

While others such as Werner (1948), Piaget (1954), and Vygotsky (1978) drew on distance concepts, it was not until Sigel's (1970) paper that psychological distance was first postulated as a developmental construct. Specifically, Sigel has described psychological distance as the individual's emerging ability to understand that an object (task, idea, etc.) can be represented by something other than the concrete object itself. He considers psychological distance as a function, in that it evolves in relation to the others and objects that constitute the individuals' environment. He examines psychological distance as an issue of learning, in that the individual develops an ability to respond to the discrepancy that new information poses. And, he details the use of psychological distance, or distancing, as an intervention in which expert others pose questions, or organize text, and so forth in ways that create an appropriate level of distance between what an individual knows and what he or she is still working to understand.

Central to this construct is the cognitive process of representing information to one's self and the ecology of the environment that enables an individual to rerepresent information to him or herself in the service of subsequent conceptual development. As such, the distance between what is known and what is still to be understood, or discrepancy, is posited as the major impetus in development. Although developmental theory has also used terms like *discontinuity* and *disequilibrium* to focus on the lack of complete isomorphism between events or states and the perception of understanding of those events, the discrepancy that characterizes psychological distance results in developmental shifts that we call change or growth. Such change takes place across the life-span in a wide variety of contexts. As such, psychological distance is linked to cognitive, social, and physiological change.

Given the dynamic (and elusive) quality of change, a construct such as psychological distance is at once appealing and synthetic. This volume (and the conference on which it is based) was organized to call attention to the pervasiveness of the psychological distance construct and to facilitate subsequent discussion of its implications for learning and development. In particular, the chapters that follow address three questions: (a) What is the role of psychological distance in individual functioning? (b) What are the cognitive demands that promote change? and, (c) What are the ecological demands that contribute to change?

In each of the chapters different models are utilized to account for the construct defined in this volume as psychological distance. The construct is an abstraction apart from the models and the research generated by the models reported in these chapters. We suggest that these individual chapters, taken together, comprise a broad understanding of a psychological phenomenon that accounts for differences in understanding; differences in performance; differences in encoding, storage, and retrieval of information; and differences that relate in the broadest sense to information processing and problem-solving. The overall picture that we are attempting to structure is based on cognitive, social, educational, linguistic, and a variety of human performance domains. The interrelation of mediating variables, relations between mediating and dependent variables, and the overall relation between objective and subjective realities are made richer by looking across these individual models with the particular organizing construct of psychological distance. Further, across the chapters, psychological distance emerges as an important variable that accounts for both competence and performance differences in human growth and understanding.

Rodney R. Cocking
K. Ann Renninger

REFERENCES

Ebbinghaus, H. (1914). *Memory: A contribution to experimental psychology*. (H. A. Ruger & C. E. Bussenius, Trans.). New York, NY: Columbia University Press. (Original work published in 1885).
Neisser, U. (1976). *Cognition and reality: Principles and implications of cognitive psychology*. San Francisco: W. H. Freeman and Co.

Piaget, J. (1954). *The construction of reality in the child.* (M. Cook, Trans.). New York: Basic Books.

Sigel, I. E. (1970). The distancing hypothesis: A causal hypothesis for acquisition of representational thought. In M. R. Jones (Ed.), *Miami symposium on the prediction of behavior 1968: Effects of early experience* (pp. 99–118). Coral Gables, FL: University of Miami Press.

Vygotsky, L. S. (1978). *Mind in society: The development of higher psychological processes.* (M. Cole, V. John-Steiner, S. Scribner, & E. Souberman, Trans.). Cambridge, MA: Harvard University Press.

Werner, H. (1948). *Comparative psychology of mental development* (revised). Chicago: Follett.

Acknowledgments

The editors would like to thank Educational Testing Service for sponsoring the Conference on The Development and Meaning of Psychological Distance in honor of Irving E. Sigel, Distinguished Research Scientist, May 1–3, 1990. Particular appreciation is extended to Gregory Anrig, Margaret Goertz, and Victor Bunderson for their help in facilitating the conference, which provided the basis for this volume. In addition, the editors also would like to acknowledge support for their work on this volume from both the National Institute of Mental Health and Swarthmore College.

Foreword

In every science, there is a need for bold ideas that weave together seemingly disparate phenomena into coherent patterns. In the presence of such ideas, a new ambition infuses the work of the day. Researchers become challenged to extend their work into directions never before explored and to draw connections never before anticipated. Scientists start thinking big and taking chances, and interesting things begin to happen.

If the need for bold ideas is true for sciences generally, it is particularly so for psychological science at the end of the twentieth century. In its lively past, psychology has had its share of vaulting theories that have compelled allegiance and encouraged productive debate. But today there is a theoretical vacuum in the field, so much so that many wonder whether the enterprise may continue as a viable, unitary discipline at all.

Almost twenty years ago, Roger Brown and Richard Herrnstein (1975) announced that "The day of grand schemes for psychology has passed." If somewhat imperious, the statement did capture the trend that was shaping then and that indeed would become dominant during the entire period since. True to Brown and Hernstein's prediction, the last two decades have seen a reckless debunking of virtually every systematic construct, theory, or paradigm that has gained the smallest of followings. There has been a collective turning away from all lines of work that presume to do more than investigate a particular phenomenon in a particular context. As has been said repeatedly in nationwide conferences and reports, this has become an era of "problem-centered" research. I have heard this dispiriting phrase repeated on countless occasions; and I recall groaning (usually silently, but not always) each time.

Solving problems—especially socially important ones—is a fine goal for scholars. But no realm of scholarship will grow without powerful constructs that can link any research problem to a broader vision. Imagine where physics would be today if Kepler had declined to use untried laws of physical motion to describe the orbits of stars and planets. Or where biology would be if Darwin had considered the notion of evolution (which dated back but was often dismissed by early Greek philosophy) too speculative for describing the raw natural observations that he made from the decks of the *Beagle* (Koestler, 1964). Note too that plenty of Kepler's contemporaries spent their lives refining astronomical measurements, just as many of Darwin's fellow naturalists spent their lives creating thick catalogues of diverse species. Not until these two took some chances to bring their particular observations into the uncertain world of transcendent ideas did their respective sciences come to life.

I am encouraged about the notion of "psychological distance" as used in this volume. In and of itself, of course, it does not constitute a comprehensive theory. Yet it does offer some unifying potential across a range of intriguing phenomena. In this volume, the notion of psychological distance brings fresh perspectives to studies of both cognitive and interpersonal processes, including the awareness of discrepancy, symbolic representation, self-regulation, social understanding, peer relations, underachievement, and adaptive thinking in educational settings. In each case, the notion is used not only descriptively but also analytically, to identify mechanisms responsible for communication and change.

In this way, the authors demonstrate that psychological distance is a construct that is well positioned to address many questions that psychologists (and especially developmental ones) are in business to ask. It handles with ease the dual nature of psychological experience, the simultaneously social and individual nature of all human action. This dualism has been often noted but rarely captured in explanatory constructs. I believe that this one has the potential to do so. As a consequence, it promises to open new avenues to our understanding of the dynamic relation between social influence and individual progress.

One example in this volume is the contribution that the construct of psychological distance makes toward clarifying the role of conflict in development. Many theories have noted conflict's role, but the meaning of "conflict" has proven slippery. Is it conflict itself or the awareness of such that makes a difference? Are the conflicts generated from within or without? What counts as a conflict? Should one include events that appear more conciliatory than conflictual? Experimentation until now has not given us good answers to these questions, at least in part because we have always been forced to operationalize conflict in a one-dimensional manner. Among the delights of this volume is the way such forced compromises are avoided. The construct of psychological distance easily handles both the intrapsychic and interpersonal dimensions of conflict. It also directly suggests the specific ways in which conflict spurs change. If this direction is pursued in further work, it could accomplish one of the major goals of developmental theory.

The appeal of any new idea lies partly in its ability to tie together other ideas that arc presently in the wind and partly in its ability to suggest insights that the other ideas have missed. On both counts, psychological distance looks promising. It is a likely candidate to promote constructive work on the most interesting problems in our field.

Psychologists of all stripes have discussed the central processes of representation, communication, and change. Our major theorists have advanced many powerful notions to account for such processes. Many of these notions have found their way into one or another chapter of this volume: mediation, optimal discrepancy, cognitive conflict, equilibration, the zone of proximal development, and so on. Psychological distancing runs like a stream through all these ideas. The stream has a strong beginning; one can hope with good reason that it will grow into a brimming river.

William Damon
Providence, RI
November 1992

REFERENCES

Brown, R., & Herrnstein, R. (1975). *Psychology* (p. vii). Boston: Little, Brown.
Koestler, A. (1964). *The act of creation.* New York: MacMillan.

List of Contributors

Jennifer A. Bivens Department of Psychology, University of Northern Iowa, 140 Baker Hall, Cedar Falls, IA 50614–0505.

Urie Bronfenbrenner Human Development and Family Studies, Cornell University, Martha Van Rensselaer Hall, Ithaca, NY 14853–4401.

Rodney R. Cocking Basic Behavioral and Cognitive Sciences, National Institute of Mental Health, 5600 Fishers Lane, Parklawn Building, Room 11C-16, Rockville, MD 20857.

William Damon Department of Education, Brown University, Box 1938, Providence, RI 02912.

Judy S. DeLoache Department of Psychology, University of Illinois at Urbana-Champaign, 605 East Daniel Street, Urbana, IL 61820.

Kurt W. Fischer Human Development, Larsen Hall, Appian Way, Harvard University, Cambridge, MA 02138.

Patricia M. Greenfield Department of Psychology, University of California, 1282A Franz Hall, 405 Hilgard Avenue, Los Angeles, CA 90024–1563.

Jerome Kagan Department of Psychology, William James Hall, 33 Kirkland Street, Harvard University, Cambridge, MA 02138.

Lynn Kratzer Department of Psychology, University of Pittsburgh, Pittsburgh, PA 15260.

Robert B. McCall Office of Child Development, 411 LRDC, University of Pittsburgh, Pittsburgh, PA 15260.

Walter Mischel Department of Psychology, 405 Schermerhorn Hall, Columbia University, 116 & Broadway, New York, NY 10027.

Lynn Okagaki Child Development and Family Studies Department, Purdue University, West Lafayette, IN 47907–1267.

K. Ann Renninger Program in Education, Swarthmore College, 500 College Avenue, Swarthmore, PA 19081–1397.

Monica Rodriquez Department of Psychology, SUNY—Albany, Department of Psychology, Albany, NY 12222.

Carolyn U. Shantz Department of Psychology, Wayne State University, 71 West Warren Avenue, Detroit, MI 48202.

Irving E. Sigel Educational Testing Service, Mail Stop 07-R, Rosedale Road, Princeton, NJ 08541–0001.

Nancy Snidman Department of Psychology, Harvard University, Cambridge, MA 02138.

Robert Sternberg Department of Psychology, Box 11A Yale Station, Yale University, New Haven, CT 06520–7447.

Jaan Valsiner Department of Psychology, University of North Carolina, CB #3270, Davie Hall, Chapel Hill, NC 27599–3270.

René van der Veer Vakgroep Algemene Pedagogiek, Rijksuniversiteit Leiden, The Netherlands.

Malcolm W. Watson Psychology Department, Brandeis University, Brown 125, Waltham, MA 02254–9110.

James V. Wertsch Department of Psychology, Clark University, Worcester, MA 01610.

PSYCHOLOGICAL DISTANCE AND DEVELOPMENTAL THEORY

1 Psychological Distance as a Unifying Theory of Development

Rodney R. Cocking
National Institute of Mental Health

K. Ann Renninger
Swarthmore College

One of the paradoxes in developmental theory is the child's simultaneous intrapsychic and interpsychic development. The child is growing in mental capacity at the same time that competence in the social world is evolving. The paradox is that while the child is struggling to define self, behaviors are also being learned whose function is to integrate self into a social network, which often means that egocentric behaviors are in conflict with sociocentric ones. The theory that is the topic of this chapter draws on processes that promote both individual and social growth into a unified theory of development.

Building on the work of Werner (1948), Piaget (1954), Vygotsky (1978), Hunt (1961), Sigel (1970), and Sigel and Cocking (1977a, 1977b) among others, psychological distance is conceptualized as either the distance between what the learner understands and what still has to be understood (intrapsychic), or ways in which others adjust information for the learner in order to be fully comprehended (interpsychic). Psychological distance is a construct pertinent to almost all dimensions of psychological research. Furthermore, it is a uniquely psychological phenomenon in that it always remains at the psychological level of analysis and cannot be reduced to strictly social or physiological processes.

In this chapter, the richness and relevance of psychological distance as a construct is highlighted. In particular, psychological distance appears to serve both organizing and explanatory functions across seemingly diverse sets of theoretical and research questions, such as differentiation of self in personality development; conceptual representation in cognitive development; dialogue in the development of communication skills; information processing in cognitive science; regulatory mechanisms in the growth of control processes; and concept formation in crossover areas of cognition, learning, and thinking skills. The chapter also addresses how psychological distance functions: whether as a mediating variable, a collateral product, a control or monitoring function, or, in some instances, how it serves as an instigator or *zeitgeber* of development.

DIFFERENTIATION OF SELF

Both perceptual discrimination and response differentiation figure prominently in the evolution of psychological complexity. Separation of self from the surrounds means that children see their behavior as distinct from other immediate events and, further, that they represent these differences to themselves, often in seemingly idiosyncratic ways. This personal mode of representation can be conceptualized in terms of both the distinctiveness of behavior vis-à-vis an event, as well as in terms of the context of the event (Sigel, 1984). Further, the differences in symbol systems and the acts of representation (talking to give a verbal description of something or in drawing pictures to give a graphic description) that are unique to the child's developmental experiences are also ways of capturing psychological differentiation (Cocking & Copple, 1987). Equally critical to psychological complexity are these two different modes of behavioral functioning and representation—event representation and symbolic functioning for encoding, retrieving, and comparing events in memory and information processing. Common to each of these mental mechanisms is an undercurrent of functional concepts driving humans toward a characteristic of event representation that simultaneously preserves the uniqueness of the individual who witnessed the event and the perceiver who encodes in a variety of modalities (e.g., olfactory, action, language) what is witnessed. Furthermore, these symbolic representations are manipulated and retrieved over time and over logistical transformations (Sigel, 1984).

Encoding, storage, retrieval, recall, and application of event information comprise the psychological activities termed representation and representational thinking (Sigel, 1991; Sigel & Cocking, 1977a). Such activities build on the individual's involvement in witnessing and processing events. To this end, then, mental representation is conceptualized as the basic mechanism or set of mechanisms for the construct of psychological distance.

Language Representation

Although theoretical debates have ensued over the relative importance of the role of language in conceptual thinking, no theory of human cognitive functioning denies that it is a prime vehicle for engaging the individual in bridging the psychological distance between palpable reality and the mental world. Even in debating the language/communication distinction among deaf and hearing individuals, the same point stands: Language is a powerful representational symbol system that facilitates various levels of functioning, including encoding, memory, and retrieval of information.

One pathway for bridging psychological distance is through the social-communication functions of language. The representational system takes on a different dimension when it serves the two, seemingly opposing, functions of simultaneously separating the individual from others, while at the same time keeping that distance within the narrow range of mutual understanding and conceptual comprehension. The social dimensions of language include the receptive/comprehension aspects, the communication aspects, and the sophisticated aspect of dialogue. Dialogue adds a time dimension that allows repeated, synchronized "turns" at interpreting and elaborating both one's own and another's commentary. Each of the social dimensions of language are variations and developments of a representational/symbol system that allows people to engage in a "meta-analysis" of how each thinks about the world. The participants, in effect, are able to say: "This is what I see in the situation, this what you see . . ." and the language system of representation becomes the vehicle for analyzing the individual differences in understanding and meaning. Language, in this sense, creates a demand to think about one's own and others' thinking and the possibility that the two are not the same. This discrepancy between two perspectives for interpreting the world is termed *psychological distance*.

Charting language as one of the symbol systems a child learns to use involves consideration of both the unmediated language of the speaker and his or her "own" language: the realization of this representational system in the "monologic" of the child. That is to say, there is the representational system of language and the individual's use of the system. Language is an interesting phenomenon for developmental psychologists because one can look at how norms are acquired (linguistics) and how rule systems are extrapolated (learning), and at the same time study how language is conceived or how it interacts with the child's logic (psycholinguistics). Each of these features of the representational system provokes psychological distance, in terms of individual differences in development and in terms of the growth of meaning.

Conceptual Representation

With the possible exception of children's transitory idiosyncratic language usage, no word has a singular meaning or represents only one object or event. In fact, representational models posit multiple pathways and multiple modalities of representation in order to embody "elasticity" of meaning.

Meaning is the basis of concept learning and in its early stages the development of meaning is driven by prototype parent–child interactions, such as parents' corrected restatements of children's ungrammatical utterances so that the child comes to use correct words and syntax (cf. Brown & Bellugi, 1969; Cocking & Potts, 1976). Parents worry about corrections at the "word" level of meaning initially (restating "fishy" when the child says "birdie" while looking into an aquarium). Noun and verb corrections in number, case, and gender constitute a grammatical level of "meaning" corrections that parents engage in as the child moves toward sentence construction. While the child is engaging in the assimilation/accommodative squeezing, pushing, and molding that comes from trying to fit new events with what is already known, the parent is motivated to help the child's representational systems fit the cultural norms of the symbol systems, as well as to fit the parent's own "accuracy" standards. The disparity between what the child is ready to use at the moment and what the child will come to use is a psychological disparity. It is this type of discrepancy or distance that stretches the elastic of the language/word symbol system for representing the specifics of a particular category (Sigel & Cocking, 1977a). It also accounts for expansion of a representational category at both the word and the category levels so that, at the word level, a word like "dog" comes to mean both fuzzy poodle *and* skinny, yappy Chihuahua, although at the category level, the category "animal" expands to include both dog and cat (cf. Rosch, 1975).

Growth in representational competence involves shifts from a literal interpretation of a concept or a problem to a more symbolic or cognitively economical, representational model of the concept/problem. Attention to the child's meaning provides the basis of adult adjustment (cf. Rogoff, 1990; Tharp & Gallimore, 1988), or distancing (cf. Copple, Sigel, & Saunders, 1984a, 1984b; Sigel & Saunders, 1979), of information that is central to young children's learning. Although understanding another's "meaning" or the psychological distance between what he or she means and what is intended is critical to shared understanding and learning, regardless of age.

The use of models to describe mechanisms of representation has recently focused on differences between mechanisms of behavioral control and mechanisms that assist in maintaining behaviors. The parallel distributed processing (PDP) model (Rummelhart & McClelland, 1986; McClelland & Rummelhart, 1985; and the PDP research group) is an example of a model focused on control mechanisms. The purpose of mapping the networks of connections is to establish the overlap and functional redundancy in the control of behavior and to identify the critical parameters controlling actions. In such a model, psychological distance refers to the discrepancies created by the possibilities and usages of multiple representational pathways for encoding information. There is a qualitative outcome in such a model that is important to the proximal and ultimate effects on behavior—effects on behavior now and over time. Information is learned, encoded, and retrieved through multiple sensory pathways (e.g. remembering both the visual and olfactory components of an experience) and at multiple levels of meaning (recalling the words, the intent of the words, and the reactions of others).

The expert–novice paradigm, on the other hand, is an example of a model focused on maintenance mechanisms and on the utilization of representational tools. The model has been applied most widely to understand problem solving and to describe how and what influences the way in which problems are analyzed and represented by individuals. Maintenance mechanisms, we suggest, are functionally related to models of meaning and how meaning is represented by the individual. Maintenance models are important in the ways they inform about cognitive economy, as in problem solving. What maintains consistency and variation in problem representation (cognitive economy) indicates how the individual transfers represented meaning across problems and across domains of behavior.

As the focus on both control and maintenance models suggests, psychological distance describes a dynamic concept, one in which there is tension between the factors (e.g., psychological, biological, cultural) or elements (e.g., prior knowledge, "g") that contribute to what is or can be represented and changed in the representation. Common to both types of models is the individual's move away from literal interpretations of events toward symbolic representations.

Dialogue

Dialogues illustrate other important dimensions of psychological distance. The dynamic aspects of representation in psychological distance are described in the shared (or nonshared) aspects of dialogue. Factors such as motivation, multiple meanings, invention, intention, deceit and lying, joking and teasing, and beliefs illustrate multiple levels of representing and multiple levels of utilizing information. The critical component of this type of symbol manipulation is its socially shared aspect. Whether for gaining mutual understanding or for other motivational, creative, or pleasureful purposes, the exchanges hinge on mutual engagement by the involved parties.

Dialogues are well documented in the developmental language learning literature, illustrating a continuity from monologues to early pretend dialogues in which the solitary child holds up both ends of the conversation. Although they illustrate certain growth processes in language learning and in the communication functions of language, such early dialogues do not reflect differences in psychological perspective that is characteristic of true dialogues. However, it is posited by distancing theory that dialogues are a functional mechanism in the growth of psychological complexity (cf. Sigel, 1969; Sigel & Kelley, 1988). Functionalists have considered such dialogues to include rehearsal and practice episodes of conversation (cf. McNeill, 1966); social developmentalists have described them as important examples of early perspective taking (or lack of it, because the child so readily agrees with himself; cf. Flavell, Green, & Flavell, 1986; Damon, 1990).

The shared intentional meanings between parent and child bring semantic analysis into the picture of how dialogues work. In this form of representation, the structure of the symbol system can remain essentially unchanged at the surface level due to multiple and special meanings that develop between two people. Intonation, for example, comes to convey meaning that becomes bound to the social or interpersonal dimension of language, and that cannot be expressed or conveyed in other ways, such as in writing. Meaning is also conveyed in the socially constructed understanding of gesticulation, clothing, and use of functional objects (cf. Lotman, 1988; Wertsch & Bivens, this volume).

When the distance between referent and symbol is mutually shared there is more room for spontaneity and flexibility. Children's word play (initially with attempts to establish sound/meaning isomorphisms such as in rhymes) extends to sophisticated word play and other types of language/meaning manipulations, such as lying, in which the representational system does not preserve the shared meanings. The converse can also occur, in which meanings are preserved when the symbols are radically altered, as in humor and puns. However, mutually "shared" does not necessarily mean that the participants are matched or co-equal in their contributions to the exchange. Rather, there is actually an optimal mismatch (Hunt, 1961), or distance, between the individual and partner in the exchange, such that they both contribute to defining the course of their dialogue-relationship (Renninger & Winegar, 1985). Sameness, agreement, and homogeneity of perspective might be said not to provide participants room to grow, and in the discrepancy model of distancing theory, such overlap and congruity are dysfunctional for development. By contrast, difference that is within a limited or optimal range of discrepancy actually facilitates development (Sigel & Cocking, 1977a).

This discussion must acknowledge the relationship of the individual to the representing process and the symbol system, in addition to what has been said about how symbol systems function for interpersonal exchanges. As previously mentioned, a critical component of the psychological distance construct is the perceiver of the event. Without falling into solipsists' logic, it is important to look at the individual vis-à-vis the event and the system that is used to encode that event. That is, the issue of internal representation is separate from an issue of felicity with the symbol system. For example, nonstandard English (NSE) may be a system used for representing events by Black children. The system is different from standard English (SE), but which system is used says nothing about the individual's internal representation of the event. On the other hand, the Hispanic youth who uses the one-to-one algorithm to translate Spanish to English to algebraic equations in order to solve algebra word problems often falls into trouble on both counts of a poor internal representation and a lack of facility in the language/math symbol systems (cf. Cocking & Chipman, 1988). Clearly, how the event/text is perceived contributes to the psychological distance it reflects.

MODELS OF INFORMATION PROCESSING

The emergence of psychological distance is addressed by two complementary models: models that explore the specifics of meaning systems (including studies of indigenous cognition) and models that promote thinking and problem solving (including studies of information processing). Each addresses the role of the perceiver's most "distant" experiences on his or her responses. Studies of category formation and categorical thinking have used research strategies to determine how new items or events are classified, or whether new categories are established to handle novel experience.

Studies of indigenous cognition inform models of information processing in terms of the specifics of the meaning systems underlying thought. In this respect, indigenous cognition is different from studies in comparative cognition. Indigenous cognition attempts to understand people's cognitive life by including research variables that capture "*their* views and *their* understanding of what *their* cognitive life is about" (Berry, Irvine, & Hunt, 1988, p. 2; Kim, in press).

Indigenous cognition recalls previous research on cognitive style that also illustrates the notion of psychological distance. Cognitive styles that are typical of a culture or a subculture are understood differently when approached as global comparison ("he's a visual vs. a verbal thinker and that's why he is so good a reading a map; she's action-oriented or an 'enactive encoder'—she can *fold* the map" or "he's a holistic rather than an analytic thinker") versus comparisons based on a multilevel framework that considers the relationship between the individual's representational system(s) and the specific meanings of those system(s).

Cognitive style, in this sense, includes variations in the "intention" of a style. Question asking and, more importantly, question answering are important subcultural differences. Native American Arapaho culture does not admit direct questions as an acceptable discourse style, and yet the youngsters are taught in Socratic methods in public school systems. The pauses in communication say as much as the words in Japanese dialogue (Azuma, 1991; Lebra, in press). The social dimension (e.g., others as questioners) is probably the critical factor in these kinds of psychological distance.

The Whorfian hypothesis was an early framework to account for a dimension of functioning we now understand as psychological distance. It was an attempt to look at the variation and invariances in information processing across one representational system—language. The hypothesis was that the variations and invariances should be predictable from "a model of the mechanics of thought" (Hunt & Banaji, 1988, p. 81).

Studies of Native American Ute cognition (Leap, 1988) and the older studies on syllogistic reasoning from Luria and Vygotsky illustrate how important context and thinking about context are on one's efforts to relate to a problem. In this sense, context is the same as its function for memory retrieval. This is "context" as it impacts upon the individual's ability to detach psychologically from the personal meaning of the event and to think about possibilities and consequences of the event.

Further aspects of indigenous cognition that are relevant to the psychological distance construct include consideration of the role of context and its effects in learning and memory cuing. Such research typically focuses on transfer of learning and ways in which either the language and/or the task might be adjusted to facilitate transfer. It focuses on the way in which the culture, the language, and the task constrain (and empower) learning.

Related context research investigates the constraints on thinking imposed by the framework or context boundaries of particular symbol systems. Comparative cognition (e.g., Serpell, 1979) has explored this arena in studies where dominant representational systems for problem execution are reversed—as in comparisons between African and Scottish children in graphic drawing and three-dimensional model-building tasks. Baratz (1969) similarly reversed nonstandard English and standard English representational systems in American children as they solved language-based problems. In all instances, the conclusion was that performance differences were due to the constraints of the representational systems children were required to utilize for performing a task and not due to the individuals' internal representations of the problems (see also Sigel & McBane, 1967). It was concluded, in these comparisons, that the representational system assigned for task performance was psychologically remote—too distant to the problem solver vis-à-vis that particular problem (but not necessarily outside his or her capabilities).

On the one hand, the role of others in processing information cannot be overlooked. Studies of indigenous and comparative cognition, as well as the numerous studies of siblings, peers, parenting, teaching, and clinical exchange, indicate that such influence is significant—even when the "other" is not physically present (cf. Mead, 1934). On the other hand, it is the individual who processes information. It is the individual who perceives, represents, and acts on information.

Psychological distance also is reflected, then, in the way in which the learner interprets and proceeds with a particular task (e.g., a math word problem, making a friend, or a maze in a video game). The student who skips over the parentheses in an algebra word problem is responding to those aspects of the task that make sense, and is, in effect, adjusting the psychological distance of the problem for him- or herself in such a way that the problem undertaken is different than the problem assigned. This so-called faulty logic (Ginsburg, 1977) is common and problematic. It often leads to or results in misunderstanding.

In general, it is possible to talk about children's knowledge as increasingly more articulated with age, and as such, enabling them to become more facile in their abilities to access a wide range of tasks (cf. Bjorkland, 1985; Fischer,

1980), albeit with some differences between them with respect to proficiency (cf. Gardner, 1983). In this sense, psychological distance is used to refer to universals in students' abilities to apprehend and apply mnemonic understanding and an increased efficiency in work with information to assigned tasks (cf. Folds, Footo, Guttentag, & Ornstein, 1990).

In fact, there are at least four ways in which to adjust tasks so that the learner is more likely to respond to the task as assigned. These include organizing the task: (a) to build on what students already know about that task; (b) to make it similar enough to other tasks in which students have previously engaged; (c) to present the task in conjunction with another task on which the student recently has been working; and/or (d) to provide closure to a set of questions on which the student has been engaged. Interestingly enough, however, each of these adjustments requires that the expert have a solid understanding of the logic and faulty rules that characterize an individual's approach to the task. Some generic notion about how, for example, fifth graders solve problems is not sufficient.

Along the same lines, Newman, Griffin, and Cole (1989) have suggested that tasks are really "strategic fictions" (p. 135). Their point is that there is no single interpretation of a task. Rather, the process of teaching/working with others involves communication of understanding(s) and an appreciation that there are always multiple understandings of any task. These authors suggest that the conditions of learning can be modified and enhanced through use of written language, category schemes, and computers and is not limited to verbal feedback or exchange with another. They suggest further that those who are facilitating learning need to recognize that cognitive change, or learning, involves changed roles as the learner becomes more expert. Such facilitation underscores a more unique or idiosyncratic aspect of psychological distance. While on the one hand the learner's actual process of representation involves universals such as an expanding knowledge base, increased mnemonic capacities, and the development of strategies, how the task is understood, on the other hand, has a more unique character, which cannot be overlooked if the adjustment of information for learning/action is meant to result in shared understanding.

Conclusions

A general assumption in cognitive theory is that perceiving and behaving are driven by the individual's striving toward conceptual coherence. The Constructivist framework is predicated on the individual's active construction of reality through accommodative processing (rather than by pure assimilation). How does such a theory account for anomalous experience? Does developmental theory posit that children see *all* experience as anomalous? What does anomalous experience do to the individual's personal epistemology and how is the construction of reality affected? The intrusions into one's concepts and the vulnerabilities of one's "loose connections" or resiliencies of the indigenous constructs all figure into new directions for research on concept formation as a basic model of information processing.

REGULATORY MECHANISMS

Information processing and the tools of representational-symbol systems, together, form the model of how reality is constructed. Context, culture, and indigenous factors such as environmental affordances mediate the constructive process; however, they do so in conjunction with regulatory mechanisms such as the individual's beliefs, interests, habits, intrinsic motivation, and meta-awareness.

Beliefs

The discourse model, based on language processes discussed previously, is posited as the evaluation system the child learns with respect to *beliefs*. As Bakhtin (1981) phrases it, events that revolve around issues of beliefs are evaluated in the internal representation of authorities—"I am me in someone else's language," so to speak (p. 315). Development, because it occurs within a social context of parents, siblings, and others who are present, may mix the boundaries of self and other. Emotions and the affective tone of events are components of represented experience. Both figure prominently in attitude formation and development. But because of powerful symbol and representational systems indigenous to culture and subculture, a mechanism of instantiation, as contrasted with processes of individuation, operates in belief frameworks by which one makes judgments during the constructive process (cf. McGillicuddy-DeLisi, 1982; McGillicuddy-DeLisi, Sigel, & Johnson, 1979). That is, as metacognitive, evaluative thinking occurs during learning and mental construction, beliefs operate as a standard against which the judgments are made; learning does not occur outside a frame of reference for the individual. Psychological distance is particularly interesting with respect to the development of attitude–belief discrepancies in people's valuing and evaluating behaviors. The questions are whether, when, and how individuals come to recognize and respond to the distance between one's personal constructs and the belief systems that seem incompatible with significant others.

Interpersonal accounts are often the primary mechanism for representing culture-specific information. In other words, beliefs as filtered through tradition may function as regulators of psychological distance. For example, certain Native Americans of Montana don't tell their traditional coyote stories in the summertime. Why? "It's tradition." There's no mysticism to the season storytelling; there's no tribal prohibition; it's just not done. Where rationale and affect run low to alter the way things are done but feelings are strong for maintaining tradition, the psychological distance for questioning and seeking justifications or explanations is low. Explanations like "My grandmother said so" or "My grandmother said a snake would get you if you told those stories in the summer" say a lot about the place of American teaching tales in people's respect for beliefs and the desire to preserve them. Such explanations also say something about the way in which information may need to be adjusted so that the receiver/individual learns it. One does not learn very much about cognition by studying beliefs, but on the other hand, we learn the historical and affective roots of people's evaluating processes vis-à-vis particular issues. These historical and affective dimensions are the very ones that are elusive to the symbol systems that humans learn. Interpersonal accounts are often the primary mechanism for representing culture-specific information. In other words, beliefs as filtered through tradition may function as regulators of psychological distance. These regulatory mechanisms speak to the individual or idiosyncratic qualities of learning and adaptation within the context of a culture or subculture. As such, they speak specifically to what does and does not vary between individuals.

Interest and Intrinsic Factors

Individual interest is yet another regulator of psychological distance. While individuals are typically well aware that beliefs influence their understanding about events, they are not necessarily aware that their own individual interest, or stored knowledge and value for a class of events, is a powerful organizer of their actions. For example, interest has been shown to both increase attention and to distract attention from tasks (e.g., solving a word problem, not thinking about the context of basketball in which the problem is embedded) as a function of how difficult the task is for that individual (see Renninger, 1992). Interest also has been shown to influence young children's attention and memory for tasks, actions with others, actions with play objects, and children's persistence under conditions of stress. In fact, it appears that for young children, play with an identified object of interest (e.g., a truck) actually leads their play with other objects for which they also have prior knowledge. It is with these objects that children explore possibilities for activity, set challenges for themselves, and develop a repertoire of actions that they carry over to subsequent tasks (Renninger, 1990).

Intrinsic motivation, on the other hand, specifies the goals that for that individual are powerful contributors to action. Intrinsic motivation presumes both that the individual is goal directed and that people decide what to do on the basis of their evaluations of possible outcomes (Deci, 1975). It differs from belief and individual interest, in that belief is a set of assumptions that may regulate an individual's actions, but beliefs are not specifically linked to goals. Similarly, interest is the stored knowledge and value with which an individual engages in activity, but the individual is not necessarily metacognitively aware of his or her interest or its subsequent influence upon activity.

Meta-awareness as a regulator of psychological distance also is unique to the individual. Meta-awareness is cognizance of particular strategies which assist understanding. This particular regulator differs from the others in that it is explicitly presented to, or modeled for, the individual by another, with the expectation that it will become one of the individuals' strategies for completing tasks. The assumption underlying the teaching of metacognitive techniques is that these strategies will eventually be internalized as their own. Such strategies facilitate task completion by lessening the psychological distance between what one understands the task to represent initially and what the process of more focused attention to the task makes possible.

Reciprocal teaching (Palincsar & Brown, 1984), for example, engages students in the process of talking about their reading (mathematics, writing, etc.) (see Campione & Brown, 1990). The process of talking and asking questions about the content of the task not only enables students to engage tasks at a level of difficulty that is appropriate for them, but provides support for further solidifying their understanding of the task (cf. Bruner, 1977). Teaching metacognitive strategies also models a process that enables students to self-consciously regulate the psychological distance of tasks that they encounter. Metacognitive training, thus, is a technique for helping learners to begin internalizing self-monitoring in their independent work with similar tasks.

Concept Formation

People do not have to adopt others' beliefs and attitudes, habits, interests, intrinsic motivation, or meta-awareness in order to comprehend what they say or to understand their intent, although awareness of these organizing principles clearly influences the individual. Concepts function to communicate shared meaning. Beliefs, as discussed thus far, are a special kind of concept. Separating how one thinks about a problem from how one feels about the problem is a contrast across affective and analytic dimensions. Concepts are built from categories of information that often have valences associated with them—how strongly one feels is the grouping principle (good/bad; powerful/weak; cutting-edge/mundane). In fact, problem solving, decision making, and reasoning are all logical thinking tasks that are influenced by the individual's concepts of the information, and that information, further, may have organized frames (concepts) associated with it that are affective, as well as conceptual. The central mechanism of concept formation is categorization based on prior experience with the task/activity. Categorization is seen by cognitive psychology as a path of cognitive economy for thinking because it reduces disparate attributes to common dimensions.

What are the variables that shape concepts? If experience gives us the material for our constructions, then frequency of experience should be related to how well-defined a concept is. The size and the breadth of a category are linked to the number of exemplars for the category. Distortions in the category are a function of how good the exemplars are (casual examples vs. prototypic exemplars). The number of categories associated with an object or event and their respective distinctiveness also affect how the categories function, either exclusively or interchangeably. Passage of time also shapes a category in terms of heightening or leveling members as examples of the category. Feedback one gets also says something about the adequacy of category membership and often forces multiple classifications. Finally, memory set is seen as influencing what remains a durable category or a durable member of a category (Neisser, 1967; Homa, 1984; Smith & Medin, 1981).

Thus, although each of these variables shape concepts, distance also contributes to how these concepts are understood. Distance can be distinctiveness in attribute, the passage of time, the relationship between category and exemplar, and so forth. The point is that conceptual reasoning is an abstracted model of cognitive functioning. Abstractions necessarily invoke a distance between the event and its representation—the representation of particular instances and the durability of the representation in memory. New directions in concept formation and categorical thinking relate to decision making and training of effective problem solving based on skills of categorization. For example, a prototype integration model would predict that by using variables of frequency and saliency, one would get better transfer of learning by training students on high-variance exemplars. The variance dimension, presumably, operates effectively because psychological distance has created the maximum tolerance limits for including new instances. Transfer is greatest, and hence most effective, when performance is capable of accounting for anomalous experience and the learner relies on what was learned for solving the problem of accounting for anomalous examples. High-variance exemplars for instruction would include affective dimensions, as well as analytic and perceptual dimensions.

CONCLUSIONS

The construct of psychological distance functions in a variety of ways, including provoking or *zeitgeber* functions, mediating functions, catalyst functions, and monitoring and control functions. More specifically, it appears that psychological distance describes both the interrelatedness of many behaviors (e.g., symbol system functioning and cognitive functioning) and the role of psychological distance as an explanatory construct for developmental change in these behaviors. In fact, in examples where psychological distance is hypothesized to be a causal agent of development it appears that the construct has potential for providing the basis for understanding ontogeny. The generative nature of the construct, however, either in terms of how it provides the basis for the next generation of cognitive research studies or in terms of how it functions in emerging new behavioral paradigms, remains an open question.

REFERENCES

Azuma, H. (1991, June–July). *Commentary on continuities and discontinuities in Asian cognitive socialization.* Conference presentation, Continuities & Discontinuities in the Cognitive Socialization of Minority Children (P. M. Greenfield & R. R. Cocking, organizers). Washington, DC.

Bakhtin, M. M. (1981). *Four essays by M. M. Bakhtin: The dialogic imagination.* In M. Holquist (Ed.). Austin, TX: University of Texas Press.

Baratz, J. C. (1969). A bidialectical task for determining language proficiency in economically disadvantaged children. *Child Development, 40*(3), 889–901.

Berry, J., Irvine, S. H., & Hunt, E. B. (1988). *Indigenous cognition: Functioning in cultural contexts.* Dordrecht, The Netherlands: Martinus Nijhoff.

Bjorkland, D. F. (1985). The role of conceptual knowledge in the development of organization in children's memory. In C. J. Brainerd & M. Pressley (Eds.), *Basic processes in memory development: Progress in cognitive development research* (pp. 103–142). New York: Springer-Verlag.

Bruner, J. (1977). *The process of education.* Cambridge, MA: Harvard University Press.

Brown, A. L., & Campione, J. C. (1990). Communities of learning and thinking, or a context by any other name. *Contributions to Human Development, 21,* 108–126.

Brown, R., & Bellugi, U. (1969). Three processes in the child's acquisition of syntax. *Harvard Educational Review, 34,* 133–151.

Cocking, R. R., & Chipman, S. (1988). Conceptual issues related to mathematics achievement of language minority children. In R. R. Cocking & J. P. Mestre (Eds.), *Linguistic and cultural influences on learning mathematics* (pp. 17–46) Hillsdale, NJ: Lawrence Erlbaum Associates.

Cocking, R. R., & Copple, C. E. (1987). Social influences on representational awareness: Plans for representing and plans as representation. In S. L. Friedman, E. K. Scholnick, & R. R. Cocking (Eds.), *Blueprints for thinking: The role of planning in cognitive development.* (pp. 428–468). New York: Cambridge University Press.

Cocking, R. R., & Potts, M. (1976). Social facilitation of language acquisition: The reversible passive construction. *Genetic Psychology Monographs, 94,* 249–340.

Copple, C., Sigel, I. E., & Saunders, R. (1984b). *Educating the young thinker: Classroom strategies for cognitive growth.* Hillsdale, NJ: Lawrence Erlbaum Associates. (Original work published 1979)

Copple, C., Sigel, I. E., & Saunders, R. (1984a). *Educating the young thinker.* New York: Prentice-Hall.

Damon, W. (1990). *The moral child.* New York: Macmillan.

Deci, E. (1975). *Intrinsic motivation.* New York: Plenum.

Fischer, K. W. (1980). A theory of cognitive development: The control and construction of hierarchies of skills. *Psychological Review, 87,* 477–531.

Flavell, J. H., Green, F. L., & Flavell, E. R. (1986). Development of knowledge about the appearance-reality distinction. *Monographs of the Society for Research in Child Development, 51* (1, Serial No. 212).

Folds, T. H., Footo, M. M., Guttentag, R. E., & Ornstein, P. A. (1990). When children mean to remember: Issues of context specificity, strategy effectiveness, and intentionality in the development of memory. In D. F. Bjorklund (Ed.), *Children's strategies: Contemporary views of cognitive development* (pp. 67–92). Hillsdale, NJ: Lawrence Erlbaum Associates.

Gardner, H. (1983). *Frames of mind.* New York: Basic Books.

Ginsburg, H. (1977). *Children's arithmetic: How they learn it and how you teach it.* Austin, TX: Pro-ed.

Homa, D. L. (1984). On the nature of categories. In G. H. Bower (Ed.), *The psychology of learning and motivation: Advances in research and theory, V.* New York: Academic Press.

Hunt, E. B., & Banji. (1988). In J. W. Berry, S. H. Irvine, & E. B. Hunt (Eds.), *Indigenous cognition: Functioning in cultural context.* Dordrecht, The Netherlands: Martinus Nijhoff.

Hunt, J. M. (1961). *Intelligence and experience.* New York: Ronald Press.

Kim, U. (in press). Individualism, collectivism, and child development: A Korean perspective. In P. M. Greenfield & R. R. Cocking (Eds.), *The development of the minority child; Culture in and out of context.* Hillsdale, NJ: Lawrence Erlbaum Associates.

Leap, W. (1988). Assumptions and strategies guiding mathematics problem solving. In R. R. Cocking & J. P. Mestre (Eds.), *Linguistic and cultural influences on learning mathematics* (pp. 161– 186). Hillsdale, NJ: Lawrence Erlbaum Associates.

Lebra, T. S. (in press). The triple message in Japanese child socialization: Position, empathy & nature. In P. M. Greenfield & R. R. Cocking (Eds.), *The development of the minority child: Culture in and out of context* Hillsdale, NJ: Lawrence Erlbaum Associates.

Lotman, Y. M. (1988). The semiotics of culture and the concept of a text. *Soviet Psychology, 26,* 52–58.

Mead, G. H. (1934). *Mind, self and society from the standpoint of a social behaviorist.* Chicago: University of Chicago Press.

McClelland, J. L., & Rummelhart, D. E. (1985). Distributed memory and the representation of general and specific information. *Journal of Experimental Psychology: General, 114,* 159–188.

McGillicuddy-DeLisi, A. V. (1982). Parental beliefs about developmental processes. *Human Development, 25,* 192–200.

McGillicuddy-DeLisi, A. V., Sigel, I. E., & Johnson, J. E. (1979). The family as a system of mutual influences: Parental beliefs, distancing behaviors and children's representational thinking. In M. Lewis & L. A. Rosenblum (Eds.), *The genesis of behavior: Vol. 2. The child and its family* (pp. 91–106). New York: Plenum.

McNeill, D. (1966). Developmental psycholinguistics. In F. Smith & G. Miller (Eds.), *The genesis of language* (pp. 15–84). Cambridge, MA: MIT Press.

Neisser, U. (1967). *Cognitive psychology.* New York: Appleton.

Newman, D., Griffin, P., & Cole, M. (1989). *The construction zone: Working for cognitive change in school.* Cambridge, MA: Cambridge University Press.

Palincsar, A., & Brown, A. L. (1984). Reciprocal teaching of comprehension-fostering and comprehension-monitoring activities. *Cognition and Instruction, 1*(2), 117–175.

Piaget, J. (1954). *The construction of reality in the child* (M. Cook, Trans.). New York: Basic Books.

Renninger, K. A. (1990). Children's play interests, representation, and activity. In R. Fivush & J. Hudson (Eds.), *Knowing and remembering in young children* Emory Cognition Series (vol. III; pp. 127–165). Cambridge, MA: Cambridge University Press.

Renninger, K. A. (1992). Individual interest and development: Implications for theory and practice. In K. A. Renninger, S. Hidi, & A. Krapp (Eds.), *The role of interest in learning and development* (pp. 361–395). Hillsdale, NJ: Lawrence Erlbaum Associates.

Renninger, K. A., & Winegar, L. T. (1985). Emergent organization in expert-novice relationships. *Genetic Epistemologist, XVI*(1), 14–20.

Rummelhart, D. E., & McClelland, J. L. (1986). *Parallel distributed processing: Explorations in the microstructures of cognition, Vols. 1 & 2: Foundations.* Cambridge, MA: MIT Press.

Rogoff, B. (1990). *Apprenticeship in thinking: Cognitive development in social context.* New York: Oxford University Press.

Rosch, E. (1975). Cognitive representations of semantic categories. *Journal of Experimental Psychology: General, 7,* 573–606.

18   COCKING AND RENNINGER

Serpell, R. (1979). How specific are perceptual skills? A cross-cultural study of pattern reproduction. *British Journal of Psychology, 70,* 365–380.

Sigel, I. E. (1969). The Piagetian system and the world of education. In E. Elkind & J. H. Flavell (Eds.), *Studies in cognitive development: Essays in honor of Jean Piaget.* New York: Oxford University Press.

Sigel, I. E. (1970). The distancing hypothesis: A causal hypothesis for the acquisition of representational thought. In M. R. Jones (Ed.), *Miami Symposium on the Prediction of Behavior, 1968: Effect of early experiences* (pp. 99–118). Coral Gables, FL: University of Miami Press.

Sigel, I. E. (1984). Reflections on action theory and distancing theory. *Human Development, 27*(3 4), 188–193.

Sigel, I. E. (1991). Representational Competence: Another Type? In M. Chandler and M. Chapman (Eds.), *Criteria for competence: Controversies in the conceptualization and assessment of children's abilities* (pp. 189–207). Hillsdale, NJ: Lawrence Erlbaum Associates.

Sigel, I. E., & Cocking, R. R. (1977a). Cognition and communication: A dialectic paradigm for development. In M. Lewis & L. A. Rosenblum (Eds.), *Interaction, conversation, and the development of language: The origins of behavior* (Vol. V, pp. 207–226). New York: Wiley.

Sigel, I. E., & Cocking, R. R. (1977b). *Cognitive development from childhood to adolescence: A constructivist perspective.* New York: Holt, Rinehart, & Winston.

Sigel, I. E., & Kelley, T. C. (1988). A cognitive developmental approach to questioning. In J. Dillon (Ed.), *Classroom questioning and discussion: A multidisciplinary study* (pp. 105–134). Norwood, NJ: ABLEX.

Sigel, I. E., & McBane, B. (1967). Cognitive competence and level of symbolization among five-year-old children. In J. Hellmuth (Ed.), *The disadvantaged child* (Vol. 1, pp. 433–453). Seattle, WA: Special Child Publications of the Seattle Sequin School.

Sigel, I. E., & Saunders, R. (1979). An inquiry into inquiry: Question asking as an instructional model. In L. Katz (Ed.), *Current topics in early childhood education* (Vol. 2, pp. 169–193). Norwood, NJ: ABLEX.

Smith, E. E., & Medin, D. L. (1981). *Categories and concepts.* Cambridge, MA: Harvard University Press.

Tharp, R., & Gallimore, R. (1988). *Rousing minds to life: Teaching, learning, and schooling in social context.* Cambridge, MA: Cambridge University Press.

Vygotsky, L. (1978). *Mind in society: The development of higher psychological processes* (M. Cole V. John-Steiner, S. Scribner, & E. Souberman, Trans.). Cambridge, MA: Harvard University Press.

Werner, H. (1948). *Comparative psychology of mental development* (rev.). Chicago: Follett.

2 Psychological Distance and Behavioral Paradigms

K. Ann Renninger
Swarthmore College

Rodney R. Cocking
National Institute of Mental Health

At the end of Chapter 1, it was suggested that the construct of psychological distance facilitates description of developmental change. How the construct provides the basis for the next generation of research studies or emerging new behavioral paradigms was left as an open question, however. One of the difficulties in anticipating such new directions is the very language with which we have to work. As behavioral scientists, we are trained to consider variation in the relations between variables and we are pretty careful about articulating what those variables are. A construct such as psychological distance challenges us to think in terms of several aspects of a person's functioning (e.g., biological, psychological, social, physical) in relation to the problems or conflicts with which he or she engages over time.

As the studies reported in this volume clearly demonstrate, psychological distance cannot be assessed once and generalized to all situations, or across individuals. Rather, we suggest that the construct is an abstraction apart from the models and research generated by these models. It is a construct that permits serious consideration of individual differences as a function of both the process and the product of cognition and ecology. In order to further examine the possibilities afforded by this construct, this chapter overviews the way that issues central to psychological distance are reflected in current models of learning and development. Following this, chapters in the present volume are used to form the basis of a discussion of psychological distance as a developmental construct. Finally, this chapter focuses on distal and proximal variables specifically, and their joint contribution to subsequent research and behavioral paradigms.

PSYCHOLOGICAL DISTANCE AND MODELS
OF LEARNING AND DEVELOPMENT

Researchers across a wide variety of research questions and contexts have begun to concern themselves with contrasts between proximal and distal causes of behavior, or psychological distance, as a means for describing variability in behavior. In this section of this chapter, some of the links between psychological distance and four of these models are articulated by way of illustrating that the construct is both in use and useful. In particular, research based on each of these models has begun to reflect shifts from a focus on the products of learning to consideration of the processes of learning. Such a shift has been accomplished through use of multiple methods and levels of analysis in research design, and acknowledgment of multi-dimensional aspects of functioning in theoretical discussions.

Learning

Learning models are emerging once again as tests of developmental theory. Cognition and cognitive variables are being returned to the status of dependent variables. An example of how the distance construct drives learning models in terms of the issues it provokes is, for example, What are the differences in "learning by being told" versus "learning by example?" This is not to imply that the comparison of these two models is dichotomous (e.g., good/better or best/worst). Rather, it appears that cognitive and developmental theories have reached a point where the questions being addressed are similar. They are both asking what happens to learners.

Although both models differ from the Piagetian (1954) constructivist model, in which learning is conceptualized as occurring by invention, common to all three models is the critical process of abstraction. All three models rely on the learner's abstracting of principles in order to benefit from experience. The principles that are extrapolated from examples may differ or overlap with the principles gleaned from what is learned from being told information over and over or by various sources. In terms of the preceding discussion, the symbol systems of the two models may be the critical difference (language and its match with internal representations). The social dimension may also be important. The distancing-inspired question under each of these models, however, focuses on how the learner comes to evaluate his or her own performance and how he or she becomes a critic of personal experience: that is, how he or she takes the learning situation and judges it by some standards. It is this kind of qualitative outcome that is important to a construct like psychological distance, and it is in this sense one would evaluate the importance of the construct—that is, in terms of proximal and ultimate effects on behavior—the effects upon behavior now and in the long-term.

Another type of learning model is analogous to the extensions of the PDP model and computational models of cognition. They include psychological modeling that is inspired by neural models from biology to describe things like the nature of memory. McClelland and Rumelhart (c.f. 1985) both state that they built a math model based on the primary processing unit—the neuron. It is the speed of processing that differentiates computers from neurons. The model posits that it is the phenomenon of parallel processing that gives humans the speed advantage over computers.

Multiple representation systems, the distribution of these systems, and parallel processing activities all derive from a basic concern of the distancing construct as well, because these focus on how experience is encoded. Further, brains "know" what to do in learning situations, and as computational models begin to focus on machine learning, the questions under study by these researchers have begun to address how humans do things that they do well. The focus of these questions derives from what previously had been described only in the psychological realm: generalization and categorization of experience.

Pattern recognition, for example, something humans do very well, is a behavior that computer scientists have chosen to model. Humans learn to distinguish same/different relations and then to generalize on the basis of these categorizations. Some of the unique human processes that are presenting special challenges to models of learning are perceptual. These processes operate differently from one another depending on whether they involve the visual or auditory system. Pattern recognition works very differently in each of these systems as they attack perceptual features that have two distinct representational realizations: words like "enough, bough, bought, through, though, cough" challenge the independence of systems, while also forcing functional questions about integration and synthesis.

Adaptation Versus Learning Models

The functional purpose of learning is typically thought of as adaptation or in the service of adaptation. What is psychologically or behaviorally remote from the individual is generally thought not to aid in adaptive functioning. New learning that is not crystallized is not as automatic nor as immediately accessible as fixed or long standing learned action patterns. Such learning is seen as tenuous and vulnerable in its early entry into repertoires. An emerging behavioral paradigm illustrates how learned behaviors and adaptive behaviors may function quite differently. It may help us to understand cognitive and learning vulnerabilities, as well as help us understand these behaviors as markers of other disease.

The animal model in biological research generally operates within a paradigm whereby interventions are judged for their beneficial or deleterious impact upon behavior. For example, primate models of changes in cognitive functioning due to human immunodeficiency virus (HIV) infection are being studied for purposes of determining if there are early mental-functioning markers that occur prior to seropositive conversion. That is, they are being studied to determine if there are any early behavioral markers that serve useful diagnostic functions. Further, such studies generally ask questions about the course of cognitive or behavioral change due to the onset of disease. In acquired immune deficiency syndrome (AIDS) dementia this means identifying which functions are most severely impaired, which ones are affected first, and so forth. The medical model, then, asks about the impact of disease on behavior. From this model we do learn significantly from studying critical components of cognitive functioning by focusing on part-processes. This study of part-processes is important in behavioral research because it is not possible to study the whole course of schizophrenia, AIDS dementia, depression, and the like.

Based on what behavioral scientists have learned about naturalistic behaviors and learned behaviors, however, the new paradigm further considers the meaning of "behavior in context." If there is a specific feature of animal behavior that has been observed in a variety of contexts and a variety of species it is that sick animals adapt as long as possible and try to mask their vulnerabilities for the purpose of survival within the troop or colony (Goodall, 1986). With the medical model, we really do not know when the onset of infection begins to affect cognitive functioning and we probably learn only about performance under advanced stages of disease. Nothing is learned about early marker functions or about the developmental features of the disease–behavior relationship.

Resiliency and vulnerability are two critical indices of the durability of learned behaviors. By attending to the focus of learning involved in adaptation, it has become possible to consider the impact of disease on cognitive functioning. If behaviors that derive from critical cognitive functions, for example, are taught to animals prior to infection induction, it is possible to look at both onset and course of deterioration of these behaviors without the adaptation confound associated with naturalistic behavioral variables that are masked by animals' compensatory adaptation. Further, the psychological distance construct gives a specific dimension to a diverse set of behaviors. For, within the distance construct, possibilities for learning can be specified, and researchers are then in a position to consider the acquisition of abstractness, symbol system accessibility, and short- and long-term memory for learned behaviors.

Transduction and Behavioral Pathways Models

In addition to using psychological distance as a way to conceptualize a class of behaviors being studied, psychological distance is pertinent to discussions about relevant/critical pathways of behavioral transmissions. It is possible to study the impact of a research construct such as psychological distance across generations of subjects using within-families or within-culture designs. Thus, for example, a transduction-pathways model would be useful for addressing new research in indigenous cognition. Questions stemming from such consideration might include those dealing with the relevant/critical pathways of behavioral transmissions, in which the distancing inspired question might be said to be: What does not change? Sigel's (cf. 1970) work on cognitive style and his distancing hypothesis predict that one approaches proximal experiences differently when the people or aspects of the event create discrepancies that the individual has to resolve. It is unlikely that humans have to "discover" each and every event anew with each generation. Rather, it is more likely the case that humans' metacognitive abilities enable them to encode critical and significant events that, in turn, promote and facilitate learning in subsequent generations by providing the critical mismatches for learning. Identifying transmission pathways would provide information about the durability of learning across generations and permit identification of those aspects of functioning that are malleable and, as such, worth targeting as sources of change. For example, from stress research we learn that stress during pregnancy affects the next generation of offspring (McClintock, 1988); although stress directly affects the mother's hormonal system, it also indirectly impacts the behavior and adaptation of the offspring.

Identifying critical experiences has been the focus of learning studies. Identifying transmission pathways may tell us about the durability of learning across generations. Differential pathways may, for example, account for differences Sternberg and Wagner (1989) have identified between everyday cognition and formal logical thinking. Of course, the domains and contexts vary, but the transmission pathways for what is learned are possibly very different also, even though the same set of skills of logic, such as Piagetian hypothetico-deductive logic, operate in both instances. Clearly, functional theories need to account for the salient and relevant pathways of transmission in order to account for performance differences in skills that have the same underlying competencies.

Homeostasis Models

A final example of how psychological distance is reflected in behavioral models is the homeostasis model. A critical aspect of homeostasis is the timing of perturbing events. Psychological distance draws on and contributes to models of homeostasis in that the actual timing of the challenge, or discrepancy, that a problem or conflict poses is critical. By such accounts, timing of experience alters the organism's developmental history. Timing of the presence of the luteinizing hormone, for example, determines the onset of ovulation, etc. Temporal relations in various levels of behavioral analyses inform about the differential importance of the event with respect to psychological, social, and physiological development, and differentially with respect to degree of impact at the different times. Concepts such as critical periods and developmental plasticity derive from this model.

Conclusions

One method to test the future of a construct like psychological distance is to ask how it stands up with respect to a variety of models. In this section of this chapter current behavioral models were presented and questions were posed that contrast proximal with distal causes of behavior and pose ways to account for behavioral variability. It appears that each of these models of learning and development reflects distance-related questions, although the models vary in the specific questions they address. Further, it appears that the issues each model addresses together with the issues addressed by each of the other models actually provide a more comprehensive understanding of processes involved in individual functioning and change than any one model can independently.

In an effort to delineate more specifically the ways in which psychological distance can be discussed as a construct for describing change, the next section of this chapter focuses on the way in which psychological distance begins to inform a discussion of psychological distance as a broad framework for conceptualizing and undertaking further study of individual variability. Specifically, each of the chapters included in this volume is used to illustrate both the breadth of the construct and its application across a variety of domains and aspects of functioning.

PSYCHOLOGICAL DISTANCE AS A
DEVELOPMENTAL CONSTRUCT

Psychological distance, as a developmental construct, draws attention to both the cognitive and ecological aspects of problem solving. Psychological distance refers to the way in which the individual equilibrates and represents information for him- or herself. Psychological distance also refers to socially shared cognition in that it is the way in which the individual engages the classes of objects, events, or ideas and the way in which others perceive and respond to this engagement. In fact, these two aspects of distancing are coordinated in the sense that they affect and inform each other. In each the focus is on the psychological distance that an individual comes to identify as a challenge, whether this challenge is facilitated by another or is self-generated.

As the chapters in the present volume suggest, psychological distance is universal. It influences problem solving across intrapersonal, interpersonal, academic, and artistic domains. It involves the self, the family, peers, the school, teachers, objects, events, and ideas. It also appears to have no cultural boundaries. In all cases, those encountering a problem must take an active role to resolve it. This involves distancing themselves from the problem in such a way that they can act on it. Recognition of conflict (e.g., novel information, a difficulty with a friend, the need to delay gratification) leads individuals to use and/or generate distancing strategies to resolve discrepancy. These strategies, in turn, result in a changed understanding of that situation or concept. Distancing strategies are not a tangible or factual set of concepts that can be taught or absorbed passively. Instead, each individual must construct an understanding of the concept him- or herself, possibly through observation, imitation, or guided interaction with others. These "others" may be peers, adults (teachers or parents), or even symbol systems such as models or media forms (e.g., photographs, pictures, video screens, television, radio, print).

Furthermore, the individual needs to be aware that there is a conflict before he or she can respond to it. Even an infant's response to novelty suggests that recognition of the conflict which novelty represents took place (see Kagan & Snidman, this volume). In fact, it appears that it is only when the individual is aware of conflict that he or she can respond to it. Such awareness, however, is often substantially facilitated through interaction with others. Shantz (this volume) reports that children, for example, seldom understand arguments and fights as more than a part of their lives. They seldom understand that they significantly alter their long-term relationship with others. She was able to get the children to reconstruct these conflicts during interviews by asking them to say what they had learned from their conflicts. The very process of having the children think back to the conflict provided them with the ability to understand the conflict in a different way. Presumably, the process of asking children to reconstruct past experiences enabled them to be more adept at social functioning than they were prior to the interview.

Certainly the process of actively bringing a task to students' awareness is basic to current research efforts in metacognition. Most such efforts, however, have been limited to students' school work in subjects such as mathematics and reading. In contrast, Okagaki and Sternberg's (this volume) PIFS curriculum is designed to draw students' attention to the interpersonal and intrapersonal dimensions of their schooling. The focus of this curriculum is based on the assumption that because the domains of intrapersonal and interpersonal functioning are not typically articulated subjects of study in school, students do not develop the reflective and contemplative capabilities necessary to succeeding in them. Ironically, from a clinical perspective, both intrapersonal and interpersonal knowledge are prerequisites for success in traditional school subjects. As Okagaki and Sternberg report, identification of strategies for acting successfully within intrapersonal and interpersonal domains introduces the students to a language for describing these domains—a language for describing the distance between what they know and could know about their social functioning. This calls students' (and teachers') attention to possibilities for how they might engage their classwork differently—information that the students (and teachers) in their studies did not generate for themselves.

A further effect of what Watson and Fischer (this volume) have labeled social priming, or current experience, is found in their work assessing children's ability to understand changes in family roles as a function of divorce. In these studies, they interviewed children about role relationships in the family. While the effect of asking the children about roles was presumably the same for children from divorced families and children from intact families, they found a significant impact of social priming on the level of the children's thinking about roles. They report that highly emotional and personal conflicts such as divorce focus children's attention on the discrepancy in their situation and the questions about roles posed by the experimenter. Thus, the children reorganized their previous understanding of roles as a function of their experience of changed roles in the family.

Skill theory (Fischer, 1980) provides a base from which to consider further to what extent the impact of prior experience leads to more detailed and synthetic understanding of, say, roles in the family, or, instead, regresses in relation to discrepancy. Watson and Fischer's findings suggest that both skill level and emotion influence the child's level of representational competence (the ability to comprehend the equivalence of various modes of representation) and their ability to regulate their emotions. Experience appears to provide a scaffold for increased representational competence. Those children whose parents were divorced were more likely to struggle with alternative notions of role ascription than were children from intact families. On the other hand, whether this experience led to skills in terms of role ascription was dependent on the level of skill the child had. With less skill, the emotional impact of the divorce depressed performance; with more skill, the emotional impact of the divorce increased performance. Such data suggest that the discrepancies that an individual is able to perceive are linked to how developed that individual's representational competence is.

Similarly, DeLoache (this volume) describes young children's emerging understanding of miniature models as a kind of developmental readiness. As she points out, abstraction is necessary to developed thought and the possibility of change. In order to understand models and what they stand for as a symbol, children must achieve psychological distance from the object, and represent it as two dimensional. In achieving psychological distance, the child assumes a dual orientation to the model/concept, which involves understanding it both in terms of what it is and what it represents. This achievement, however, involves many successive rerepresentations prior to the one that can be observed as reflecting this dual orientation.

The real issue, in some sense, is whether individuals perceive the discrepancies that are inherent in their present situation and to what extent they meet the expectations that others have for them in this regard. As Valsiner and van der Veer's (this volume) discussion of Vygotsky's thinking about this process of "growing through" makes clear, it is reasonably easy to observe the presence of well-formed psychological functions. It is nearly impossible to directly observe those that are only approximations of a final form. In some sense, individuals can be described as always in the process of growing through. There is always psychological distance between what they know and what they have yet to understand.

It appears also, for example, that the presence of psychological distance is not always a sufficient condition for change. McCall and Kratzer's study (this volume) of underachievers suggests that their lack of persistence in the face of challenges, lack of self-confidence, and fear of failure are the result of inadequate social distancing experiences. By this they mean that underachievers have either not been aware that conflicts were present or for some reason could not respond to such challenges. They appear to lack an understanding of the reciprocity of relationship, whether this is with peers, parents, or schools.

Certainly, Wertsch and Bivens (this volume) underscore the importance of children's participation in interaction for developing crucial representational abilities. Through social interaction with both adults and peers, children are forced to reexamine their own concepts in contrast with those of others. The notion of calling attention to conflict through distancing is typically an effective strategy for helping students in the process of developing conceptual understanding. This process eventually enables them to shift from dependence on other-regulation to self-regulation. Presumably, the challenges or conflicts to which, for example, the underachiever is responding are at a level of discrepancy that is optimal for him or her. It appears to be the mismatch of the expectations of the institutional, familial, and social others that are not met. At this time, as McCall and Kratzer point out, the literature is far from conclusive about who as an underachiever will respond eventually to social pressures and expectations and why this occurs. It may be, for example, that underachievement requires specific kinds of distancing for change to take place.

Sigel (this volume) does suggest that there is a kind of responsibility shared by participants (the child and the text, the child and an adult other, the child and peer others, etc.) in creating, or calling attention to, psychological distance. As he points out, distancing strategies affect children's intellectual and social characteristics. Here distancing strategies refer to an individual's ability to understand the implications or alternative representations of a situation, conflict, or problem. Distancing techniques, however, also refer to an adult or expert others' use of questions, juxtaposition of texts, etc. to facilitate increased levels of representational competence among individuals. Thus, while the process of change is driven by the psychological distance to which one is ready to respond, it is not exclusively cognitive, nor primarily driven by adult instruction. Rather, as in the case of the underachievers, it seems that there may be a need to appreciate differences between individuals in terms of what comes to be understood as appropriate distancing, if that distance is to be linked with change.

In fact, as Mischel and Rodriqucz (this volume) report, the same psychological processes that allow for effective delay with preschool middle-class children also seem to apply to populations of high-risk children. Those children who know effective strategies for self-control are those who are more likely to exert self-control. They have also found that both children's knowledge of self-control strategies and the use of these strategies are reliably related to a range of adaptation and coping skills (see Rodriguez, Shoda, Mischel, & Wright, 1989). Here, the critical aspect of learning involved in self-control, for example, was not age of the individual, but rather a shared knowledge of the strategies—shared, that is, with the experimenter, an expert-other, the society, etc. At issue, then, is the question of who is in a position to decide what the psychological distance is for the learner and the question of what might be required to better assess the nature of psychological distance in the first place and the techniques to be employed in subsequently "adjusting" that distance. Clearly, calling attention to a conflict or problem does not always lead to change.

The means for distancing information may well influence what is perceived as a conflict and, in turn, the concepts that are being developed. Greenfield (this volume), for example, cites the role of cognitive socialization (influence of cultural tools on the development of skills for processing and communicating information) in the development of representational competence. She reports that the real-time nature of television and video games interferes with the reflective functions of distancing strategies, undermining more traditional aspects of representational competence. She points specifically to the player as both consumer and producer of the environment. In this case, the player contributes to creating challenges or conflicts on which he or she then works. The dual roles of the player as both player and producer essentially eliminate more conventional notions about using distancing techniques for increased representational competence—at least for the already skilled person.

Representational competence is generally characterized by the individual's move from a concrete understanding of the object as object to an understanding that includes implications for that object such as anticipating what could happen to it, thinking back (hindsight) to what it could be, and/or transformation into a symbol (cf. Sigel, 1986). Given Greenfield's findings, it may be more accurate to think about psychological distance, especially as it relates to intervention, as having a content that is predictable—thus enabling the use of distancing techniques. At more sophisticated levels of understanding (such as that of the video game players), psychological distance might be more accurately described as involving both unpredictable as well as predictable content. Not only does knowledge contribute to how psychological distance is perceived and responded to, but it appears to influence the nature of the content, and as a consequence the change(s), that can be facilitated, or at least how such facilitation might occur. For the novice, distancing techniques, or methods that might be employed to push the individual to reconceptualize his or her understanding of a class of objects or events, may well be optimal. For the more informed learner, distancing techniques may need to be individualized: informed by the particulars of content and the specifics of the individual's prior questions and learning in the given domain. It may also be the case that for the skilled individual, psychological distance is more likely to be self-generated than facilitated by another, given that it is at this point the individual has internalized a mode of resolving and posing discrepancies for him or herself.

The place of individual differences in a discussion of a construct about change is also raised, albeit differently, by Kagan and Snidman's (this volume) study of children's temperament. They report that inhibited and uninhibited characteristics appear to be unchanged influences on functioning over time. Findings such as this provide a lens for further considering what is optimally discrepant (Hunt, 1961) for both inhibited and uninhibited individuals, in turn providing information about how intervention using distancing might be provided to facilitate further conceptual development. It raises other questions about the nature of challenges or conflicts as well. Furthermore, it suggests that psychological distance refers to the possibility of change, but not necessarily to probability of change as a function of environment.

As Bronfenbrenner (this volume) points out, acknowledgement of the reciprocity of the individual and his or her environment "not only allows for, but even anticipates *synergistic effects* as a predominant characteristics of human development" (p. 20). Rather than proceeding with the assumption that the processes influencing development operate in some uniform way, regardless of the characteristics of the person or the environment, he admonishes us to recognize the reciprocity of these processes in shaping human development and psychological outcomes. At this time, then, it appears that the role of psychological distance in development is, at very least, dependent on how much adjustment both the individual and his or her environment can make, which is, in turn, probably related to age and/or pathology.

FROM MODELS TO PARADIGMS

In the first section of this chapter, it was concluded that the distancing-inspired questions of each model, if undertaken by researchers using the other models, would serve to clarify the way in which psychological distance contributes to and accounts for variability in behavior, or change. In the second section of this chapter, the discussion of psychological distance as presented in each of the other chapters in this volume was used to provide a more synthetic description of psychological distance as a developmental construct. The next step in going from the construct level of analysis to models that utilize the construct in the context of various research problems is to proceed to a third level of analysis. Thus, in this section of the chapter, it is suggested that a broad framework such as psychological distance that builds on multiple perspectives of an event, issue, etc., offers a rich interpretation of data—an interpretation necessary both to account for individual variability in behavior and to address problems that extend beyond the confines of the laboratory.

Distance as a Relative Construct

In chapter 1, Cocking and Renninger describe psychological distance as a theoretical construct used to explain individual psychological growth. In that chapter, development of the individual is contrasted with development that is instigated or mediated through social processes. In this analysis, therefore, distance could be construed as a dichotomy between proximal, intrapsychic, and the more distal, interpsychic growth. Cocking and Renninger further suggest that development, rather than being reduced to a dichotomy, spans a continuum in which cognitive representational processes and understanding of referents are relatively proximal or distal to the individual, just as the social agents that or who assist in the distancing process could be regarded as more or less proximal or distal. From this perspective, then, the distancing construct can be thought of in terms of proximal or distal relations of particular variables to the individual. This framework is a level of analysis separate from the models from which specific research hypotheses are derived.

Two recent accounts point to the need for psychological literature to address the implications of the relative proximal–distal relations of variables. Flavell, Flavell, Green, and Korfmacher (1990) have addressed this concern in the relationship between young children's cognitive development and what they think about their represented worlds. Specifically, Flavell et al. have asked questions about young children's understanding of what they view on television. They suggest that previous studies have made the tacit assumption that children distinguish between the proximal images on a TV screen and the distal referents they portray (1990, p. 401). They suggest, further, that the representation and the things represented can be analyzed along a continuum, which in this volume we term the distancing construct. Some of the research models in this volume characterize the representation–referent disparity as a discrepancy model. The point is that the development of symbolic functioning studied within a model that contrasts appearances (internal interpretations) with reality can also be analyzed along the proximal–distal dimension of the distancing construct. In this case, Flavell et al. state that young children (3-year-olds) whose attention is focused on the salient, proximal image of the TV screen can tell you a great deal about what they see, and at the same time, because they know little about mental representation, they regard the stimulus as real and palpable, rather than as a representation of a distal referent. Most importantly, Flavell et al. found that the specific context defined the reality for the child's answers with respect to the reality of images and their referents. That is to say, context-related and context-free queries in child research constitute a variable that can be cast along the psychological distance dimension. In this case, proximal interpretations of events are literal. Such findings are consistent with Luria's (1932) classic studies of analogical reasoning in which it was found that specific instances and personal experience of events overrode generalizable principles based on logic.

A second example of issues in the psychological literature that need to be addressed at a different level of analysis is the conflictual findings between comparative cognitive research and indigenous cognition (Cocking, in press). Performance variables, cited in the previous chapter (Cocking & Renninger, Chapter 1, this volume) have been shown to yield differences among different cultural groups because of the performer's familiarity with the task or the materials (Serpell, 1979; Baratz, 1969). In comparative psychology different cultural groups are asked to perform on identical tasks, presumably as a methodological control. Indigenous cognitive studies, by contrast, require the experimenter to determine the the specific cognitive ability that is to be measured and then to utilize a task appropriate to that culture. The methodological control in these studies is in terms of meaningfulness of the task. For the purposes of this chapter, however, the difference between these two approaches to understanding cultural differences in cognition can be analyzed in terms of psychological distance. The dependent variable of the comparative psychologist, according to the indigenous model, is psychologically remote or distant to the meaning system of the performer.

Ecological Validity and Psychological Distance

One resolution of the differences among models or methodologies is to adopt a different level of analysis. Taking the case of the relations between representational skills and a cognitive task, one could use the following model to represent the relations among the component skills and a proximal variable under study. Figure 2.1 represents how a developmental psychologist might look at relations between the component skills of an Anglo child asked to represent an experience by drawing a picture (Goodnow, 1977) or an African child to build a three-dimensional model (Serpell, 1979). The individual component variables each have a relation to the proximal variable. Further, each has an empirically derived relation to every other variable.

This same analysis can be used to address how the components relate to the same variable when it is cast as a distal variable, again looking for the individual relations to the distal variable and for the interrelationship among the vari-

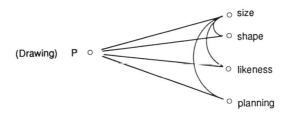

FIG. 2.1. Model used to represent relations among component skills and a proximal variable.

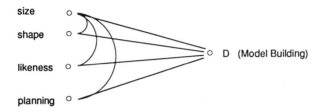

FIG. 2.2.   Model used to represent relations among component skills
and a distal variable.

ables. In the previous example, it this would mean looking at the child's performance on both the proximal and distal tasks, such that Anglo children would
both draw and build three-dimensional models, and the African child would be
asked to perform both tasks as well (Fig. 2.2).

The two components of the model, taken together, give an overall picture of
the relation for the same variable when regarded as a proximal and as a distal
variable. (Proximal and distal are terms that are relative to the performer, so for
the Anglo child in Serpell's studies the P of Fig. 2.2 becomes D to denote its representational status relative to drawing.) This overall relation between the proximal and distal functioning of the same variable is what Brunswik (1947/1956)
called ecological validity. By addressing the subjective and objective meanings
of a variable, context is both defined by its relation to the event and is accounted
for as a contribution to performance (Fig. 2.3).

Examples from the chapters that follow illustrate how different models have
been utilized to account for the construct defined in this volume as psychological
distance. The construct is an abstraction apart from the models and the research
generated by the models reported in these chapters. We are further suggesting
that the individual chapters, taken together, comprise a broader understanding of
a psychological phenomenon that accounts for differences in understanding;
differences in performance; differences in encoding, storage, and retrieval of
information; and differences that relate in the broadest sense to information
processing and problem-solving. The overall picture that we are attempting to
structure is based on cognitive, social, educational, linguistic, and a variety of
human performance domains. The interrelations of mediating variables, relations
between mediating and dependent variables, and the overall relations between
objective and subjective realities are made richer by looking across these individ-

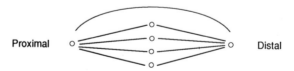

FIG. 2.3.   Model used to represent relations among component skills
and the same variable regarded as both a proximal and a distal variable.

ual models with the particular organizing construct that is the topic of this book. Further, we believe that by considering another framework that integrates these diverse domains and performances, psychological distance emerges as an important variable in accounting for both competence and performance differences in human growth and understanding.

REFERENCES

Baratz, J. C. (1969). A bidialectical task for determining language proficiency in economically disadvantaged children. *Child Development, 40*(3), 889–901.

Brunswik, E. (1956). *Perception and the representative design of psychological experiments.* Berkeley, CA: University of California Press. (Original work published 1947)

Cocking, R. R. (in press). Research models of continuities and discontinuities. In P. M. Greenfield & R. R. Cocking (Eds.), *The development of the minority child: Culture in- and out-of-context.* Hillsdale, NJ: Lawrence Erlbaum Associates.

Fischer, K. W. (1980). A theory of cognitive development: The control and construction of hierarchies of skills. *Psychological Review, 87,* 477–531.

Flavell, J. H., Flavell, E. R., Green, F. L., & Korfmacher, J. E. (1990). Do young children think of television images as pictures or real objects? *Journal of Broadcasting & Electronic Media, 4,* 399–419.

Goodall, J. (1986). *The chimpanzees of Gombe: Patterns of behavior.* Cambridge, MA: Belknap Press of Harvard University Press.

Goodnow, J. J. (1977). *Children drawing.* Cambridge, MA: Harvard University Press.

Hunt, J. M. (1961). *Intelligence and experience.* New York: Ronald Press.

McClelland, J. L., & Rummelhart, D. E. (1985). Distributed memory and the representation of general and specific information. *Journal of Experimental Psychology: General, 114,* 159–188.

McClintock, M. K. (1988). *Pheromones behavior and the regulation of fertility.* National Institute of Mental Health Report (Grant MH-47188). Unpublished manuscript.

Luria, A. R. (1932). *The nature of human conflicts: Or emotion, conflict and will.* New York: Liveright.

Piaget, J. (1954). The construction of reality in the child. (M. Cook, Trans.). New York: Basic Books.

Piaget, J. (1954). *The construction of reality.* New York: Basic Books.

Rodriquez, M. L., Shoda, Y., Mischel, W., & Wright, J. (1989 April). *Delay of gratification and children's social behavior in natural settings.* Paper presented at the meeting of the Eastern Psychological Association, Boston.

Serpell, R. (1979). How specific are perceptual skills?: A cross-cultural study of pattern representation. *British Journal of Psychology, 70,* 365–380.

Sigel, I. E. (1970). The distancing hypothesis: A causal hypothesis for acquisition of representational thought. In M. R. Jones (Ed.), *Miami symposium on the prediction of behavior 1968: Effects of early experience* (pp. 99–118). Coral Gables, FL: University of Miami Press.

Sigel, I. E. (1986). Early social experience and the development of representational competence. In W. Fowler (Ed.), *Early experience and the development of competence* (pp. 49–65). *New Directions for Child Development, No. 32.* San Francisco: Jossey-Bass.

Sternberg, R. J., & Wagner, R. K. (1989). Individual differences in practical knowledge and its acquisition. In P. Ackerman, R. J. Sternberg, & R. Glaser (Eds.), *Learning and individual differences* (pp. 255–278). New York: Freeman.

3

The Encoding of Distance: The Concept of the Zone of Proximal Development and Its Interpretations

Jaan Valsiner
Developmental Psychology Program, University of North Carolina

René van der Veer
Vakgroep Algemene Pedagogiek, Rijksuniversiteit Leiden,
The Netherlands

All development involves the construction of distance between the present and the past, and overcoming the distance from the present to the future. It is usually that latter process—the constant forward move from what can be known in the present to what cannot yet (but might) become known in the next moment that has been difficult for psychologists to conceptualize. This theoretical weakness seems to become increasingly widespread in contemporary psychology with its accentuated empiricistic emphasis on inductive knowledge assembly, which is not paralleled by an equal focus on rigor of deductive argumentation. In the theoretical realm of contemporary psychology the tyranny of eclecticism governs, which increases the imminent danger of psychology becoming a non-science at best, and non-sense at worst (see Cairns, 1986; Smedslund, 1979; Toulmin & Leary, 1985). Ironically, extensive proliferation of empiricism in psychology leads psychologists to worse (rather than better) possibilities to understand psychological phenomena (see Thorngate, 1990).

There are very few theoretical constructs in the active use of psychologists in the present day that can help us to conceptualize the process of development from the present to the future. It is therefore not surprising that the rather metaphoric concept that Lev Vygotsky brought into the focus of attention of psychological discourse in early 1930s, and that has become widely known in contemporary psychological discourse as "zone of proximal development" (Cole, John-Steiner, Scribner, & Souberman, 1978, p. 86) or as "zone of potential development" (Simon & Simon, 1963, p. 31), has been captivating the minds of many a contemporary researcher. Indeed, that concept gives hope for understanding the issue of development as it takes place at the intersection of the person and the social world (Laboratory of Comparative Human Cognition, 1983; Lee, 1987;

Minick, 1987; Wertsch, 1984). It seems to match well with the ever-louder voices in psychology that claim to fit under the "ecological," "interactionist," "transactionist," "constructivist," "deconstructionist," "organismic," and "systemic" labels, each of which denotes a denomination that is trying to establish its social legitimacy within the convent of science.

The concept of "zone of proximal development" poses a number of theoretical problems that need to be addressed quite separately from the ongoing social discourse that tries to fit a multitude of approaches under the somewhat mystical umbrella of that concept. First, it entails a reference to a "zone"—essentially a field-theoretical concept in an era of psychology that has largely forgotten the gargantuan efforts by Kurt Lewin to adopt topology for purposes of psychological discourse. Second, the understanding of "development" has been highly varied in contemporary psychological discourse, ranging from loosely formulated ideas about "age-group differences" (or "age effects") to narrowly definable structural transformation of organisms in irreversible time and within context (e.g., Brent, 1984; Valsiner, 1987, 1989). Finally—to complicate the matters even further—contemporary psychologists have to wrestle with the qualifier of "proximal" (or "potential", or "nearest"), as it is the connecting link between the field-theoretic "zone" and the concept of "development" in this complex term.

The goal of this chapter is to analyze the different forms that the culturally organized (constrained) reasoning of psychologists at different time periods has given to the concept of "zone of proximal development." We will start this analysis by outlining the history of the concept, from the time (1932/1933) when Vygotsky began to use it on the basis of the ideas expressed in international psychology of the time (Vygotsky, 1933/1935, p. 119). In order to contrast Vygotsky's version of the concept with its later transformations, we will use the abbreviation ZBR (from Russian: *zona blizhaishego razvitia*) throughout this chapter. As we proceed to analyze the contemporary redefinitions of the concept, we will use the favorite abbreviations of different authors who have used the concept (e.g., ZPD, Zo-ped).

THE HISTORY OF THE CONCEPT:
VYGOTSKY AND PAEDOLOGY

The beginnings of Vygotsky's use of the ZBR concept constitute an interesting story in themselves. In 1931, the laboratory in Moscow at the Academy of Communist Education where Vygotsky's group had been involved in their empirical research program on cultural-historical theory was closed under increasing ideological pressure (see Joravsky, 1989; Valsiner, 1988 for analyses of the social context of psychology in the U.S.S.R. in 1931). This led to the dispersion of the group of empirical investigators, some of whom moved to Kharkov as a break-away "Kharkov School" of "activity theory" (e.g., Leontiev, Zaporozhets); others found places at different other institutes in Moscow. Vygotsky, while staying mainly in Moscow, took up lecturing at the Leningrad State Pedagogical Institute (see Van der Veer & Valsiner, 1991). This lecturing was mainly associated with the discipline of paedology (known as "child study movement" in American literature), all the more so that Vygotsky had redefined that discipline for himself as that of an interdisciplinary synthetic science of development (Vygotsky, 1931a, 1931b, 1931c). His vision for paedology entailed the emergence of qualitatively new developmental science with its own methodology, on the basis of different disciplines that had been investigating issues of children. Vygotsky was actively involved in the organization of paedology in the Soviet Union. He was at the time a professor of paedology at the Moscow State Pedagogical Institute and at the Moscow Medical Institute. Vygotsky's role in the paedology in the U.S.S.R. in the early 1930s was prominent. This important position in paedology later served as the ideological pretext for blacklisting his work (e.g., Rudneva, 1937). The shadow of paedology remained as a negative ideological factor in discrediting Vygotsky's work even in the 1950s—his involvement with the discipline needed to be explained away as insignificant occasional "error" at the reintroduction of his work to Soviet psychology (Kolbanovskii, 1956).

A detailed analysis of the emergence and use of the concept of ZBR is given elsewhere (Van der Veer & Valsiner, 1991, chapter XII). Here we trace the specific ways in which Vygotsky's previous development of theory (the "cultural-historical theory") and his new concentration on theoretical paedology, together with its applications in educational contexts, gave rise to his use of the ZBR concept.

ROOTS OF ZBR IN THE "CULTURAL-HISTORICAL THEORY"

It can be argued that the logic of development of Vygotsky's cultural-historical theory led to the need to conceptualize the developmental processes that operate in the domain of present-to-future transformation of the functioning structure of the psychological system. Different investigations (Leontiev, 1932; Luria, 1928; Vygotski, 1929) within the cultural-historical framework, together with the root idea of the person "freeing" him or herself from the confines of the given situation through sign-based mediation and instrumental action, had demonstrated the possibilities of children's further progress beyond their present level of psychological functioning. However, the actual processes by which these possibilities become realities in ontogeny were not yet charted. It may be reasonable to characterize the cultural-historical focus on the role of mediation of psychological processes in 1927–1931 as primarily microgenetic in its emphasis. Most of the empirical studies that are known from that period were based on microgenetic experimentation and involved comparisons of age groups (mostly cross-sectional in nature). Since Vygotsky's cultural-historical ideas emerged in the context of his fascination with Wolfgang Köhler's experiments on problem solving in primates and those of Jean Piaget in children (e.g., Vygotsky & Luria, 1930), it is not surprising that the microgenetic focus dominated over the on-togenetic one in the analysis of development. It was only at around the time when paedology became the dominant theme in Vygotsky's own thinking that the need for ontogenetic analysis of how different psychological processes became re-structured (i.e., his emphasis on "crises in development" at different ages—Vygotsky, 1933/1984, pp. 318–339, 368–385).

The major link between cultural-historical theory and paedology was Vygotsky's manuscript, *The history of development of higher psychological functions* (Vygotsky, 1931/1983). The central issue that framed this linkage was the possibility (afforded by the "method of double stimulation"—the main con-tribution of the cultural-historical theory to methodology) to study the emergence of "free will" in ontogenesis (Vygotsky, 1931/1983, pp. 290–291). The issue of intentional control of psychological functions had been the central divider of the "higher" and "lower" levels of psychological organization; now Vygotsky set himself the task of tracing the synthesis of higher processes prospectively in ontogeny. Of course, in his sociogenetic perspective, the meaning of "free will" of the individual was set up in a context-bound way—emphasizing the internal reconstruction of externally given social suggestions. That internal reconstruc-tion takes the form of the child's construction of psychological tools to be capable of volitional management. The free will (which actually is "free" only in a limited sense, as it involves the recognition of the limits of use of already developed action strategies) indicates the possibility for the child to transcend the structure of the given social setting. The developing child becomes increasingly free in the sense of going beyond the given setting in children's play, adolescents' fantasizing (Vygotsky, 1931e, p. 455), and social interaction with others (Vygotsky, 1931d, pp. 16–17).

This developing context-bound free will is socially instructed by way of the rearing efforts of the "social others" with whom the child is interdependent. These efforts are informed by the goals these other persons surrounding the child have set themselves. The crucial issue for Vygotsky in 1931 became to which psychological functions—the ones that can be observed already to be present, or the ones that are in the process of emerging—should the efforts of "will-rearing" be directed. His answer (Vygotsky, 1931/1983, p. 295) was clear—at the latter and not at the former. It is at this juncture in Vygotsky's thinking that his dialectical theoretical core of understanding of development meets his applied focus on the teaching–learning process (as it guides the child toward overcoming the present state of being, through a process of relying on presently existing psychological functions in the service of developing novel ones). Similar ideas were expressed by Vygotsky's collaborators in different contexts. Zaporozhets

(1930, p. 232) criticized IQ-testing methods for their "blindness" to study the process of further intellectual development of the child, and Luria explained the same idea through the use of neurophysiological language:

> The rearer is not compelled to wait until the maturing nervous system leads to the overcoming of the early diffuse nature of the neurodynamic processes—he is confronted with the possibility to include these neurodynamic processes in the highest psychological systems of behavior, and through that re-organize these [processes] not from "below" but from "above". (Luria, 1931, p. 28)

In order to understand the emergence of the ZBR use in Vygotsky's discourse, it is important to bear in mind the consistent emphasis on developing psychological processes that form the holistic dynamic structure of the child's personality. Vygotsky's effort to explain human ontogeny led him to bring together the developmental theory and traditions of paedology. This duality of focus—on developmental theorizing and paedological (test-based "diagnostic") applications—was obvious already in 1931. In the same manuscript where the basic idea of social rearing of not-yet-developed processes is expressed, we can trace the roots of thinking that later serve as illustrations for his ZBR concept (chapter XIV, "The problem of cultural age," Vygotsky, 1931/1983: the distance between individual and socially assisted performance).

Vygotsky argued against the "measurement of intelligence" by way of documenting the psychological (mental) functions that have already finished their course of development (1931/1983, pp. 308–309). Using the comparison with a clinician who on the basis of observable symptoms can diagnose the underlying causes of a disease, he explained the need of mental testing to go beyond mere documentation of the observable symptoms to the explication of the underlying causal system. Indeed, the traditional definition of intelligence by way of what intelligence tests measure would equal a physician's statement that the patient has influenza because the thermometer measures the body temperature to be above normal. Psychology has had a long history of semantic transformation of its measurement-based descriptive concepts into causal concepts attributed to be "behind" these measurements (latent variables or traits). Vygotsky recognized that theoretical impasse well before he started to use the ZBR concept. Ironically, as we see later, that concept itself has undergone transformation from a descriptive to a causal one since the 1930s.

To summarize: By about 1931, Vygotsky had reached the theoretical necessity to conceptualize the "making of the future" in human ontogeny. All the ideas that would later play relevant roles in the use of the ZBR concept were already in use in his thinking: the need to concentrate on the social facilitation of developing functions, the role of play and fantasy in helping the person to "go beyond the present," and the relevance of social suggestions and interaction in the internalization process. However, Vygotsky had been playing with these ideas without a unifying concept—and it is that function that the term of ZBR seems to have performed in Vygotsky's own history of ideas.

THE BEGINNINGS OF THE ZBR CONCEPT IN VYGOTSKY'S DISCOURSE

Some time in 1932–1933, Vygotsky started to use the ZBR notion. Because most of Vygotsky's creativity in these years took the form of numerous redundant and poorly survived lecture stenograms/notes (rather than completed manuscripts), we may be never able to document the exact earliest use of the term. It is clear that he used ZBR explicitly during 1933 in his various lectures and presentations in paedology.

The earliest documented mention of ZBR can be found in a lecture given in Moscow at Epshtein Institute of Experimental Defectology on March, 17, 1933. The title of the published version of that oral speech—"On the paedological analysis of the pedagogical process" (Vygotsky, 1933/1935, pp. 116–134)— reflects the context in which the use of that concept came into being. It reinstates the major theoretical idea of timing instructional intervention in conjunction with the first mention of the concept (in conjunction with expression of indebtedness to the work of Ernst Meumann):

> Investigations led paedologists to the idea that one should determine at least a double level of child development, namely: first, the level of actual development of the child, i.e., that what already matured to the present day; and, secondly—the zone of his nearest development, i.e., those processes in the further development of these same functions which, as they are not mature today, still are on their way already, are already growing through and already tomorrow will bear fruit; already tomorrow transfer to the level of actual development. (Vygotsky, 1933/1935, p. 120)

It becomes clear from this very first verifiable mention of the ZBR concept by Vygotsky that his use of the term was a mediational device for bringing together different lines of his ideas. The botanical metaphor of "growing through" indicates his focus on the opposition of the presently observable (already formed) and presently not yet observable (not yet formed) functions.

Further crucial textual evidence for Vygotsky's synthesis of the structure of developmental processes with the issues of paedological diagnostics of the "levels of development" comes from the recently published version (Vygotsky, 1933/1984, p. 264) of his lecture at the Leningrad Pedagogical Institute on March 23, 1933. Most probably, his oral presentation on that date was turned into a written text in late 1933 or early 1934 (as the first mention of this text is dated at 1934—see Vygotsky, 1934, p. 323).

In the first part of this text, Vygotsky emphasized the qualitative structural reorganization (dialectical synthesis) nature of the developmental process. He described the course of child development as characterized by periods of calm or uneventful advancement that are separated from one another by times of crises. The latter are the relevant periods for development, as the ontogenetic progression takes a catastrophic form and resembles "revolutionary breakthroughs" (Vygotsky, 1933/1984, p. 249). The exact beginning and end points of the crises cannot be noticed in any exact way, but the periods during which the actual transformation of the psychological structure take place can be pinpointed because of their seemingly disorganized and chaotic nature. Six crisis periods in child development were outlined by Vygotsky: those of newborn age, 1st, 3rd, 7th, 13th, and 17th year. It is during these periods that the emergence of higher levels of psychological organization take place. Vygotsky was always ready to view developmental change as a process of dialectical synthesis (see Van der Veer & Valsiner, 1991), and the crisis periods in ontogeny guided him to look for relevant developmental phenomena.

It is in his description of the dialectical synthesis process during crisis periods that Vygotsky elaborates upon the idea of unity of evolution and involution (taken from J. M. Baldwin), which he explicitly alluded to in numerous other presentations:

> The progressive development of child's personality, continuous building of the new that was so clearly expressed in all stable age periods, as if fade away or stop during crises periods. The extinction and contraction, disintegration and decomposition of the previously formed processes that characterized the child of the given age move to the frontal plane. The child during the critical periods does not so much acquire, but loses what was attained before. (Vygotsky, 1933/1984, p. 251)

The process involution dominates over that of evolution during the age periods of crises. However, each crisis has its own culmination point (*kulminatsionnaia tochka*) that is the locus at which the dialectical synthesis is accomplished. Vygotsky's idea of crisis periods in human ontogeny as expressed in 1933 is continuous with the ideas of qualitative breakthrough points in a reader's reaction to literary texts in his writings of the years 1916–1925 (see Van der Veer & Valsiner, 1991). What is clearly different from his earlier application of the idea of dialectical synthesis, however, is a consistent emphasis on the structure of processes of a psychological kind that are assumed to become linked with one another in novel ways at the crisis periods, thus leading to the emergence of a novel (qualitatively higher) structure of psychological functions. The psychological processes (which were not charted out in explicit detail by Vygotsky) were considered to form two "lines": those that "were more or less immediately linked with main novel formations" were called central lines of development, while other (particularistic) processes of development at a given age were delegated to adjunct status (Vygotsky, 1933/1984, p. 257). The same psychological function— speech, for instance—may play an adjunct role in development in infancy, become central in early childhood, and again become adjunct in the following age periods. The actual dialectical synthesis at crisis periods leads to the reorganization of the structure of central and adjunct psychological functions in ways that give rise to novel functions on the basis of loss and reorganization of the previous ones. Unfortunately, Vygotsky never gave a concrete example of how this dialectical synthesis takes place, given a specific structure of psychological functions. Instead, he moved to emphasize the role of the social situation of development for each qualitative transition. If we can know the social situation of development at the beginning of a developmental period, then we can proceed to study how in that situation new psychological functions come into being (Vygotsky, 1933/1984a, pp. 258–259). Surely that emphasis opened wide the possibility of discussing the importance of social assistance in the development of the individual child. The immediate leap by Vygotsky from the issues of structural transformation of psychological functions to the emphasis (but no elaboration) of the role of the social situation of development can be viewed as the beginning of all the later confusion that the ZBR and ZPD concepts have had to be subjected to in scientific discourse.

Finally, Vygotsky brought the ZBR concept into his argumentation—but in conjunction with "applied issues" (1933/1984, pp. 260–268). It is here that the "diagnosis of the level of development" becomes clearly linked with an emphasis on heterochrony in the development of different psychological functions (1933/1984, p. 262). Because the time points of the final formation of different psychological functions differ, at any given moment some of these processes are nearing their respective moments of formation, while others have already become formed. The task for diagnosis of development was defined by Vygotsky here in terms similar to his lecture in Moscow the week before—as the analysis of not-yet-emerged but now-developing processes (aside from the already actualized ones). It is from the position of this methodological imperative that Vygotsky continued to talk about the ZBR, linking it with the issues of teaching–learning as a practical application of that imperative (1933/1984, p. 265).

The third relevant presentation involving the introduction of the ZBR concept took place 2 months later—when Vygotsky gave a presentation on the development of everyday and "scientific" concepts at Leningrad Paedological Institute on May 20, 1933 (Vygotsky, 1933/1935, pp. 96–115). The topics covered in that presentation parallel the ones that have been available for quite a while (Vygotsky, 1934, chapter 6; in English, Vygotsky, 1962, 1986, 1987). The main focus of the presentation was the issue of how school-learning-based "scientific concepts" are linked in their development with the "everyday" concepts (referring to the work of Shif, 1935). In that process, the "scientific" concepts that are introduced in school were claimed to run ahead of the development of everyday concepts, but at the same time be based on the latter. Hence it is important to fit the presentation of scientific concepts in school with the previous potential readiness (based on the development of everyday concepts) of the child—the scientific concepts are introduced from above to reorganize the present structure of everyday concepts that have developed previously from below—to paraphrase Luria's ideas reported before.

To summarize: Within the 2-month period (March–May 1933) Vygotsky was observed to pick up the concept of ZBR and use it actively in different contexts. In all of these uses the concept remained a descriptive one, marking the emphasis on the study of developing (as opposed to already developed) psychological functions. The need for a descriptive term to mediate that emphasis was already present in Vygotsky's cultural-historical thinking about paedology as the science of development. However, the label "paedology" was used in the Soviet Union at the time to denote a highly heterogeneous child study movement that had imported many of its methods from Europe and North America. It is in his disputes with his contemporary paedologists that the ZBR term was used extensively by Vygotsky for rhetorical purposes.

VYGOTSKY'S USES OF THE ZBR CONCEPT IN DIFFERENT CONTEXTS

If we consider Vygotsky's use of the ZBR concept as a rhetoric mediating device for his disputes with his contemporaries, it may become easier to understand why the use of this concept occurs in different contexts, and why there was never a clear effort to clarify the term in theoretical ways. In the final 15 months of his life, Vygotsky made frequent (but often passing) use of the ZBR concept. The extant texts of Vygotsky provide us with a potpourri of examples of the use of the ZBR concept. If we look back at the corpus of statements about ZBR that is available in Vygotsky's manuscripts and published work, three directions are discernible. First, ZBR was explained in the language of "difference score" between the "assisted" and "individual" achievement conditions (Vygotsky, 1933/1935; also detailed description of his examples in Van der Veer & Valsiner, 1991; Vygotsky, 1933/1984, pp. 244–268). Second (as a generalized extension of the first line), the emphasis in explaining ZBR was on the general (nonquantitative) difference between the child's capability in socially assisted contexts (Vygotsky, 1934, chapter 6; 1933/1935, pp. 3–19) and in individual ones (without the direct reference to the "difference score" notion). In both cases, however, these explanatory efforts were meant to communicate a major theoretical idea— child development is at any given time in the difficult-to-observe process of emergence, which is masked by (easily visible) intermediate outcomes (= actual level of development). It is easy to see how both the "difference score" and "social assistance" versions of the ZBR are reflections of the same process description of development that we outlined earlier. The first stems from Vygotsky's rhetorical effort to redirect paedologists' diagnostic efforts from the test-based analysis of outcomes of development to the estimation of the potentials of further development. The second is a practical issue of how to link the teaching–learning process with development in the context of schooling.

The third line in Vygotsky's use of the ZBR concept takes it out of the immediate social situation to the object-mediated world. In one of his lectures at

Leningrad Pedagogical Institute in 1933 devoted to play, Vygotsky claimed for play a status similar to teaching–learning in interdependence with development. Explicitly, he argued that play creates the ZBR:

> In play the child is always higher than his average age, higher than his usual everyday behavior; he is in play as if a head above himself. The play contains, in a condensed way, as if in the focus of a magnifying glass, all tendencies of development; the child in play as if tries to accomplish a jump above the level of his ordinary behavior.
>
> The relationship of play to development should be compared with that of teaching-learning to development. Changes of needs and consciousness of more general kind lie behind the play. Play is the resource of development and it creates the zone of nearest development. Action in the imaginary field, in imagined situation, construction of voluntary intention, the formation of the life-play, will motives—this all emerges in play and . . . makes it the nineth wave of preschool age development. (Vygotsky, 1933/1966, pp. 74–75)

The seeming discrepancy between the interpersonal nature of teaching–learning and largely individual focus of play as creators of the ZBR can be overcome simply by pointing out that Vygotsky was speaking about preschool-age children's development in the context of play, and of school-age children's development in conjunction with teaching–learning. However, this is a minor issue that may merely help us to organize the myriad of ideas that Vygotsky played with. More importantly, the equal role of play and teaching–learning in the creation of ZBR fits exactly with the general theoretical background (described earlier) on the basis of which Vygotsky moved on to the concept of ZBR. Because Vygotsky's main emphasis was on development of the structure of psychological functions, the different contextual conditions for that development come together in the domain of personal experience (*perezhivanie* in Russian—better translated as the process of experiencing and state of "living-through"). The notion of experience was suggested by Vygotsky as the unit of analysis in psychological theorizing about personality, in exact parallel to the use of word meanings as units of analysis of thinking (Vygotsky, 1933/1984, pp. 382–383). In the process of personal experience, the capability of a developing child to "raise above himself" under conditions of social assistance, and through "self-help" of rule- or role-play, become equivalent. Thus, the ZBR concept was used by Vygotsky to emphasize the process of construction of the future structure of the functions on the basis of the present experience by the child.

THE MECHANISM THAT CREATES ZBR: IMITATION

For Vygotsky, the use of the ZBR concept was descriptive rather than explanatory. Its use emphasized the need to conceptualize the causal system of development, which links the present with the future. ZBR was consistently used to remind paedologists about the need to proceed beyond the world of appearances (documentation of results of development) to analysis of proto-functions and mechanisms that lead their development. ZBR could not function in that explanatory role. Instead, Vygotsky turned to the idea of imitation and emphasized that this is the mechanism that underlies development (Vygotsky, 1933/1984, p. 263; 1933/1935, p. 49; 1933/1935, p. 109). Vygotsky argued that only human children are capable of imitation of others (in contrast to the apes studied by Wolfgang Köhler), and that the capability for imitation made it possible for ZBR to exist. In other terms, Vygotsky perceived the process of imitation as the mechanism of development.

It should be clarified here that the meaning of the term "imitation" was taken by Vygotsky in a wide sense that is close to James Mark Baldwin's "persistent imitation" concept (Vygotsky, 1935, p. 13; cf. Baldwin, 1892). That concept implies "imitation" of the (socially given) models beyond copying them (rather than merely producing an exact copy, at best). Thus, "persistent imitation" equals constructive experimentation with the given model, and its transformation into a novel form—both in actions directed toward the model and in the resulting internalization of understanding of the model.

If persistent imitation is the basic process that operates on the functions within the ZBR at any given time, then the three different categories of explanations of ZBR that Vygotsky gave in different places become united. Processes of imitation are involved in all cases—when the "difference score" notion is used, Vygotsky makes the point of linking the diagnostic aspect of ZBR with the "ideal mental age of the class," the level of teaching-demands on learners in the class that matches the given children's ZBR (Vygotsky, 1933/1935, p. 47). Knowing a particular child's ZBR in the sense of the difference score, and that of the given class, allows the paedologist to set up optimal conditions for the work of imitation. Likewise, any social situation creates the opportunities for imitation. The child constructs these opportunities for him or herself in creating rule-based play for him or herself. In a similar vein, adolescents and adults also create these opportunities for their self-development in their fantasy worlds.

IRREVERSIBILITY OF TIME AND ZBR: SOME IMPLICATIONS

We have reached an essential point—Vygotsky's ZBR concept was used descriptively to cover different phenomena that are derived from the same underlying causal system. The causal system, however, was insufficiently specified by him. On the one hand, Vygotsky followed the lead of the sociogenetic thinking of Baldwin, Janet, and others in attributing the role of the "moving force" of development to imitation. Thus, the ZBR concept became an external description of the "field," the boundaries of which coincided with what the child at a given time can imitate. On the other hand, Vygotsky developed the idea of heterochronic emergence of different psychological functions, among which some have already become formed by the present moment, and others are still in the process of formation. It is toward the latter that any goal-directed effort of guiding development must be aimed. In other words, teaching–learning runs ahead of development not in the literal sense of one process preceding the other in time, but in the sense that at this time (meaning the present) the process of teaching–learning is functionally interdependent with the developmental processes that are emerging but have yet to become established.

Hence a methodological paradox emerges: Although the teaching–learning process "creates" the ZBR (Vygotsky, 1933/1935, p. 134; 1935, p. 16) in the present, there is no way in which anybody can study that process directly, within the present. Efforts to characterize the ZBR empirically require a translation of the focus from a simultaneous coverage of developmental processes into comparison of successive outcomes of formation of these processes (see Fig. 3.1).

In Fig. 3.1 we have tried to graphically depict this translation. Different psychological functions (a–f) develop in heterochronic ways, each of them reaching the state of "recognizable final form" at different moments in ontogene-

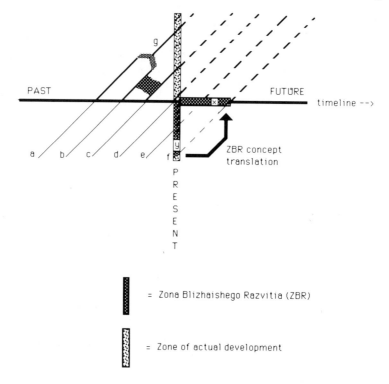

Fig. 3.1. The projection of the present to the nearest future in Vygotsky's ZBR concept.

tic time (horizontal time line). The development of these functions caɪ observed before they reach their final form, but their further development integration of already formed functions a and b into a new one, g) can be observed subsequently.

At the PRESENT "slice" of time, it is relatively easy to observe the presence of those psychological functions that are well formed (d, c, g), but it is impossible to directly observe those (f, e) that are only in the process of approaching their recognizable final forms. While the immediate focus is the ZBR (y axis in Fig. 3.1), there is no way of accessing it. Vygotsky tried to solve this paradox by believing that in the socially aided process of trying to solve novel problems the investigator can get a glimpse of the nearest future course of the development of the psychological functions involved in that process. Following that line of reasoning, one can only know about the content of y if one guides the functions involved (e, f) toward their future final forms. Thus, the "hidden" PRESENT (y) becomes translated into "nearest" FUTURE (x) ("ZBR concept translation" in Fig. 3.1).

Here is the paradox that stands in the way of empirical use of Vygotsky's ZBR ✶ concept: It refers to the hidden processes of the present that may become explicated in reality only as the present becomes the (nearest) past, while the (nearest) future becomes the present. However, any empirical research effort (including Vygotskian "teaching experiments" using the "method of double stimulation") can take place only within the present (given the constraint of irreversibility of time). It is for that reason that the ZBR concept could not be specified by Vygotsky in any more detail than a general emphasis on the need to pay attention to the processes of development that are constructing the new "present" that is currently "future"—on the basis of the functional organization of the child in the actual present. ZBR was a powerful rhetorical device in Vygotsky's dialogue with contemporary paedology. It pointed to the need to study processes of development on-line, but provided very little opportunity for an explicit theory of the developmental process.

The second complication with the ZBR concept is that Vygotsky turned out to become a hostage to the loss of emphasis on dialectical synthesis. As emphasized earlier (and elsewhere: Van der Veer & Valsiner, 1991), the theme of dialectical synthesis is present in Vygotsky's thinking from his adolescent years until his death. This theme was clearly present in his description of the developing phenomena to which the ZBR concept was applied as well (play, social interaction and internalization, concept formation). However, in no place in Vygotsky's texts where he uses the ZBR concept is that concept made dialectical in itself. For example, when a child demonstrates the availability of a "higher" psychological function in a socially guided problem solving situation, it is known that this function is not available to the child in his individual problem-solving effort. If, from that contrast, we infer that the child in the near future becomes capable of using that function individually, then we think of the development of that function in terms of its mere transposition from the interindividual to the intraindividual domain. No dialectical construction of novelty is implied here. If it were implied, we could expect a psychological function that is evident in present-time socially aided problem solving to lead to a different individual function in the near future (i.e., to emergence of novel form in psychological functions in the process of internalization). If Vygotsky were to remain consistent with his dialectical world view and allow for this possibility in his use of the ZBR concept, then the future state of an individual's psychological functions could not be previewed through diagnostic uses of socially aided problem-solving contexts. Instead, Vygotsky would have had to confess that the nearest-future state of development cannot be predicted from the child/social context interaction, although the latter undoubtedly plays a role in the synthesis of (unpredictable) future of the psychological functions. Again, Vygotsky's use of ZBR in his dialogue with paedologists did not lead him to spell out these (quite agnostic) implications of the ZBR concept. In this sense, Vygotsky's ZBR falls out of the line with most other ideas of his theoretical heritage.

FROM ZBR TO ZPD: CONTEMPORARY
TRANSFORMATIONS OF THE CONCEPT

As we showed, Vygotsky's concept of ZBR is linked with a difficult paradox that irreversibility of time sets up for any developmental theoretical construct. Since this concept has been picked up by many contemporary investigators, these theoretical problems of the concept are at times acutely felt in the literature. Some recent discussions (Paris & Cross, 1988; Valsiner, 1985; Wertsch, 1984; Winegar, 1988) bring out a number of problems that contemporary psychologists face while trying to construct their concepts along the lines of ZBR. Thus it is worthwhile to analyze how these conceptual problems are handled by many researchers whose discourse includes the use of "zone of proximal development" (ZPD, or Zo-ped) terminology.

Contemporary psychologists' persistent imitation of Vygotsky's ZBR concept has led to different parallel (and occasionally linked) lines in the development of the ZPD. Winegar (1988) has outlined three main lines in the history of ZPD uses. The first line involves the relative assessment of children's performance (assisted versus individual problem-solving). The second line concentrates on the use of ZPD in settings of interactive learning and joint actions. Finally, Winegar has outlined some uses of ZPD in the context of more theoretical efforts in developmental psychology. All of these lines emerged in the web of the respective social situations of the researchers who have set themselves varied goals in their research efforts, and hence arrived at different versions of the ZPD concept. Characteristically, many of them tend to use the umbrella label of "Vygotskian" (or "neo-Vygotskian") in the presentation of their directions of the use of the ZBR-derivate concepts.

Line 1: From ZBR to Dynamic Measurement of Abilities

Given Vygotsky's active explanations of the ZBR concept in the terminology of traditional paedological testing, it is not surprising that contemporary researchers have developed the ZPD concept further along similar lines (Brown & French, 1979; Campione & Brown, 1987). The mediator's role of Alexander Luria in the inception of this line is noteworthy (see Wozniak, 1980). The fit of ZPD with dynamic assessment of learning potential makes it possible to adopt the overwhelmingly dominant use of the interindividual reference frame and set up studies of "individual differences". At the same time, the dynamic assessment focus allows the investigators to keep in mind different facets of the child's learning process (Day, 1983). Still, the learning process is seen as a property of the child. The child, while confronted with a specified task and given hints (social suggestions) of how to solve it, moves toward a solution. After the solution, the child can be observed to transfer the strategies to new tasks, and the efficiency of the transfer is viewed as the basis for statements about wider or narrower ZPD of different children (Brown & Ferrara, 1985, p. 284). The ZPD concept becomes interpreted in terms of child's readiness, and its narrower use is that of an interindividual differences metric (Campione, Brown, Ferrara, & Bryant, 1984, pp. 78–79). It is therefore not surprising that from an interactionist theoretical perspective, the question of whether it is better or worse to have narrow or wide ZPD starts to provide ambivalent answers (see Paris & Cross, 1988).

The interest in the learning process and in the transfer of what has been learned by the child is framed within the individual–ecological frame—the experimenter's prompts in the problem-solving situation are a (social) part of the task setting, rather than an equal "third factor" that regulates the child/task environment interaction (see Valsiner, 1987; 1989). The dynamic assessment use of ZPD combines the individual–ecological and interindividual reference frames, with the latter playing the primary role in the investigators' reasoning. The individual differences focus of this line has extended the conventional paedological side of Vygotsky's ZBR notion, without further advancement of the embryonic developmental theory behind it.

Line 2: From ZBR to Interactive Learning— Scaffolding and Beyond

Historically the emphasis on scaffolding (Wood, 1980; Wood, Bruner, & Ross, 1976) has accentuated the external–interactional nature of children's guided learning. As Griffin and Cole (1984, p. 47) have pointed out, the scaffolding metaphor "leaves open questions of children's creativity." The emphasis is on the way in which children go beyond the constraints specified by the scaffolding. Instead, it is the adult's relinquishing of control over aspects of joint activity that becomes relevant:

Adult and child together were achieving success on a task, but the nature of their individual contributions varied with the child's level of ability. Once the child could be lured into some form of task-relevant activity, however low level, the tutor could build around him a supporting structure which held in place whatever he could manage. That supporting activity served to connect the child's activity into the overall construction and to provide a framework within which the child's actions could lead to and mean something more general than he may have foreseen. As the child mastered components of the task, he was freed to consider the wider context of what he could do, to take over more of the complementary activity. (Wood, 1980, pp. 281–282)

Here it is clear that the central notion of Vygotsky's ZBR—that of the child's persistent imitation that develops the emerging psychological functions—is not captured in the scaffolding metaphor. The tutor does not "work at" creating any new functions in the "depth" of the child's mind, but merely makes sure that the heterochrony in the maturation of functions is overcome in particular task solution settings. If a given task can be accomplished by action sequence X–Y–Z, and the ability to perform Y is not yet matured, the tutor helps the child to accomplish Y, thus making it possible for the child to solve the task. Once the ability for Y matures, the tutor withdraws the support for Y, as the child can now accomplish the whole task individually.

Scaffolding assumes maturational emergence of abilities heterochronically—those abilities that are not yet matured cannot participate in the problem solving, and therefore the tutor must scaffold these aspects of action that rely upon these abilities. Here the teaching–learning does not proceed "ahead of development" (in Vygotsky's favorite words), but rather tries to fit in with the maturational schedule of established abilities. Indeed, in the explicit elaboration of the ZPD concept, scaffolding links it with the "child's hypotheses" in a task situation as well as the "adult's discovery of child's mastery" (Wood, 1980, p. 284), without any notion of the presently emerging psychological functions. An equally clear indication of this is evident in Bruner's (1985) coverage of the similarity between scaffolding and ZPD:

If the child is enabled to advance by being under the tutelage of an adult or a more competent peer, then the tutor or the aiding peer serves the learner as a vicarious form of consciousness *until such time as the learner is able* to master his own action through his own consciousness and control. When the child achieves that conscious control over a new function or conceptual system, it is then that he is able to use it as a tool. Up to that point, the tutor in effect performs the critical function of "scaffolding" the learning task to make it possible for the child, in Vygotsky's word, to internalize external knowledge and convert it into a tool for conscious control. (Bruner, 1985, pp. 24–25, italics added)

In sum, the scaffolding version of ZPD follows the individual–ecological reference frame—because (from the child's perspective) the social scaffolds that the tutor builds around the child's task-oriented actions are merely human additions to the task. These social additions—like the prompts given by the tester in a dynamic assessment situation—make the execution of the child's presently available capabilities possible under complex task conditions (e.g., Greenfield, 1984, p. 119; Cazden, 1983, p. 42; Zukow, 1986). It does not concentrate on having impact on those psychological functions that are not yet presently available, but might come into being in the near future. Even if the actual prompting or scaffolding by the more experienced partner may have some impact on the development of latently emerging psychological functions, the theoretical use of the ZPD terminology is not set up to capture the process of such impact. In sum, both the dynamic assessment (line 1) and scaffolding (line 2) perspectives on the ZPD have restored the social context around the individual child's development in its manifest forms. However, these perspectives have not specified the interdependence of the context and the developmental processes.

Line 3: ZPD as a Component in Theoretical Systems

Contemporary psychology seems to be in a crisis—on the one hand, its theoretical repertoire is static and common-sensical, but the need for construction of developmental (dynamic) theoretical systems to account for complex psychological phenomena is growing. Emphasis on structure and dynamic processes has become rare in contemporary psychology. As was observed in the description of the first two lines of interpretation of the ZPD concept, the concept has been used either in rather general ways, or in conjunction with the structure of action on some highly specific task. Very few efforts have been made to construct theoretical frameworks that locate ZPD in a structured theoretical context. Furthermore, sometimes theoretical efforts in present-day psychology serve as convenient umbrella systems to allow the investigators to carry out a myriad of empirical studies without much innovation in the theoretical sphere.

Sometimes Vygotsky's role in the history of ZPD notions in psychology is attributed to his supposed "activity-theoretic" orientation. As we have shown elsewhere (Van der Veer & Valsiner, 1991), the representation of Vygotsky as one of the originators of Soviet "activity theory" constitutes a historically recent exaggeration of the realities in Soviet psychology in early 1930s. The actual roots of the activity-theoretic perspectives in Russian psychology go back to the work of Aleksandr Lazurskii (e.g., Lazurskii, 1906, chapter 5; 1916) and his disciple Mikhail Basov (Basov, 1929; Basov & Kazanskii, 1931). Vygotsky's role in the advent of Soviet activity theory was certainly of secondary nature, and fitted poorly with his emphasis on the primacy of semiotic mediation of human psychological processes. Hence it is accurate to view contemporary researchers who have set up their versions of the ZPD or Zo-ped concepts as advancing beyond the limits of a "Vygotskian" approach toward a potentially new synthesis of ideas.

THE FIRST ADVANCEMENT: WERTSCH'S SEMIOTIC
VIEW OF ACTIVITIES IN ZPD

Wertsch takes his ZPD notion beyond Vygotsky's ZBR in two directions—toward an activity-theoretic domain (largely Leontievian) and toward semiotic (Bakhtinian) domains. In the first domain, the link of the ZPD concept with the notion of situation definition and goal structures of partners in the asymmetric caregiver–child interaction sets up contexts for empirical investigations and takes the concept to novel domains (Wertsch, 1984, 1985). His first elaborations of the ZPD concept took the form of analysis of adult–child joint actions (McLane, 1987; Saxe, Gearhart & Guberman, 1984; Wertsch & Hickmann, 1987; Wertsch, Minick, & Arns, 1984). However, at the same time, the recognition of Vygotsky's original emphasis on semiotic mediation and internalization has led to the focus on intrapersonal processes that retain their cultural roots in internalized versions—as internal dialogic processes (Wertsch, 1985; Wertsch & Stone, 1985). The internalization process proceeds through points of intersubjectivity that are present within the ZPD. These points allow the child to experience the joint action situation definition, and carry it over (appropriate it) into the internal sphere (Wertsch, 1985, pp. 162–163).

To summarize, Wertsch has accomplished what Vygotsky himself failed to accomplish—the synthesis of the ZPD concept with the idea of semiotic mediation of higher psychological functions (see especially Wertsch & Minick, 1990). By rejecting Vygotsky's strong emphasis on word meaning as the unit of analysis, and extending it toward text-semiotic mediation through Bakhtin's ideas (see Wertsch & Bivens, this volume), the ZPD concept is substantively enhanced.

SECOND ADVANCEMENT: ACTIVITY-CONTEXTUAL
APPROACH

The emphasis on the "mutual construction of culture and person" (Cole, 1985) that has for many years been unifying the work of the Laboratory of Comparative Human Cognition (LCHC) (see LCHC, 1982) becomes encoded in the concept of Zo-ped (Griffin & Cole, 1984; LCHC, 1983). Cole extends the ZPD concept to the domain of collectively organized activity—it becomes viewed in general as the "structure of joint activity in any context where there are participants who exercise differential responsibility by virtue of differential expertise" (Cole, 1985, p. 155). In that joint activity, an individual person indeed develops from present to future on the basis of ideal models of the future, and of the past (as the ideas of Nikolai Bernshtein are brought together with the Zo-ped concept—Griffin & Cole, 1984, pp. 48–49). However, the emphasis on collective shared activities leads Cole into the theoretically central adoption of the Soviet focus on activity theory in general terms, and of the concept of leading activity in particular. This extension of Vygotsky's ideas to the domain of activity theory leads to the establishment of a hybrid theory. Cole's emphasis on development concentrates on the ongoing activity that is transformed in ontogeny:

> . . . as an alternative to internal, individual stage approaches to the study of development, leading activities provide for a notion of societally provided progressions, the sort of context-selection mechanisms . . . . Second, the "leading" notion provides a framework for uniting several important aspects of development: Variations in the frequency of experiences can be related to changes in kind of psychological activity. Changes in leading activities can be related to the reorganization of constituent actions and operations internally and interpsychologically. The appearance of new leading activities provides for the emergence of new functional systems. As a new leading activity appears, it provides for the reorganization and internalization of prior stages by transforming them into the everyday, in contrast to the new leading activity. (Griffin & Cole, 1984, p. 51)

Although an explicit emphasis here is made upon internal operations and internalization, the major focus remains on the different kinds of activities in which the child is embedded. This is in line with the functional (or cultural) practice perspective on specific cognitive processes (LCHC, 1982), a standpoint that avoids the problems of mental generalization. This is accomplished by concentrating upon the person–social world fusion. Any society, for example, provides guidance in that it provides an age-graded sequence of activities through which an individual moves. Moreover, the child is always a participant in a myriad of culturally organized activities, and the latter guide the child's development of individual activity patterns. The Zo-ped is "dynamically achieved by the *child and others in a social environment"*, (LCHC, 1983, p. 335, original italics); it belongs to the interaction between the child and the "social others," rather than to the child him or herself.

THIRD ADVANCEMENT: ROGOFF'S THEORY OF "FUSION" OF PERSON AND CULTURE

Barbara Rogoff's consistent emphasis (Rogoff, 1982, 1986, 1987, 1990) on the cultural guidance of children's participation in social settings that guides their cognitive development has led to an interesting development of the ZPD concept. Starting from an interest in neo-Gibsonian "ecological psychology" on the one hand, and Leontiev version of Vygotsky's perspective on the other (see Rogoff, 1982), she has moved to view ZPD as a framework in which the "stretching" of the child's skill and understanding takes place (see Rogoff, 1986, pp. 27 and 31). The "event" (interactive setting) that is constructed jointly by the active (goal-oriented) child and the other person who is more knowledgeable about the cultural ways of acting than the child (but equally goal-oriented) becomes the "unit of analysis" of the guided participation process as the context for human development. The use of "event" (activity) as a "unit" leads to a clear recognition of variability as being central for development (Rogoff, 1990, p. 30), as it necessarily emerges in the asymmetric (in roles, linked with knowledge and skills) but is simultaneously a joint action process where "challenges" (e.g., "comfortable-yet-challenging" tasks; Ellis & Rogoff, 1986, p. 315), "constraints," and "support" are constructed. This joint action process is guided by meanings and purpose (Rogoff, 1990, p. 29), and can be studied adequately only in the dynamic form of processes that lead to the unfolding of events. This emphasis on the developing child as an active "cultural apprentice" who actively develops mental and instrumental means is linked with the ZPD:

> Children enlist involvement of caregivers in their own activities and attempt to enter into caregivers' activities according to their interests. Such interaction is likely to fit the characteristics of guided participation for pragmatic reasons—the adult limits the amount of responsibility according to the child's skill, and the child insists on a role that *is interesting and, hence, within the child's zone of proximal development.* (Rogoff, 1990, p. 100, italics added)

In other terms, Rogoff's ZPD is a dynamic region of sensitivity to learning experiences in participation contexts where the participants have actively set up their roles (see also Rogoff, 1987). On the side of the adults, the responsibility for performing aspects of tasks comes to the adjustment of social support to the range of ZPD (Rogoff, 1990, p. 109). Rogoff's emphasis on the children's active seeking of assistance and structure from adults is fully in line with Vygotsky's original emphasis (in the cultural-historical theory). At the same time, Rogoff avoids clear structured elaboration of internal psychological functions in the child (and actively denies the need of the internalization concept—a key to Vygotsky's theoretical heritage; see Rogoff, 1990, pp. 195–197). This leads Rogoff's theory to be very close to the reduction of any psychological processes to the undifferentiated notion of situated activity (e.g., Lave, 1988). However, closeness to the fusional reductionism of person to cultural activity settings is not absolute in Rogoff's theory. Her emphasis is on role- and meaning-based actions by the child in environments where the "social other" need not be immediately present (Rogoff, 1990, pp. 186–187). This return to Vygotsky's idea that play creates the ZBR allows her to escape the theoretical trap of all-encompassing contextual determinism.

Rogoff's theoretical orientation has emerged in conjunction with a program of explicit microgenetic research on dynamic joint problem-solving settings where both the child and the "more experienced social other" pursue their goals (Ellis & Rogoff, 1986; Rogoff & Gardner, 1984). Rogoff has also been emphasizing the shift in the structure of social guidance in ontogeny (Gardner & Rogoff, 1982; Rogoff, Malkin, & Gilbride, 1984), and the internalized bases for the use of cultural skills such as memorization devices (Rogoff & Mistry, 1985) and planning strategies (Rogoff, Gauvain, & Gardner, 1987). All this leads Rogoff's perspective to stand out as a unique conceptual system that unites the activity-theoretic tradition of LCHC on the one hand, and the psychological processes orientation of Vygotsky's cultural-historical emphasis on the other.

FOURTH ADVANCEMENT: INTERACTIVE CONTEXT FOR THE "SYMBOLIC ANIMAL"

Within the European intellectual framework, the Yugoslav research tradition (Ivic, 1978) has emphasized the symbol-constructive nature of the human development process. This semiotic advancement of Vygotsky's ideas is somewhat parallel to that of Wertsch, but moves in its own productively unique direction as it sets up the study of semiotic analysis of iconic systems (figural, nonverbal phenomena that occur in symbolic play and dreaming) in their own right (Ivic, 1988, 1989). This line of advancement of Vygotsky's ideas takes the intrapsychological functions as the internalized experiences and sets those up for specific investigation. The social nature of the psychological world of the person is extended from the verbally encoded semiotic systems to the nonverbal (figurative) codes. Socially shared joint activity is important as the domain within which developmentally relevant novel intrapsychological phenomena are constructed. ZPD emerges here as a concept to describe the mechanisms of internalization—construction of intrapsychological novelty (Ivic, 1989, pp. 5–7).

The notion of ZPD in the work of the Institute of Psychology of Belgrade University is set up not only theoretically. It has been used to analyze early ontogeny of interaction in ways that utilize dyadic units of measurement (Ignjatovic-Savic, Kovac-Cerovic, Plut, & Pesikan, 1988). The main aim for this empirical elaboration is to retain the complementarity of the adult–child joint action in different contexts defined in respect to the child's process of development. The latter aim leads the researchers to view the ZPD in relation to other domains (or zones) of experience: Zone of Actual Development, Zone of Future Development, and Zone of Past Development (see Ignjatovic-Savic et al., 1988, p. 110). The developmental process proceeds by "moving" some aspects of joint activity from the Zone of Future Development to ZPD, and subsequently to Zone of Past Development. Phenomena from these different zones can be observed in microgenetic task settings intermittently—reminding otherwise all too enthusiastic "Vygotskians" that not every aspect of joint action is actually productive for further development. Along similar lines, different parallel processes involving the dynamic coordination of these zones create the possibility for a wide range of developmental courses, because the child's social environment is necessarily heterogeneous. This undermines the use of the ZPD concept as a means for predicting a child's future (a pervasive pastime of child psychologists) and calls for the investigation of the child's representative social "resources":

The conceptualization of the ZPD as an interactive phenomenon implies changes in the practice of using ZPD as a diagnostic tool for the assessment of the child's development. If we assess the child in the interaction with a competent adult this does not necessarily have to be a good basis for the prediction of his future development if his everyday interactions are not of that kind. On the other hand, when the child is with an incompetent adult, we can underestimate his developmental potential. Of course, if the child is growing only with this person his developmental future would be very close to what was predicted on the basis of the assessment. Fortunately, children enter in interaction with more than one person. So the best way to assess the child's present state and his future is to find a representative sample of his learning environment. The clue to prediction would be typical, predominant interaction. (Ignjatovic-Savic, 1989, p. 7)

This spatially (as seen in the focus on representative range of environments) and temporally (different zones operating intermittently and in mutual coordination) organized perspective on ZPD extends Vygotsky's original ideas in a productive way. It is the strong emphasis on the study of processes of development (both onto- and microgenetic) that this perspective implies. As such, it is antithetical to the assessment orientation (line 1 as given above) and subsumes the scaffolding traditions as special cases within a general theoretical field.

FIFTH ADVANCEMENT: COCONSTRUCTION OF FUTURE THROUGH BOUNDED INDETERMINACY

Developmentalists are usually theoretically confused about the issue of determinacy versus indeterminacy in the processes of ontogeny. In an effort to bypass that impasse, Valsiner (1987) has proposed a general theoretical perspective that views development as organized by "bounded indeterminacy." The psychological processes are viewed as developing by sets of interpersonal (and subsequently intrapersonal, semiotic) constraint systems that determine the direction of the nearest future development. These constraint systems are constantly reorganized by the coconstructive efforts of the developing person and his or her social others in particular environmental settings. The constraint systems are viewed as containing two kinds of zones at every time moment of the present—the Zone of Freedom of Movement (ZFM), which defines the set of possibilities that can be actualized at the given time, and the Zone of Promoted Actions (ZPA), which includes the set of possibilities that actualization of which is promoted at the time by the persons involved in the interaction. It is obvious that the ZFM notion continues the field-theoretic traditions of Kurt Lewin (see Valsiner, 1984, 1985, 1987).

Valsiner has also made an attempt to integrate the ZPD concept into the field-theoretic system of explaining social-cognitive development. ZPD becomes a zone that denotes the range of possible nearest-future transformations of present psychological processes, conditional on the present organization of the ZFM/ ZPA structure (Valsiner, 1987, chapter 4). It is obvious that ZPD in that system becomes subservient to the present-state field-theoretic explanation and is oriented toward explaining the social roots of individuals' experiences (see criticism by Van Oers, 1988). Furthermore, ZPD in Valsiner's (1985) theoretical construction is presented as empirically unaccessible:

> The ZPD is a concept pertaining to the realm of what kinds of further developmental accomplishments are possible for the given child at the given time in ontogeny, under condition of others' assistance. Therefore it is impossible to determine the empirical boundaries of ZPD in actuality. If the boundaries of ZPD are determined inductively, on the basis of empirical observations, the result of such study is the actualization of some subset of the ZPD, from which it is not possible to determine the full set of ZPD that was existing before the given sub-set was studied (and actualized by the study). Once the child has learned to read with grandmother's help (proving that reading under the conditions of instruction that the grandmother used while testing the child, was indeed in ZPD when the teaching started), it would be impossible to find out whether the same function (reading) could have been within the ZPD set with the help of somebody else, using different methods of teaching (e.g., mother, father, teacher). For the purposes of the study of the boundaries of ZPD, the child will not re-learn the important function (reading) with the help of another instructor. What has been learned with the help of an instructor in a certain way, cannot be learned again as a totally novel function, with the help of another instructor. This basic nature of development renders the full extent of ZPD in principle empirically unverifiable. (Valsiner, 1985, p. 31)

Valsiner's limitation of the ZPD concept to a status conditional of his other zone terms constitutes an effort to clarify the otherwise largely metaphoric (umbrella-type) use of the term in contemporary developmental psychology. His application of the ZPD concept encounters difficulties similar to those that Vygotsky faced (and that were depicted in Fig. 3.1).

GENERAL CONCLUSIONS: THEORETICAL DEVELOPMENT BEYOND ZPD?

We have overviewed the history of Vygotsky's ZBR concept, as well as that of its derivates under the label of ZPD. Recent concerns about the status of the concept (Paris & Cross, 1988; Shotter, 1989; Winegar, 1988) may begin to make better sense in the light of the mindscape covered here. Indeed, the ZBR/ZPD concept has been widely used as a metaphor, and its operationalization has been complicated when attempted. But of course not every theoretical concept in psychology needs operationalization and measurement, and arguments against turning ZPD into another measured characteristic have substance (Valsiner, 1987; Winegar, 1988). Of course, metaphors can be as confusing as they can be helpful. It seems that a wide and indiscriminate use of the ZPD concept, without a clear explication of its meaning, allows contemporary psychology to be more globally fascinated by sociogenetic ideas than by developing specific notions that could explain the social nature of individual psychological development. Still, locating that social nature to be exemplified by the ZPD without further specifying its nature can be a theoretical impasse that creates another "black box" type of explanation in a science that historically has been plagued by a myriad of such explanations.

Starting with Vygotsky, the ZBR/ZPD concepts have helped investigators to concentrate their attention on the social-developmental aspect of psychological functions, not permitting them to forget that in the most general sense development moves from present to future through the child's interdependence with the social world. At the same time, the concept has generated an additional conceptual difficulty—it has translated issues of presently emerging psychological functions into empirically observable forms that could emerge in the near future. However, the ZPD concept remains unconnected with the actual processes that underlie the emergence of novelty. In this respect, both Vygotsky's ZBR and the different versions of its advancement as ZPD remain inconclusive. The use of the ZPD concept has provided an easy alternative to tackling the complicated issues of how the child's encounter with the external world becomes functional in bringing new psychological functions into being. The interactive process of creating and comprehending novelty is not explained by a mere reference to a function "being in" the ZPD at the given moment or "coming into" it in the future. The actual mechanisms of the process by which the culture and individual meet in the novelty-constructing process of development remain uncharted, while our fascination with the "zone of proximal development" remains a widely used cliche that yet has to lead to theoretical innovation in contemporary psychology.

ACKNOWLEDGMENTS

The editorial suggestions of Ann Renninger were very helpful in bringing this chapter into its final form. The authors are also grateful to Terry Winegar, Jeanette Lawrence (and other colleagues and students at Melbourne University), and Michael Cole for their input in the writing of this manuscript.

REFERENCES

Baldwin, J. M. (1892). Origin of volition in childhood. *Science, 20,* 286–287.
Basov, M. I. (1929). Ocherednyie problemy psikhologii. *Estestvoznanie i marksizm, 3,* 55–82.
Basov, M. I. & Kazanskii, N. G. (Eds.). (1931). *Deti u stanka.* Moscow-Leningrad: Gosuchpediztat.

Smedslund, J. (1979). Between the analytic and the arbitrary: A case study of psychological research. *Scandinavian Journal of Psychology, 20,* 129–140.

Thorngate, W. (1990). The economy of attention and the development of psychology. *Canadian Psychology, 31,* 262–271.

Toulmin, S., & Leary, D. E. (1985). The cult of empiricism in psychology, and beyond. In S. Koch & D. E. Leary (Eds.), *A century of psychology as science* (pp. 594–616). New York: McGraw-Hill.

Valsiner, J. (1984). Construction of the zone of proximal development in adult-child joint action. *New Directions for Child Development, 23,* 65–76.

Valsiner, J. (1985). Theoretical issues of child development and the problem of accident prevention. In T. Gärling and J. Valsiner (Eds.), *Children within environments: Toward a psychology of accident prevention* (pp. 13–36). New York: Plenum.

Valsiner, J. (1987). *Culture and the development of children's action.* Chichester: Wiley.

Valsiner, J. (1988). *Developmental psychology in the Soviet Union.* Brighton, England: Harvester Press.

Valsiner, J. (1989). *Human development and culture.* Lexington, MA: D. C. Heath.

Van der Veer, R., & Valsiner, J. (1991). *Understanding Vygotsky: A quest for synthesis.* Oxford: Basil Blackwell.

Van Oers, B. (1988). Activity, semiotics and the development of children. *Comenius, 32,* 398–406.

Vygotsky, L. S. (1929). The problem of the cultural development of the child. *Pedagogical Seminary and Journal of Genetic Psychology, 36,* 415–434.

Vygotsky, L. S. (1931a). K voprosu o pedologii i smezhnykh s neju naukakh. *Pedologia, 3,* 52–58.

Vygotsky, L. S. (1931b). Pedologia i smezhnyie s neiu nauki. *Pedologia, 7–8,* 12–22.

Vygotsky, L. S. (1931c). Psikhotekhnika i pedologia. *Psikhotekhnika i psikhofiziologia truda, 2–3,* 173–184.

Vygotsky, L. S. (1931d). Kollektiv kak faktor razvitia anomal'nogo rebenka. *Voprosy Defektologii, 1–2,* 8–17.

Vygotsky, L. S. (1931e). *Pedologia podrostka.* Moscow-Leningrad: Gosuchpediztatel'stvo.

Vygotsky, L. S. (1934). *Myshlenie i rech.* Moscow-Leningrad: GIZ.

Vygotsky, L. S. (1933/1935). *Umstvennoie razvitie detei v protsesse obuchenia.* Moscow-Leningrad: Gosudarstvennoie Uchebno-pedagogicheskoie Izdatel'stvo.

Vygotsky, L. S. (1933/1966). Igra i ee rol' v psikhicheskom razvitii rebenka. *Voprosy Psikhologii, 12*(6), 62–76.

Vygotsky, L. S. (1931/1983). *Sobranie sochinenii. Vol. 3. Problemy razvitia psikhiki.* Moscow: Pedagogika.

Vygotsky, L. S. (1933/1984). *Sobranie sochinenii. Vol. 4. Detskaia psikhologia.* Moscow: Pedagogika.

Vygotsky, L. S. (1962). *Thought and language.* Cambridge, MA: MIT Press.

Vygotsky, L. S. (1986). *Thought and language* (2nd ed.). Cambridge, MA: MIT Press.

Vygotsky, L. S. (1987). Thinking and speech. In R. W. Rieber and A. S. Carton (Eds.), *The collected works of L. S. Vygotsky. Vol. 1. Problems of general psychology* (pp. 39–285). New York: Plenum.

Vygotsky, L. S., & Luria, A. R. (1930). *Etiudy po istorii povedenia.* Moscow-Leningrad: Gosudarstvennoie izdatel'stvo.

Wertsch, J. V. (1984). The zone of proximal development: Some conceptual issues. *New Directions for Child Development, 23* (pp. 7–18). San Francisco: Jossey-Bass.

Wertsch, J. V. (1985). *Vygotsky and the social formation of mind.* Cambridge, MA: Harvard University Press.

Wertsch, J. V., Minick, N., & Arns, F. (1984). The creation of context in joint problem solving. In B. Rogoff & J. Lave (Eds.), *Everyday cognition* (pp. 151–171). Cambridge, MA: Harvard University Press.

Wertsch, J. V., & Stone, C. A. (1985). The concept of internalization in Vygotsky's account of the

genesis of higher mental functions. In J. V. Wertsch (Ed.), *Culture, communication and cognition: Vygotskian perspectives* (pp. 162–179). Cambridge, England: Cambridge University Press.
Wertsch, J. V., & Hickmann, M. (1987). Problem solving in social interaction: A microgenetic analysis. In M. Hickmann (Ed.), *Social and functional approaches to language and thought* (pp. 251–266). Orlando, FL: Academic Press.
Wertsch, J. V., & Minick, N. (1990). Negotiating sense in the zone of proximal development. In M. Schwebel, C. A. Maher, & N. S. Fagley (Eds.), *Promoting cognitive growth over the life span* (pp. 71–88). Hillsdale, NJ: Lawrence Erlbaum Associates.
Winegar, L. T. (1988). Child as cultural apprentice: An alternative perspective for understanding Zone of Proximal Development. *Genetic Epistemologist, 16*(3), 31–38.
Wood, D. J. (1980). Teaching the young child: Some relationships between social interaction, language, and thought. In D. R. Olson (Ed.), *The social foundation of language and thought* (pp. 280–296). New York: Norton.
Wood, D., Bruner, J., & Ross, G. (1976). The role of tutoring in problem solving. *Journal of Child Psychology and Psychiatry, 17, 2,* 89–100.
Wozniak, R. H. (1980). Theory, practice and the "zone of proximal development" in Soviet psycho-educational research. *Contemporary Educational Psychology, 5,* 175–183.
Zaporozhets, A. V. (1930). Umstennoie razvitie i psikhicheskie osobennosti oirotskikh detei. *Pedologia, 2,* 222–234.
Zukow, P. G. (1986). The relationship between interaction with the caregiver and the emergence of play activities during the one-word period. *British Journal of Developmental Psychology, 4,* 223–234.

Brent, S. (1984). *Psychological and social structures.* Hillsdale, NJ: Lav

Brown, A. L., & French, L. A. (1979). The zone of potential deve intelligence testing in the year 2000. *Intelligence, 3,* 255–273.

Brown, A. L., & Ferrara, R. A. (1985). Diagnosing zones of proxin Wertsch (Ed.), *Culture, communication, and cognition: Vygotskian pe* Cambridge, England: Cambridge University Press.

Bruner, J. S. (1985). Vygotsky: A historical and conceptual perspective. ... ᴊ. ᴠ. ᴡᴇrᴛscʜ (Ed.), *Culture, communication, and cognition: Vygotskian perspectives* (pp. 21–34). Cambridge, England: Cambridge University Press.

Cairns, R. B. (1986). Phenomena lost: Issues in the study of development. In J. Valsiner (Ed.), *The individual subject and scientific psychology* (pp. 97–111). New York: Plenum.

Campione, J. C., Brown, A. L., Ferrara, R. A., & Bryant, N. R. (1984). The zone of proximal development: Implications for individual differences and learning. *New Directions for Child Development, 23,* 77–91.

Campione, J. C., & Brown, A. L. (1987). Linking dynamic assessment with school achievement. In C. S. Lidz (Ed.), *Dynamic assessment: An interactional approach to evaluating learning potential* (pp. 82–115). New York: Guilford Press.

Cazden, C. B. (1983). Peekaboo as an instructional model: Discourse development at home and at school. In B. Bain (Ed.), *The sociogenesis of language and human conduct* (pp. 33–58). New York: Plenum.

Cole, M. (1985). The zone of proximal development: Where culture and cognition create each other. In J. V. Wertsch (Ed.), *Culture, communication, and cognition: Vygotskian perspectives* (pp. 146–161). Cambridge, England: Cambridge University Press.

Cole, M., John-Steiner, V., Scribner, S., & Souberman, E. (Eds.). (1978). *L. S. Vygotsky: Mind in society.* Cambridge, MA: Harvard University Press.

Day, J. D. (1983). The zone of proximal development. In M. Pressley & J. R. Levin (Eds.), *Cognitive strategy research* (pp. 155–175). New York: Springer.

Ellis, S., & Rogoff, B. (1986). Problem solving in children's management of instruction. In E. Mueller & C. Cooper (Eds.), *Process and outcome in peer relationships* (pp. 301–325). Orlando, FL: Academic Press.

Gardner, W., & Rogoff, B. (1982). The role of instruction in memory development. *Quarterly Newsletter of the Laboratory of Comparative Human Cognition, 4,* 1, 6–12.

Greenfield, P. (1984). A theory of the teacher in the learning activities of everyday life. In B. Rogoff & J. Lave (Eds.), *Everyday cognition* (pp. 117–138). Cambridge, MA: Harvard University Press.

Griffin, P., & Cole, M. (1984). Current activity for the future: The Zo-ped. *New Directions for Child Development, 23,* 45–63.

Ignjatovic-Savic, N. (1989, August). *Problems of operationalization of Vygotsky's theory.* Paper presented at the 12th International School Psychology Colloquium, Ljubljana.

Ignjatovic-Savic, N., Kovac-Cerovic, T., Plut, D., & Pesikan, A. (1988). Social interaction in early childhood and its developmental effects. In J. Valsiner (Ed.), *Child development within culturally structured environments. Vol. 1. Parental cognition and adult-child interaction* (pp. 89–158). Norwood, NJ: Ablex.

Ivic, I. (1978). *Covek kao animal symbolicum.* Beograd: Nolit.

Ivic, I. (1988, June). *Semiotic systems and their role in ontogenetic mental development.* Paper presented at the 3rd European Conference on Developmental Psychology, Budapest.

Ivic, I. (1989, September). *Social interaction: Social or interpersonal relationship.* Paper presented at the Annual Conference of the Italian Psychological Society, Trieste.

Joravsky, D. (1989). *Russian psychology: A critical history.* Oxford: Basil Blackwell.

Kolbanovskii, V. N. (1956). On the psychological views of L. S. Vygotsky (on the occasion of 60 years from his birth). *Voprosy psikhologii, 5,* 104–113.

oratory of Comparative Human Cognition. (1982). Culture and intelligence. In R. J. Sternberg (Ed.), *Handbook of human intelligence* (pp. 642–719). Cambridge, England: Cambridge University Press.

Laboratory of Comparative Human Cognition. (1983). Culture and cognitive development. In W. Kessen (Ed.), *Handbook of child psychology. Vol. 1. History, theory and methods* (pp. 295–356). New York: Wiley.

Lave, J. (1988). *Cognition in practice*. Cambridge, England: Cambridge University Press.

Lazurskii, A. F. (1906). *Ocherk nauki o kharakterakh*. St. Petersburg: I. N. Skorokhodov.

Lazurskii, A. F. (1916). Lichnost' i vospitanie. *Vestnik Psikhologii, Kriminal'noi Antropologii i Pedologii, 12*(2–3), 4–13.

Lee, B. (1987). Recontextualizing Vygotsky. In M. Hickmann (Ed.), *Social and functional approaches to language and thought* (pp. 87–104). Orlando, FL: Academic Press.

Leontiev, A. N. (1932). The development of voluntary attention in the child. *Pedagogical Seminary and Journal of Genetic Psychology, 40,* 52–83.

Luria, A. R. (1928). The problem of the cultural behavior of the child. *Pedagogical Seminary and Journal of Genetic Psychology, 35,* 493–506.

Luria, A. R. (1931). K probleme nevrodinamicheskogo razvitia rebenka. *Pedologia, 2,* 18–29.

McLane, J. B. (1987). Interaction, context, and the zone of proximal development. In M. Hickmann (Ed.), *Social and functional approaches to language and thought* (pp. 267–285). Orlando, FL: Academic Press.

Minick, N. (1987). Implications of Vygotsky's theories for dynamic assessment. In C. S. Lidz (Ed.), *Dynamic assessment: An interactional approach to evaluating learning potential* (pp. 116–140). New York: Guilford Press.

Paris, S. G., & Cross, D. R. (1988). The zone of proximal development: virtues and pitfalls of a metaphorical representation of children's learning. *Genetic Epistemologist, 16,* 1, 27–37.

Rogoff, B. (1982). Integrating context and cognitive development. In M. E. Lamb & A. L. Brown (Eds.), *Advances in developmental psychology* (Vol. 2, pp. 125–170). Hillsdale, NJ: Lawrence Erlbaum Associates.

Rogoff, B. (1986). Adult assistance of children's learning. In T. E. Raphael (Ed.), *The contexts of school-based literacy* (pp. 27–40). New York: Random House.

Rogoff, B. (1987). Joint socialization of development by young children and adults. In M. Lewis & S. Feinman (Eds.), *Social influences and socialization in infancy* New York: Plenum.

Rogoff, B. (1990). *Apprenticeship in thinking*. New York: Oxford University Press.

Rogoff, B., Malkin, C., & Gilbride, K. (1984). Interaction with babies as guidance in development. *New Directions for Child Development, 23,* 31–44.

Rogoff, B., & Gardner, W. (1984). Adult guidance of cognitive development. In B. Rogoff & J. Lave (Eds.), *Everyday cognition* (pp. 95–116). Cambridge, MA: Harvard University Press.

Rogoff, B., Gauvain, M., & Gardner, W. (1987). The development of children's skills in adjusting plans to circumstances. In S. Friedman, E. Scholnick, & R. Cocking (Eds.), *Blueprints for thinking: The role of planning in cognitive development* (pp. 303–320). Cambridge, England: Cambridge University Press.

Rogoff, B., & Mistry, J. (1985). Memory development in cultural context. In M. Pressley & C. Brainerd (Eds.), *Cognitive learning and memory in children* (pp. 117–142). New York: Springer.

Rudneva, E. I. (1937). *Pedologicheskie izvrashchenia Vygotskogo*. Moscow: Gosuchpedizdatel'stvo.

Saxe, G. B., Gearhart, M., & Guberman, S. R. (1984). The social organization of early number development. *New Directions for Child Development, 23,* 19–30.

Shif, Z. I. (1935). *Razvitie nauchnykh poniatii u shkol'nika*. Moscow-Leningrad: Gosuchpedizdat.

Shotter, J. (1989). Vygotsky's psychology: Joint activity in a developmental zone. *New Ideas in Psychology, 7*(3), 1–20.

Simon, B., & Simon, J. (Eds.). (1963). *Educational psychology in the USSR*. London: Routledge & Kegan Paul.

4 Distancing Theory From a Distance

Urie Bronfenbrenner
Cornell University

As the title implies, this author came to distancing theory from a distance. Over a decade ago, when I first began to evolve an ecological paradigm for human development, I knowingly took what turned out to be a long, albeit adventurous, detour. Having defined the process of development as a joint function of organism–environment interaction, I chose, in further explication of the model, to begin with what I saw as a necessary prior task of conceptualizing the environmental terms in the ecological equation, deferring, as I put it, "for the time being" a corresponding formulation on the side of the human organism (Bronfenbrenner, 1979). Alas, "for the time being" turned out to be almost a decade. Moreover, once I began to give substance to the formless figure of the person, the effort had an unanticipated result; it led to a reformulation and elaboration of earlier conceptions regarding the structure of the environment and its role in the developmental process (Bronfenbrenner, 1989a, 1989b, 1990a, in press).

A DEVELOPING ECOLOGICAL PARADIGM

This reflective change came about in the following way. I had begun by asking the question: "What characteristics of the person are most likely to influence the subsequent course and outcomes of development?" Interrelating theoretical considerations with empirical evidence led to the formulation of the concept of what I called *developmentally instigative characteristics,* defined as personal qualities that "set in motion, sustain, and enhance processes of progressively more complex interaction with persons, objects, or symbolic elements present in the immediate environment" (Bronfenbrenner, in press). Within this broader definition, four types developmentally instigative characteristics were distinguished:

1. Personal stimulus characteristics. These are qualities of the person that invite or discourage reactions from the environment of a kind that can disrupt or foster processes of psychological growth: for example, a fussy versus a happy baby, attractive versus unattractive physical appearance, or hyperactivity versus passivity. Half a century ago, Gordon Allport (1937), borrowing a term originally introduced by Mark A. May (1932), spoke of such characteristics as constituting "personality" defined in terms of its "social stimulus value."

2. Selective responsivity refers to individual differences in reaction to, attraction by, and exploration of particular aspects of the physical and social environment.

3. Structuring proclivities. These go beyond individual differences in selective responsiveness to include the tendency to engage and persist in progressively more complex activities—for example, to elaborate, restructure, and even to create new features in one's environment, not only physical and social, but also symbolic.

4. Directive beliefs. This final class of developmentally instigative characteristics reflects the growing capacity and active propensity of children as they grow older to conceptualize their experience. It encompasses the child's evolving conceptions about the relation of the self to the environment. The construct differs from the more familiar notions of locus of control and self esteem in viewing such orientations not solely as developmental outcomes but as dynamic forces shaping the course of future psychological development—hence the qualifying term, directive.

Further discussion of developmentally instigative characteristics of the person appears in the sources cited earlier. They are mentioned here only because of their serendipitous effect in suggesting a new, additional way of conceptualizing and analyzing the ecological environment in terms of analogous developmentally instigative elements at each sequential systems level ranging from the micro to the macro. For example, the definition of the microsystem, the immediate setting in which development ultimately occurs, has been expanded to read as follows [the added portion is indicated by italics]:

A *microsystem* is a pattern of activities, roles, and interpersonal relations experienced by the developing person in a given face-to-face setting with particular physical, social, and symbolic features *that invite, permit, or inhibit, engagement in sustained, progressively more complex interaction with the immediate environment.* (Bronfenbrenner, 1990a, p. 106)

What does the addendum mean in concrete terms? The answer to this question is best conveyed by a concrete example. A decade ago, Theodore Wachs (1979) published a seminal paper in which he showed a consistent pattern of relationships between certain features in the physical environment of infants during the first 2 years of life, and their cognitive development over this same period. From among the many findings of this study, the focus for the present purpose is on those physical features of the environment that turned out to be most frequently and strongly associated with better cognitive functioning. These included a physically responsive environment, presence of sheltered areas, "the degree to which the physical set-up of the home permits exploration," low level of noise and confusion, and "the degree of temporal regularity" (p. 30).

In summary, it would appear that there are two general developmentally instigative characteristics, in this instance not of the person but of the physical environment, that can affect the course of cognitive development—one for better, the other for worse. On the constructive side are objects and areas that invite manipulation and exploration, whereas the instability, lack of clear structure, and unpredictability of events undermine developmental processes. As I have documented elsewhere (Bronfenbrenner, 1986, 1989a), these same two vectors continue to exert their opposing effects at older ages as well.

But if there are developmentally instigative characteristics of the physical environment, are there not developmentally instigative characteristics of the social environment as well—that is, analogous characteristics of other persons that "invite manipulation and exploration", or exhibit "lack of clear structure" or "unpredictability" of behavior that also shape the course of future development, again for better or for worse?[1]

SIGEL'S SCIENCE WITH PRESCIENCE

Such contemporary concepts were already emerging in Sigel's work two decades ago. It was in 1970 that he published his first, now-classic paper on the distancing hypothesis, formally stated as follows:

Acquisition of representational competence [the ability to represent the environment in symbolic form] is hypothesized as a function of life experiences that create temporal and/or spatial and/or psychological distance between self and object. "Distancing" is proposed as the concept to denote behaviors or events that separate the child cognitively from the immediate behavioral environment. (Sigel, 1970)

---

[1]A recent example comes from a synthesis of biological and social science around the concept of "social zeitgebers" (Ehlers, Frank, & Kupfer, 1988). These are proximal events or broader social changes that disrupt the circadian rhythms that become established in intimate human relationships such as those between mother and infant or husband and wife. Interruptions of these rhythms have been shown to operate as triggers setting off both mild and more serious mental disorders.

Sigel foresaw not only the important questions, but also the important answers. As the first requirement for the development of representational competence, he stipulated the necessity of "a relatively orderly, structured, and sequential environment" (1970, p. 14), thus anticipating Wachs's findings by almost a decade. Moreover, in these early years, Sigel already had the difficulty of separating the physical from the social environment in the actual experience of the developing child. Thus, in stipulating his first condition, he noted that it was the parents who provided, or failed to provide, the order, structure, and sequence in the child's environment.

From this comprehensive initial orientation, Sigel proceeded in two directions. First, in accord with his basic hypothesis, he sought to identify and gauge the developmental impact of concrete parental behaviors that created "psychological distance between self and object" for the child. In his view, the primary domain in which such dissonance was most likely to be communicated was in the sphere of linguistic behavior. It took a decade of this work before, in Sigel's judgment, there was adequate evidence to support the stated hypothesis (Sigel, 1982). Even then, a key question remained to be addressed. The data showed that parents varied considerably in the extent to which they engaged in distancing strategy. What could account for this variation?

It was in answer to this question that Sigel and McGillicuddy-DeLisi embarked on a second major research endeavor—the study of parental belief systems as determinants of parental behavior (Sigel, 1986; Sigel & McGillicuddy-DeLisi, 1984; Sigel, McGillicuddy-DeLisi, Flaugher, & Rock, 1983; Sigel, McGillicuddy-DeLisi, & Johnson, 1980). The principal results of this work have recently been summarized by Sigel:

> We have come a long way with the Distancing theory model. Our family studies, involving mostly preschool children, reaffirmed our findings and our theory that distancing strategies do relate to children's intellectual and social characteristics, especially those involving abstract thinking, mathematical reasoning and reading. . . . Thus the Distancing Hypothesis is no longer a hypothesis, but in my view, it is now a model for studying the ontogenesis of representational competence.
>
> What is also of particular interest is that we discovered relationships between beliefs and behaviors. It is quite clear that parents who believe children learn through their thinking reasoning and the like use distancing strategies quite consistently. However, parents who have other beliefs do not use such strategies. (Sigel, 1990b, p. 114)

Sigel was among the first not only to recognize the importance of parental beliefs for developmental processes and outcomes; he also anticipated a number of other key features of what were later to be referred to as ecological models for research on human development. For example, during the 1980s, a series of publications (Bronfenbrenner 1986, 1988, 1989a, 1990a, in press; Bronfenbrenner and Crouter, 1983) laid out an array of such models, ranging from the most simple to the most complex, called a *process–person–context model*. The last provided for the simultaneous assessment of variation in developmental processes and outcomes as a joint, interactive function of characteristics of the developing person and the environment. The model was first described in the revised edition of the "Handbook of Child Psychology," published in 1983 (Bronfenbrenner and Crouter, 1983). In the very same year Sigel, together with his colleagues (Sigel et al., 1983), published a study in which exactly this kind of model was not only independently conceptualized but effectively implemented. The authors hypothesized, and demonstrated, that distancing strategies were differentially effective in furthering intellectual development as a joint function of the nature of the cognitive task (i.e., context) and the characteristics of the child (in this instance, normal vs. learning disabled children).

FROM DISTANCING TO RECIPROCATION

Some of the findings obtained by Sigel and his colleagues are disappointing in that they fail to provide strong support for stated hypotheses; others are more disturbing, for they document relations that run counter to those posited. In this concluding section of my chapter, I suggest that by working from the perspective of an ecological paradigm, not only may some of these paradoxes be resolved, but the effort at resolution may lead to new, more precise, and, perhaps, even more powerful hypotheses regarding the processes that foster cognitive development.

The effort takes as its point of departure an especially disappointing and puzzling finding. Instead of treating distancing as a single variable existing along a linear continuum, Sigel broke it up into three contrasting levels, with provision for variation within each one. For example, at the lowest level, distancing involved such concrete, essentially didactic parental behaviors as naming, or asking the child to name, a particular object; describing obviously portrayed features in a picture; or identifying similarities between objects at a low level of inference. By contrast, at the highest level, the concepts presented were more abstract, and the inferences more remote.[2] The existence of such separate measures made it possible to examine the effect of individual differences among parents behaving at low, intermediate, and high levels of distancing strategy.

Correlations between these measures and assessments of children's cognitive development yielded a disconcerting pattern of results that continues to puzzle Sigel and his colleagues to the present day. Witness the following passage from his most recent chapter, prepared for the volume on the Development and Meaning of Psychological Distance.

---

[2]A more detailed presentation of these measures can be found in Sigel (1982, 1986).

Consistently over the years working with families of young children we have found that teachers', and parents', use of didactic controlling strategies tend to have a negative impact on children's representational competence. However, to our surprise, outcomes for high level strategies, i.e., those creating cognitive demands to reason, to evaluate, to think logically do not seem to have the same strong set of findings. This poses some challenges to the theory since it is also counter-intuitive. Should not engaging the child in "demands" for high level thinking provide a basis for representation competence? (Sigel, 1990a)

Although Sigel does not offer an answer to this question, he clearly does not mean it to be purely rhetorical, for it emerges from other data as well. For example, a somewhat similar pattern of results was obtained in a study by Dornbusch and his colleagues (1987) on the relation of parenting styles to school performance. For the purposes of their study, the investigators constructed questionnaire measures for the three familiar parental styles introduced by Baumrind (1966, 1971): authoritarianism, permissiveness, and authoritativeness. As hypothesized, the two former variables showed a negative relationship to school grades, whereas the association for authoritativeness was positive. The positive relationship for the latter factor, however, was much weaker in magnitude than the negative associations for the other two factors.

On the basis of an ecological paradigm of development, this pattern of differential magnitudes in the predictive power of positive versus negative parental behaviors is to be expected (Bronfenbrenner, 1990b). The argument takes as its point of departure the first of several propositions, emerging from ecologically oriented research, that specify processes at the proximal level influencing human development (Bronfenbrenner 1989a, 1990a, in press). Shorn of more formal language, the proposition may be stated as follows:

Proposition 1. Children's development takes place as a function of their participation in progressively more complex, mutually responsive reciprocal activity, on a regular basis over an extended period in the child's life, with one or more other persons with whom the child develops a strong, mutual, irrational emotional attachment, and who is committed to the child's well-being and development. (Bronfenbrenner, 1989b)

Several corollaries follow from this proposition. First, the converse of the proposition also holds; that is, any pattern of behavior on the part of the parent, or of the child, that interferes with reciprocity of response would tend to impede developmental processes and reduce favorable outcomes. Two of Baumrind's parental styles provide examples of such impairment operating at opposite poles. Permissiveness, with its laissez-faire orientation, leads both to reduced parental initiative and parental response. At the opposite extreme, *authoritarianism,* with its rigid orientation, decreases the parent's capacity for differential response to the child's actions. The findings of Sigel and his colleagues regarding the negative impact of didactic modes of both parental and teacher behavior are clearly consistent with the latter principle.

But why should the positive effects of authoritativeness in Dornbusch's research, or of high-level distancing strategies in Sigel's work, be so much weaker? Several plausible answers to this question follow from elements stipulated in Proposition 1. The first, and most important, of these elements is the requirement of reciprocity of response. To introduce an older concept from the psychology of learning into a contemporary ecological frame, the responses of parent and child must be contingent on each other. As documented elsewhere (Bronfenbrenner, 1986, 1989a), when such sequential reciprocity in parent–child behavior is used as a predictive measure, the observed relationships are considerably higher than those obtained using assessments of one-sided behavior, be it that of the parent or the child. The lower correlations obtained for authoritativeness by Dornbusch et al. (1987) and for high-level distancing by Sigel and his colleagues are consistent with this generalization.

A second relevant element of Proposition 1 is paradoxically identified by its absence. Thus, there is nothing in the proposition requiring that the process of interaction be driven primarily by cognitive demands on the child conveyed by distancing strategies on the part of the adult, and expressed through language rather than action. To be sure, there is the stipulation that the interaction be such as to allow for "progressively more complex activity," but this complexity is viewed as evolving from the activity itself, with both parties contributing to "raising the ante," typically spontaneously rather than by design.

Finally, the elements contained in Proposition 1 explicitly go beyond the cognitive sphere in identifying as a contributing factor the existence of an emotional tie between the child and the adult.

In sum, to the extent that Proposition 1 has some validity (as it seems to have in the light of the research evidence), it would appear that the processes facilitating cognitive development in childhood are not exclusively cognitive in nature nor primarily driven by adult instruction through questions and answers. In its social manifestations, the process is a joint enterprise, motivated and shaped from both sides. Hence, its strategies must be such as to provide opportunities and encouragement for dual participation in the context of an affective relationship.

Where does all this leave distancing theory, let alone its practical application in the family and the classroom? Does it mean that the constructive impact of distancing strategies is at best minimal? The answer to the latter question is clearly, "No." The basis for that answer is found in Sigel's research results comparing the effects of distancing strategies in two groups: a sample of 60 children ages 3–5 who had been diagnosed as having a language or communication disorder (but no hearing difficulties), and a matched control group of normally functioning youngsters (Sigel, 1986; Sigel et al., 1983).

The analysis of the relation between distancing strategies and assessments of the child's cognitive competence revealed a striking contrast. Although for the normal children, the correlations were typically nonsignificant and low in magnitude, the coefficients for the communicatively impaired children were consistently higher. Moreover, with the latter group, significant results were found not only for the negative impact of didactic styles but also for the positive effect of high-level distancing strategies.

Such findings are of course nicely in accord with the basic postulates of an ecological paradigm for human development. Lying at the core of the paradigm is the principle that the processes shaping development vary systematically as a joint function of the characteristics of the person and of the environment. This means that the same process can have different effects depending on the characteristics of the child. In the present instance, it would appear that distancing strategies are indeed effective when employed with children who are impaired in language and communication skills.

As documented in the research reviews already cited, other investigations employing an ecological model have revealed a similar pattern of findings regarding the influence of the characteristics of the child on developmental processes and outcomes. To cite but one example, Crockenberg (1981) found that the effect of social support to mothers on the development of mother–infant attachment was more pronounced for mothers who had an irritable infant rather than an easy baby.

DISTANCING IN CONTEXT

The question still remains, however, whether distancing strategies can also produce substantial effects with normal children. The demonstration of this possibility with Sigel's data would require expansion of a process–person–context model beyond the point that he has taken it thus far. In the studies published to date, the model, in its most complex form, has involved the analysis of variations in process as a joint function of the sex of the parent and of the child (Sigel, 1982). In this analysis, the possible confounding influences of social class and sibling composition were also controlled for by entering these variables as prior steps in a regression equation. This has of course become standard research practice. But the procedure is in fact based on assumptions that can be seriously questioned both on theoretical and methodological grounds (Bronfenbrenner, in press). If the assumptions are invalid, as they often are in relation to human development, controlling variables by prior entry in a linear regression model can not only produce misleading results, but can also mask the influence of major sources of variation in developmental processes and outcomes.

What are these potentially invalid assumptions, and the major sources of variation that can be overlooked? The answer to this question is based even more on theoretical than methodological grounds. Thus, the standard regression procedure requires the assumption that the primary relationships under investigation operate in the same way and to the same degree with respect to each of the of the factors being controlled. In the case of developmental research, this means that the processes influencing development are presumed to operate in the same way irrespective of the characteristics of the person or the environment. It is precisely this tacit assumption that is challenged by the ecological paradigm.

The assumption also has its methodological analogue in statistical theory; in that context it is known as "the assumption of homogeneity of regression." When the assumption is not justified, the use of statistical controls can produce distorted results that have no correspondence in reality. Only if the regressions are homogeneous (i.e., if the process operates in the same way in each domain of the model) can the conventional regression model be applied as a valid method of statistical control.

And if not, what can be done? Both on theoretical and statistical grounds there is the same simple answer: Each process must be examined separately in the context or population in which it occurs.

Let us now apply this principle and procedure to the present case, using social class as the control factor under consideration. Entering this variable in the regression equation before the measure of distancing strategy makes the assumption that the latter will have the same impact in furthering cognitive competence at each social class level. In the present instance, there are grounds to question this assumption. Appropriately enough, one of those grounds is found in Sigel's original paper introducing the distancing concept (Sigel, 1970). In that short but seminal work, he traces the origin of his concept to an unexpected finding obtained when he undertook to replicate one of his earlier experiments on representational thinking in a predominantly Black, lower-class sample. In his own words:

> We assumed that in view of our previous research social class might not really be a very relevant variable, so I blithely proceeded to present [the stimuli] in the usual format to these children. I discovered that they had difficulty in classifying the pictures. They tended to associate them by chaining, frequently thematically rather than on the basis of class membership or common properties. Items selected tended to bear little or no functional relationship to previous or subsequent choices . . . . Why did these children have such difficulty in simple, free classification tasks? (Sigel, 1970, p. 104)

Sigel's formulation of the distancing hypothesis represented the first step in his effort to answer this question 20 years ago. Since that time, he has taken many steps that have brought him, and us, closer to the goal. To come closer still, Sigel could take the data already available on communicatively handicapped and normal children and analyze them not only by sex of parent and sex of child but also separately by successive social class levels. As a trial hypothesis, one might expect that the relationships between parental distancing strategies and cognitive outcomes will turn out to be stronger for children in lower-class than in middle-class families, and that, contrary to the previously observed pattern, this trend will be even more pronounced for normal children than for the communicatively handicapped.

This hypothesis is founded both on theoretical and empirical grounds. As a way of illustrating both at the same time, I turn to one of the first, and best, examples that I have been able to find of research that meets the requirements of a process–person–context model. The study was carried out by Cecil Mary Drillien (1957, 1964), a physician and Professor of Child Life and Health at the University of Edinburgh. In her investigation, she analyzed the relation between the quality of mother–child interaction and the development of the child simultaneously as a joint function of the characteristics of the child and of the environment. The principal environmental factor systematically included in the research design was social class, stratified by three levels. In a parallel trichotomy, children were differentiated by birth weight into three groups, designated by VLBW (very low, 4 lb or less), LBW (low, more than 4 up to 5 lb), and normal (NRM, over 5 lb). The developmental outcome was an index of problem behavior observed when the children were between 3 and 5 years of age. The index was based on the frequency of behavior disturbances, such as hyperactivity, overdependence, timidity, and negativism. Finally, the measure of process was an assessment of the quality of maternal behavior. It took the form of a composite rating based on the mother's responses to interviews conducted in the home during the early preschool period. Regrettably, for purposes of statistical analysis, Drillien collapsed her rating scale to a two-point dichotomy of what she called "satisfactory" versus "unsatisfactory" maternal care.

To make their multiple messages more readily perceptible, the tabled results are presented in the form of a histogram (Fig. 4.1). The bars depict variation in mean scores for the degree of problem behavior (observed and rated when the children were between 3 and 5 years of age) as a joint function of maternal care, social class, and level of birth weight.

The picture emerging from an examination of Fig. 4.1 reveals some of the special strengths of a process–person–context model. As a background for understanding these more distinctive features, it is helpful to take note of findings of a more conventional sort. It is clear that the quality of maternal care is the most powerful predictor of children's problem behavior; in general, good treatment appears to reduce substantially the degree of behavioral disturbance in all children, including those of lowest birth weight. It is only when we also take into account the contextual dimension of social class that we begin to reap some of the benefits of the more complex process–person–context design. For example, perhaps most welcome is the paradoxical but encouraging finding that the quality of maternal care has an even greater impact in poor families than among the well-educated and well-to-do. Thus, it is among children from the least privileged families group that poor maternal care does the most damage and quality care

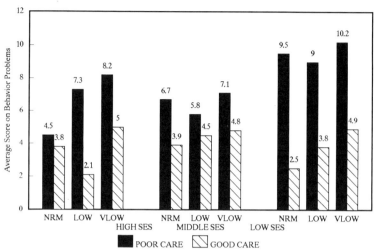

Figure above each bar is the average number of problem behaviors for each group as defined by birth weight, quality of care, and social class.

FIG. 4.1.   Problem behavior at age 3–5 years, by birth weight, mother care, and class.

does the most good. Over and above theoretical considerations, it is on the basis of findings like this that the hypothesis positing a greater impact of distancing strategies on children from lower class families is founded.

But what about the further, paradoxical prediction, deviating from the previously observed general trend, that the greater benefits of distancing strategies at this socioeconomic level will be even more marked for normal children than for the communicatively handicapped? The basis for this prediction, both conceptually and empirically, is also illustrated in Drillien's results. Thus far we have not fully exploited the yield of a process–person–context model, but have confined ourselves to one of its dual components—a process–context design. Within that framework, we have observed that the same level of quality care is not equally effective in every social context, but varies inversely with the degree of socioeconomic deprivation. The invocation of the full model, however, introduces a sobering note. Once we take into account the differential characteristics of the person, we discover that the special benefits of such care at the lowest socioeconomic level are not as great for children of lowest birth weight as for those of normal weight, and the degree of problem behavior in the former group continues to be greater than in the latter, despite good quality care. Weight handicap appears to have the opposite effect, however, in families living in more comfortable circumstances; here it is the child of moderately low birth weight who benefits most from maternal attention. How do we account for this reversal?

A plausible explanation emerges once one looks at the distribution of quality care across both birth weight and social class (not shown). In the most disadvantaged homes, it is the children of the lowest birth weight who most often receive poor quality care. By contrast, in families living in more comfortable circumstances, it is youngster who was born underweight who receives more attention from its mother, and the child of normal birth weight who is somewhat neglected.

This turnabout suggests that in families living under adequate socioeconomic conditions, most mothers give special attention to a low-birth-weight baby; by contrast, when living conditions are poor, mothers may often be so overcome by their stressful situation as to be unable to provide the extra care that such an infant requires.

It is findings of this kind, revealed through application of a process–person–context model, that provide the basis for the differential predictions set forth in the proposed guiding hypothesis.

BELIEF OR DISBELIEF?

Expansion of this same model in yet another direction may speak to another of Sigel's concerns. The low correlations between high-level distancing and cognitive outcomes obtained for normal children were not the only source of surprise and disappointment. A similar pattern appeared for the relation between belief and behavior, this time for the sample as a whole. In the words of the authors, "The failure to find consistent relationships between beliefs and behaviors is discouraging" (Sigel et al., 1983, p. 49). In the hope of obtaining stronger effects through the use of aggregate measures, the investigators grouped belief statements into a series of five broader clusters, but even this procedure "produced almost no significant results or discernible patterns of relationship" (p. 50).

However, in the overarching conceptual model that guided all of these analyses, belief systems were treated solely as mediating variables—initial links in a two-step causal chain in which parental conceptions give rise to parental behaviors that, in turn, facilitate the child's cognitive growth. But an ecological paradigm foresees yet another possibility. One of its defining properties is that it not only allows for but even anticipates synergistic effects as a predominant characteristic of human development. In keeping with this expectation, a process–person–context model not only permits but requires examination of the possibility that two or more of its elements can produce an effect greater than would be expected from their sum. For example, in Drillien's study, the combination of low birth weight and disadvantaged socioeconomic status had greater negative impact than would have been expected from the separate effects of each.

The possibility of synergistic effects also means that any element of the model can function not only as a mediator, but also as a moderator that enhances or diminishes the impact of other elements in the model. Thus, there is the possibility that the developmental importance of positive belief systems lies primarily not in facilitating the use of distancing strategies but in enhancing the constructive impact of such strategies on children's cognitive development. An initial test of this hypothesis is readily carried out by analyzing the relation between distancing behaviors and cognitive outcomes separately for two groups of families differentiated by the degree of positive parental beliefs.

CONCLUSION

It is of course possible that conducting the kinds of analyses here suggested will not alter the picture provided by the present findings, but I believe that such an outcome is unlikely. My faith is based mainly not on the efficiency of the proposed research models but on the power of a theoretical paradigm. That paradigm unifies two research approaches, and sets of findings, that have typically remained separate, in part because of the failure to formulate them conceptually and thus become aware of their potential complementarily. Proposition 1, presented earlier, offers a conceptualization of the first principle. The second may be stated as follows:

Proposition 2. The reciprocal processes that shape human development, and their psychological outcomes, vary systematically as a joint, interactive function of the biological and psychological characteristics of the person and of both the immediate and broader environmental context in which the person lives.

The process–person–context model provides for the simultaneous operationalization of both of these key principles. In discussing Sigel's seminal work in the context of an ecological paradigm and its implementation, my motive has been less an aim than a modest hope—the hope that application of such more differentiated conceptual paradigms and research designs will lead to even fuller realization and appreciation of Sigel's signal contributions to developmental theory and knowledge.

REFERENCES

Allport, G. W. (1937). *Personality: A psychosocial interpretation* (p. 54). New York: Holt.

Baumrind, D. (1966). Effects of authoritative parental control on child behavior. *Child Development, 37,* 887–907.

Baumrind, D. (1971). Current patterns of parental authority. *Developmental Psychology Monograph, 4,* 1–103.

Bronfenbrenner, U. (1979). *The ecology of human development.* Cambridge: MA: Harvard University Press.

Bronfenbrenner, U. (1986). Ecology of the family as a context for human development. *Developmental Psychology, 22,* 723–742.

Bronfenbrenner, U. (1988). Interacting systems in human development: Research paradigms: present and future. In N. Bolger, A. Caspi, G. Downey, & M. Moorehouse (Eds.), *Persons in context: Developmental processes* (pp. 25–49). New York: Cambridge University Press.

Bronfenbrenner, U. (1989a). Ecological systems theory. In R. Vasta (Ed.), *Six theories of child development* (pp. 185–246). Greenwich, CT: JAI Press.

Bronfenbrenner, U. (1989b April). *The developing ecology of human development: Paradigm lost or paradigm regained?* Paper presented at a symposium on Theories of child development; Updates and reformulations. Biennial Meeting of the Society for Research in child Development, Kansas City, MO.

Bronfenbrenner, U. (1990a). The ecology of cognitive development [condensed version]. *Zeitschrift fr Sozialisationsforschung und Erziehungssoziologie, 2,* 101–114.

Bronfenbrenner, U. (1990b). *On making human beings human.* Unpublished manuscript.

Bronfenbrenner, U. (in press). The ecology of cognitive development. In K. W. Fischer & R. Wozniak (Eds.), *Thinking in contexts.* Hillsdale, NJ: Lawrence Erlbaum Associates.

Bronfenbrenner, U., & Crouter, A. C. (1983). The evolution of environmental models in developmental research. In W. Kessen (Ed.), *History, theory, and methods,* Volume 1 of P. H. Mussen (Ed.), *Handbook of child psychology* (4th ed.), pp. 357–414). New York: Wiley.

Crockenberg, S. B. (1981). Infant irritability, other responsiveness, and social support influences on the security of infant-mother attachment. *Child Development, 52,* 857–865.

Dornbusch, S. M., Ritter, P. L., Leiderman, P. H., Roberts, D. F., and Fraleigh, M. J. (1987). The relation of parenting style to adolescent school performance. *Child Development, 58,* 1244–1257.

Drillien, C. M. (1957). The social and economic factors affecting the incidence of premature birth. *Journal of Obstetrical Gynecology, British Empire, 1,* 1008.

Drillien, C. M. (1964). *The growth and development of the prematurely born infant.* Edinburgh and London: E. & S. Livingston Ltd.

Ehlers, C. L., Frank, E., & Kupfer, D. J. (1988). Social zeitgebers and biological rhythms. *Archives of General Psychiatry, 45,* 948–952.

May, M. A. (1932). The foundations of personality. In P. S. Achilles (Ed.), *Psychology at work* (pp. 81–101). New York: McGraw-Hill.

Sigel, I. E. (1970). The distancing hypothesis: A causal hypothesis for the acquisition of representative thought. In M. R. Jones (Ed.), *Miami Symposium on the Prediction of Behavior. 1968: Effects of early experiences* (pp. 99–118). Coral Gables, FL: University of Miami Press.

Sigel, I. E. (1982). The relationship between parental distancing strategies and the child's cognitive behavior. In L. M. Laosa & I. E. Sigel (Eds.), *Families as learning environments for children* (pp. 47–86). New York: Plenum.

Sigel, I. E. (1986). Reflections on the belief-behavior connection: Lessons learned from a research program on parental belief systems and teaching strategies. In R. D. Ashmore & D. M. Brodzinsky (Eds.), *Thinking about the family: Views of parents and children* (pp. 35–65). Hillsdale, NJ: Lawrence Erlbaum Associates.

Sigel, I. E. (1990a, May). *Issue and questions regarding the relationship between distancing and representational competence.* Paper prepared for the Conference on the Development of Psychological Distance, held at the Educational Testing Service, Princeton, NJ.

Sigel, I. E. (1990b). Journeys in serendipity: The development of the distancing model. In I. E. Sigel & G. H. Brody (Eds.), *Family research: Methods, cases, and approaches: Vol. 1. Normal families* (pp. 87–120). Hillsdale, NJ: Lawrence Erlbaum Associates.

Sigel, I. E., & McGillicuddy-DeLisi, A. V. (1984). Parents as teachers of their children: A distancing behavior model. In A. D. Pelligrini & T. D. Yawkey (Eds.), *The development of oral and written language in social contexts* (pp. 71–92). Norwood, NJ: Ablex.

Sigel, I. E., McGillicuddy-DeLisi, A. V., Flaugher, J., & Rock, D. A. (1983). *Parents as teachers of their own learning disabled children* (ETS RR 83-21). Princeton, NJ: Educational Testing Service.

Sigel, I. E., McGillicuddy-DeLisi, A. V., & Johnson, J. E. (1980). *Parental distancing, beliefs, and children's representational competence within the family* (ETA RR 80-21). Princeton, NJ: Educational Testing Service.

Wachs, T. D. (1979). Proximal experience and early cognitive intellectual development: The physical environment. *Merrill-Palmer Quarterly, 25,* 3–41.

II   PSYCHOLOGICAL DISTANCE AS A COGNITIVE DEMAND

5 Temperamental Contributions to Styles of Reactivity to Discrepancy

Jerome Kagan
Nancy Snidman
Harvard University

Events that are not assimilable immediately are both a common experience and one of the most significant provocations to change in psychological and physiological processes. Uncertainty and wariness are typical English words to describe the state produced by unfamiliarity that is not understood at once, while surprise is chosen to convey the belief that comprehension was relatively rapid. The variation in reactivity to unfamiliarity is usually ascribed either to past experience and, therefore, to cognitive preparation for the event or to endogenous variation in those brain systems that are activated by novelty. Because most child psychologists prefer to minimize endogenous variation, developmental investigations of this domain usually focus on the relation between the child's knowledge and the new experience, as well as the motivational properties of discrepancies that are only moderately different from the child's schemata and concepts. Scientists who work with animals, on the other hand, are more interested in the biological bases for intra- or interspecific variation in reactivity to unfamiliarity and emphasize the role of neurotransmitters—especially norepinephrine—on the alerting response to novelty.

The renaissance in research on human temperamental categories has led a small number of developmental scholars to join comparative investigators in analyses of the contribution of the young child's physiological functioning to his or her initial reaction to novelty. At least two of the Thomas and Chess (1977) temperamental qualities—approach/withdrawal and ease of adaptation to new situations—refer to this idea.

THE ROLE OF TEMPERAMENT

Over the last 12 years our laboratory at Harvard has been studying temperamental variation among children in their reactivity to unfamiliar experiences. Although all intact children detect most variations on their knowledge, there is extraordinary variation in the behavioral responsiveness and style of reaction that accompany that process, especially when the variation is not easily assimilable. The first phase of that work revealed that 2-year-old children vary in their tendency to approach or to avoid unfamiliar people and objects. About 15%–20% of young, Caucasian children are consistently shy and timid in the face of novelty, and 25%–30% usually approach the same unfamiliar events, often in an affectively spontaneous manner. There is moderate, but significant, preservation of these two styles—called inhibited and uninhibited to the unfamiliar—from 21 or 31 months of age through $7\frac{1}{2}$ years. About three fourths of the children retained their expected classification, and the children who were most extreme initially were most likely to maintain their behavioral style. Although some of the originally inhibited children no longer displayed an extreme degree of restraint and caution when they were $7\frac{1}{2}$ years old, the majority had still not acquired the unusually spontaneous demeanor characteristic of the uninhibited child. In addition, a smaller number of uninhibited children—about 10% of the original group—became shy as the result of intervening environmental stress (Kagan, Reznick, & Snidman, 1988; Kagan, 1989).

It is important to note that these results were found for children who had been selected originally to be either extremely inhibited or uninhibited. Preservation of these two styles in less extreme children is far less common. Further, it has been suggested that these two groups of children do not fall on a continuum, but represent two categorical types. The two types of children share a genotype, an environmental history, and a set of correlated behavioral and physiological characteristics. Some support for this claim comes from study of a third longitudinal cohort of Caucasian, middle-class children who were not selected initially to be extreme on any quality and were observed at 14, 20, and 48 months (Kagan, Reznick, & Gibbons, 1989). These are the typical youngsters that developmental psychologists study in their research. There was no preservation of the inhibited or uninhibited style from 14 or 20 months to age 4 for the entire sample. However, when the analysis was restricted to those children who were either inhibited or uninhibited originally—the top and bottom 20% of the distribution—there were significant differences in behavior and physiology between the two extreme groups. This implies that the constructs inhibited and uninhibited refer to qualitative categories of children, in the same sense that beagles and terriers represent two qualitatively different strains of canines.

A second basis for the claim that the two groups are qualitatively different derives from the fact that they are characterized by distinctive physical and physiological characteristics. More inhibited than uninhibited children are blue-eyed and ectomorphic while more uninhibited children are brown-eyed and mesomorphic. In addition, inhibited children show greater reactivity in the target organs of the sympathetic nervous system, the skeletal motor system, and the hypothalamic–pituitary–adrenal axis (Kagan et al., 1988.) Specifically, inhibited, compared with uninhibited, children are more likely to display a cardiac acceleration and pupillary dilation to mild cognitive stress, higher salivary cortisol levels in the morning, and greater muscle tension. A composite physiological index based on these biological variables gathered at $5\frac{1}{2}$ years correlated with indexes of inhibited and uninhibited behavior at every age of assessment (correlations between .6 and .7). A recent assessment of these children at 10–11 years of age revealed that the inhibited children showed greater facial cooling on the right, compared with the left, side of the face. Because sympathetic activity is enhanced on the right compared with the left side, this difference implies greater sympathetic reactivity among the inhibited children.

PREDICTION FROM INFANCY

We are now in the third year of a project designed to determine whether selected characteristics of the young infant predict inhibited and uninhibited behavior in the second year. The rationale for the procedures is based on discoveries by physiologists suggesting that the amygdala and its varied projections to the hypothalamus, corpus striatum, central gray, and cortex are important participants in the avoidant behavior many animal species display to novelty (Dunn & Everitt, 1988). For example, if neurons in the amygdala of the rat are destroyed chemically, the animals lose their typical avoidant reaction to novel foods. Because all classes of sensory information eventually synapse on neurons in the amygdala, and the amygdala influences behavior to novel events, many of the behavioral characteristics that differentiate inhibited from uninhibited children could be a partial consequent of differences in thresholds of excitability in varied sites of the amygdala and its projections to targets that participate in an animal's reaction to unfamiliar events.

Support for this last statement comes from the work of Adamec and Stark-Adamec (1986), who reported that house cats who typically withdraw to novelty have lower thresholds of excitability in an area close to the basal amygdala, as well as projections to the ventromedial hypothalamus than do less fearful cats. Further, the behavioral differences between the two groups of cats emerge early during the second postnatal month, and are relatively stable thereafter, suggesting genetic differences between the two groups. Work with rhesus monkeys conducted in Suomi's laboratory (1987) reveals stability of the two contrasting behavioral types and similar physiological profiles. The possibility of a genetic contribution to the profiles of inhibited and uninhibited children is enhanced by the independent research of Matheny (1989), as well as an ongoing study on a large number of twins being conducted at the Institute of Behavioral Genetics at the University of Colorado (Robinson, Kagan, Reznick, & Corley, in press).

An important clue to the responses in young infants that might predict the inhibited or uninhibited children comes from the work of LaGasse, Gruber, and Lipsitt (1989). These investigators found that newborns who displayed an increase in sucking rate (because they decreased the temporal interval between sucking bursts) when the water they were ingesting through a nipple suddenly changed to sucrose were more likely to be inhibited 2 years later than newborns who showed a minimal increase in sucking rate following the change in taste. This result is in accord with contemporary understanding of the brain. The sensory information contained in the change from water to sucrose stimulates the amygdala, which could lead, in turn, to the increase in sucking rate. This variation in increased sucking might be attributable to differences in the excitability of the relevant nuclei in the amygdala and the projections to the motor centers serving this response. In addition, there is evidence indicating that newborn infants who fret or cry easily to unfamiliar stimulation are more likely to become fearful than less irritable infants (van den Boom, 1989).

In light of this discussion it seems reasonable to assume that an early predictor of the two temperamental groups might be a combination of motor activity and crying following encounters with unfamiliar, or changing, stimuli in various modalities.

Sample

The subjects were 102 Caucasian infants born at term without pre- or perinatal complications to mothers between 20 and 40 years of age who had been carefully screened for excessive smoking, alcohol, and coffee consumption during pregnancy. In addition, over 90% of the parents had attended or graduated from college. Thus, this sample is unusually homogeneous with respect to the good health of the mother and infant, as well as the social class and economic advantage of the family. The infants were seen in a laboratory session at 2, 4, 9, and 14 months of age; this chapter deals with the child's behavior at 4, 9, and 14 months.

4-Month Assessment

The battery at 4 months contained a series of six episodes: (a) a 60-sec baseline with the mother looking down at the infant, (b) presentation of a series of three-dimensional objects, (c) presentation of three different mobiles, (d) recordings of three different consonant vowel syllables spoken by a female voice at three different levels of loudness, (e) an additional set of three dimensional objects, and (f) a second baseline period.

Classification of the Infants

Study of the videotaped laboratory sessions revealed two obvious qualities on which infants varied. One quality was degree of motor activity during the stimulus episodes, as reflected in vigorous movements of the limbs, arching of the back, tongue protrusions, and motor tension in the arms and legs. The second differentiating quality was fretting and crying to the stimuli. About half of the infants fretted briefly on less than 15% of the trials (one fourth never fretted at all), while the remaining half of the infants fretted or cried to more than 25% of the trials or cried intensely on a few trials and were difficult to soothe.

A coder with no knowledge of the child's later behavior assigned each infant to one of two motor activity groups based on frequency and vigor of motor activity. Sixty percent of the infants were classified as low and 40% as high on motor activity. The former group displayed a motor act on an average of 15% of the 28 stimulus trials, and the high motor group on an average of 40% of the trials. The latter group was also more likely to arch the back and extend the limbs in momentary spasticity during stimulus presentations. These classifications agreed, for 80% of the sample, with the proportion of trials on which a limb movement, back arch, or tongue protrusion occurred, as judged by an independent set of three coders who did not evaluate vigor of movement or motor tension. The final classification of the remaining 20% of the infants was based on a consensus between two coders following a reexamination of the videotapes and reference to the proportion of trials on which motor activity occurred.

A coder also assigned each infant into one of three fret–cry groups based on frequency and intensity of fretting or crying, as well as the ease of being soothed when the child became distressed. The correlation between this three-category judgment and the proportion of crying or fretting trials coded by an independent set of coders was .8. Each infant was assigned subsequently to a low ($n = 52$) or a high ($n = 42$) fret–cry group based on a combination of the category judgment and the proportion of fret–cry trials.

Each infant was classified subsequently into one of four groups: high motor–high cry; low motor–low cry; low motor–high cry; and high motor–low cry, based on the criteria described. The proportions of infants in each of these four groups were 23%, 37%, 22%, and 18%, respectively.

Assessments of Fear

Ninety-four of the infants returned at 9 and 14 months for a laboratory assessment of vulnerability to fear to unfamiliar events. The 9-month battery was administered in two settings in which unfamiliar events were presented by unfamiliar females across 16 different episodes. The mother was always with the infant.

A fear reaction was defined operationally as the occurrence of fretting or crying in response to encounter with an unfamiliar event or failure to approach an unfamiliar woman or an unfamiliar object in a large playroom. At 9 months the three events that most often produced a fear reaction were: (a) the mother assumed a frown while she displayed a moving toy to the child, (b) a puppet head appeared on either the right or left side of the child's visual field accompanied by a taped female voice speaking a nonsense phrase in a voice with either a happy or an angry emotional tone, and (c) the female examiner uncovered a rotating toy and spoke a nonsense phrase in an angry tone with a frown on her face. Forty-five percent of the infants showed either no or one fear reaction, 35% showed two or three fear reactions, and 20% showed four or more fear reactions.

The battery at 14 months consisted of 17 different episodes. Twelve had been part of the 9-month battery while five were new. The events that most often generated a fear score were: (a) an unfamiliar woman opened the cabinet in a playroom revealing a metal robot and after remaining quiet for a minute invited the child to approach the robot; failure to approach was coded as fear; (b) the rotating toy and puppet procedures administered at 9 months were re-administered; (c) the child fretted and refused to accept in his or her mouth a dropper containing liquid. Forty-eight percent of these children showed no or one fear reaction, 20% showed two or three fear reactions, and 32% showed four or more fear reactions. The fear scores had high intercoder reliability ($r = .9$) because the criteria were discrete and objective.

Stability and Prediction of Fear

The fear scores were stable from 9 to 14 months ($r = .44; p < .0001$), and only 11% of the infants changed from high fear (four or more fears) to low fear (zero or one fear) or from low to high fear across the 5-month period. An analysis of variance of the fear scores at 9 and 14 months with the four different 4-month profiles as independent factors revealed a significant effect at both ages ($F = 2.7$, $p < .05$ at 9 months; $F = 7.8$, $p < .001$ at 14 months). The difference in fear score between the high motor–high cry and low motor–low cry groups was statistically significant at both ages. Not one of the 22 high motor–high cry, but 14 of the 35 low motor–low cry infants displayed a low degree of fear (zero or one fear) at both ages (chi square = 9.6; $p < .0001$). The other two groups displayed intermediate levels of fear at both ages and at 14 months were significantly different from both the high motor–high cry and low motor–low cry groups.

DISCUSSION

Because the predictive relation between 4-month reactivity to unfamiliar events and later fearfulness was not due to prematurity, illness, or distress associated with economic disadvantage, it is reasonable to suggest that it reflects the preservation of variation in physiological processes that might be partially genetic in origin. Although it is not possible to specify the relevant physiological mechanisms, one speculative explanation implicates circuits that include the amygdala and its varied projections. The basolateral area of the amygdala receives sensory input from the thalamus and cortex and sends projections to the ventromedial striatum and, as a result, excited motor activity. The central nucleus of the amygdala, which receives input from the basolateral area, projects to the cingulate and central gray, which mediate distress calls in cats and monkeys, and, by extrapolation, fretting and crying in human infants. Therefore, infants who were born with a low threshold of reactivity in both the basolateral and central areas might be expected to show greater increases in motor activity and more frequent crying to discrepant or unfamiliar stimuli than infants with higher thresholds.

The fact that infants differ in their behavioral responsiveness to change in their surround suggests that scientists should attend to temperamental factors, as well as the child's prior knowledge, when assessing behavior to events that are transformations of past experience. It is probably difficult at the present time to separate these two independent processes. Thus, inferences about an older child's psychological profile, based on his or her behavioral response to discrepancy, should be guarded unless the investigator has good reason to believe that the absence (or presence) of a specific response is due to variation in acquired knowledge. The extremely quiet 6-year-old who refuses to answer an examiner's questions might be an inhibited child rather than one who lacks the relevant knowledge.

Continua Versus Categories

These results imply, although they do not prove, that some temperamental profiles should be treated as categories. Inhibited children, who make up a small proportion of the population, are characterized by a set of correlated characteristics that are independent in a large, unselected population: high motor activity and high crying at 4 months, high fear at 9 and 14 months, and large cardiac accelerations, motor tension, and pupillary dilation to cognitive stress at older ages. These variables are only positively correlated in this small group of children, and not in a large group of unselected children. As a result, a factor analysis of these continuous dimensions might not reveal either of the two temperamental groups. Stated more formally: (a) If each of n dependent variables has more than one origin, (b) and these origins are independent, (c) but one origin is common to all of the variables for a small proportion of the population, (d) then the correlations among the variables will be low and a factor analysis will not reveal a factor that represents the small number of subjects who are characterized by high (or low) levels on all the variables, even though there is a category of individuals who are high (or low) on the dependent variables.

The physicist Pierre Duhem, in an essay called "Quantity and Quality"

(1954), noted that most scientists strive to describe their data in mathematical statements. Because mathematics assumes continuous magnitudes as a primary axiom, there has been a bias among psychologists to classify natural phenomena in terms of continuous dimensions. This premise leads easily to the assumption that every phenomenon in nature can be understood eventually as the result of the addition of continuous magnitudes. The explanation for the boiling of water relies on continuous magnitudes of heat and pressure within a pot. But Duhem adds that nature also consists of qualities that cannot be formed simply by adding quantities. He recalls Diderot asking facetiously, "How many snowballs would be required to heat an oven?"

Max Planck (1936) provides an additional example of the importance of taking into account origins when one is classifying phenomena. Consider the following two mathematical statements: $\sqrt{2}$ and 1.41421. If one takes magnitude as the criterion for classification, the two forms are similar. This frame is analogous to looking only at the contemporary behavior of a group of children. However, if one relies on origins as the basis for classification, the two forms are different, for $\sqrt{2}$ is an irrational number while 1.41421 is a rational number that can be expressed as the ratio of two integers. With respect to origin, these two forms are qualitatively different and do not lie on a continuum. We believe a similar argument is appropriate for inhibited and uninhibited children who begin life with qualitatively different biological dispositions.

The senior author cannot help noting the satisfaction derived from this corpus of data. About 30 years ago when Kagan and Moss (1962/1983) discovered that shy, timid behavior was the only quality preserved from the first 3 years of life to adulthood, they were uncertain as to the reason for the unusual degree of stability of this characteristic. They were friendly to an interpretation that awarded much of the power to early experience in the home. The current temperamental interpretation of this stability has an esthetic appeal because of its theoretical coherence and initial correspondence to known physiological processes. T. S. Eliot ends *Four Quartets* with a theme appropriate to this change in view.

> We shall not cease from exploration
> And the end of all our exploring
> Will be to arrive where we started
> And know the place for the first time.

ACKNOWLEDGMENTS

This research was supported in part by a grant from the John D. and Catherine T. MacArthur Foundation. The authors thank Susan Krupp, Hilary Sokolowski, Annie McQuilken, Jane Gibbons, and Lynn Goldsmith.

REFERENCES

Adamec, R. E., & Stark-Adamec, C. (1986). Limbic hyperfunction, limbic epilepsy, and interictal behavior. In B. K. Doane & K. E. Livingston (Eds.), *The Limbic System* (pp. 129–145). New York: Raven.

Duhem, P. (1954). *The aim and structure of physical theory* (P. Weiner, Trans.). Princeton, NJ: Princeton University Press.

Dunn, L. T., & Everitt, B. J. (1988). Double dissociations of the effects of amygdala and insular cortex lesions on condition taste aversion, passive avoidance and neophobia in the rat using the excitotoxin ibotenic acid. *Behavioral Neuroscience, 102,* 3–9.

Kagan, J. (1989). Temperamental contributions to social behavior. *American Psychologist, 44,* 668–674.

Kagan, J., Reznick, J. S., & Snidman, N. (1988). Biological bases of childhood shyness. *Science, 240,* 167–171.

Kagan, J., Reznick, J. S., & Gibbons, J. (1989). Inhibited and uninhibited types of children. *Child Development, 60,* 838–845.

Kagan, J., & Moss, J. (1962). *Birth to maturity.* New York: Wiley. (Reprinted by Yale University Press, New Haven, CT, 1983.)

LaGasse, L., Gruber, C., & Lipsitt, L. P. (1989). The infantile expression of avidity in relation to later assessments. In J. S. Reznick (Ed.), *Perspectives on behavioral inhibition.* Chicago: University of Chicago Press.

Matheny, A. P. (1989). Children's behavioral inhibition over age and across situations. *Journal of Personality, 57,* 215–236.

Planck, M. (1936). *The philosophy of physics* (W. H. Johnston, Trans.). London: Allen & Unwin.

Robinson, J. L., Kagan, J., Reznick, J. S., & Corley, R. (in press). The heritability of inhibited and uninhibited behavior. *Developmental Psychology.*

Suomi, S. J. (1987). Genetic and maternal contributions to individual differences in rhesus monkey biobehavioral development. In N. A. Krasnegor, E. M. Blass, M. A. Hofer, & W. P. Smotherman (Eds.), *Prenatal development: A psychobiological perspective* (pp. 397–420). San Diego, CA: Academic.

Thomas, A., & Chess, S. (1977). *Temperament and development.* New York: Brunner/Mazel.

Van den Boom, D. C. (1989). In G. A. Kohnstamm, J. E. Bates, & M. M. Rothbart (Eds.), *Temperament in childhood* (pp. 299–318). New York: Wiley.

6 Distancing and Dual Representation

Judy S. DeLoache
University of Illinois at Urbana-Champaign

One of the foremost achievements of early human development is "representational competence" (Sigel, 1970). Children come to realize that a variety of culturally defined symbol systems represent or stand for other objects, events, or ideas. They learn that pictures, numbers, and maps have referents, that they stand for something other than themselves.

This representational insight or competence does not come easily. This point is obvious in the case of abstract symbol systems, such as letters and numerals. Everyone expects that almost all children will have to be explicitly taught over a long period of time to read and do math.

The challenge facing the young child is not quite so readily apparent or acknowledged with other, less abstract symbol systems. For example, photographs and many other pictures bear a high degree of physical resemblance to their referents, leading to the common assumption that their referential function is transparent. It is not, however. Although very young children and even infants can recognize pictured information, they do not understand the role of pictures as representations of reality (Burns, 1990; DeLoache and Burns, 1989). As Sigel has noted, picture comprehension is "deceptively simple"; recognizing a depicted object is not the same thing as understanding that the picture is a representation of that object.

Another example of a symbol that can have a high degree of similarity to what it represents is a scale model. The research summarized in this chapter investigates young children's understanding of scale models, that is, their understanding that a model stands for or represents another space (DeLoache, 1987, 1989a, 1989b, 1990, 1991; DeLoache, Kolstad, & Anderson, 1991). Except for size, the models used in this research look very much like the larger spaces they stand for.

As we will show, 2.5-year-old children have rather remarkable difficulty achieving representational insight with scale models, remarkable both because the model–room relation is almost completely opaque to this age group and because the same relation is almost completely transparent not only to adults, but also to children just a few months older. Reasons for why this insight is so difficult to achieve are explored. It should be noted at the outset that the contribution of this research lies in what it reveals about symbolic functioning in general, not in the importance of understanding scale models in the child's everyday life. Young children rarely if ever encounter actual models in which there is referential specificity, that is, in which the symbolic object represents a specific other reality and the specific elements map onto specific, corresponding elements in the represented reality.

The representational toys with which young children spend a great deal of time do not have this specificity. Their replica toys rarely represent anything in their immediate environment or direct experience. A little boy may have a fleet of vehicles, but none of them is a model of his father's Oldsmobile or any other car the child has ridden in. Neither Barbie nor Raggedy Ann is likely to be a faithful representation of any little girl's mother. The contribution of this research lies in what it reveals about the early development of symbolic awareness in one domain and what that suggests about development in other domains.

YOUNG CHILDREN'S UNDERSTANDING OF SCALE MODELS

A dramatic developmental difference was recently reported in young children's reasoning from a scale model to a full-sized room (DeLoache, 1987). In this research, a young child (a 2.5- or 3.0-year-old) watched as a miniature toy was hidden somewhere in a scale model of a room. Then the child was asked to find a larger, analogous, toy concealed in the corresponding place in the room itself. For example, the child might observe a tiny toy dog being hidden behind the miniature couch in the model and then search for a larger toy dog that was hidden behind the full-sized couch in the room. (In this and all the subsequent model studies, half the children observed the larger toy being hidden in the room and then searched for the miniature toy in the model. This variable never makes any difference, so for ease of communication, the case in which the hiding event occurs in the model is always referred to.) To succeed in this task, children must: (a) recognize the correspondence between the model and the room; (b) map the elements of one space onto those of the other; and (c) use their knowledge of where the miniature toy was hidden to figure out where the larger toy must be.

The original study is described in some detail, because all the other research to be summarized here follows the same basic format. Each experimental session began with an extensive orientation phase during which the experimenter introduced the two toys that would be hidden as "Big Snoopy" (a stuffed dog 15 cm high) and "Little Snoopy" (a plastic dog 2 cm high). She explicitly described and demonstrated the correspondence between the room and the model ("Big Snoopy's big room" and "Little Snoopy's little room") and between all the individual items in them. The model (71 cm $\times$ 65 cm $\times$ 33 cm) was situated in a small room next to the larger room (4.80 m $\times$ 3.98 m $\times$ 2.54 m) it represented, aligned in the same spatial orientation. The model contained miniature versions of all the items of furniture in the room (e.g., couch, chair, dresser, pillows, etc.), arranged in the same relative spatial positions. The surface appearance of most of the objects in the two spaces was highly similar (e.g., the same fabric covering the miniature and full-sized couches).

Each trial involved three parts:

1. Hiding event. The child watched as the experimenter hid the miniature toy in the model, with a different hiding place used for each trial. The experimenter always called the child's attention to the act of hiding, but she never referred to the hiding place by name: "Look, Little Snoopy is going to hide here." The child was told that the other toy would be hidden in the corresponding place in the room: "Now Big Snoopy is going to hide in the same place in his big room."

2. Retrieval 1. Without retrieving the toy he or she had seen being hidden, the child was led into the adjoining room and asked to find the analogous toy. On every trial, before permitting the child to search, the experimenter provided a reminder of the correspondence between the two hiding places: "Remember, Big Snoopy is hiding in the same place as Little Snoopy." If the toy was not found on the first search, the child was encouraged to continue searching other locations (although only the first search was counted). If necessary, the experimenter gave increasingly explicit hints until the child found the object (the point being to maintain the child's motivation for the task). After retrieving the toy, either on the first or a prompted search, the child was taken back to the model.

3. Retrieval 2. Next, the child was asked to retrieve the original toy that he or she had observed being hidden at the beginning of the trial. The child was again prompted to continue searching if the first search was incorrect, and the trial always concluded with the child's retrieving the toy. Retrieval 2 was thus a standard memory trial, and it was crucial for interpreting the data. If the child was successful on Retrieval 2, then any problems with Retrieval 1 could not be due to simple forgetting or lack of motivation.

There were 32 subjects in the initial study, 16 in the 2.5-year-old group ($M = $ 31 months) and 16 in the 3.0-year-old group ($M = $ 38 months). The sample for this and all subsequent studies was predominately middle-class and white.

The results revealed a dramatic difference in the performance of these two

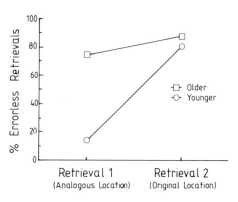

FIG. 6.1. Percentage errorless retrievals achieved by the two age groups in the original model study. From: DeLoache, J. S. (1987). Rapid change in the representational functioning of very young children. *Science, 238,* 1556–1557. Copyright 1987 AAAS. Reprinted by permission.

groups of children only a few months apart in age. Figure 6.1 shows the proportion of errorless retrievals. (An errorless retrieval is defined as the child searching first at the correct location.) The depicted interaction of age and retrieval was highly significant. The Retrieval 2 data indicate that both age groups remembered where the original object was hidden. (This high level of performance is comparable to that reported in previous research on young children's memory for location [DeLoache, 1985].)

The Retrieval 1 data show that the older children used their knowledge of the location of the toy they saw being hidden to infer where the analogous toy was hidden. Having seen the miniature dog being placed under the floor pillow in the model, they headed right for the larger pillow in the room. This inference came so easily that their success in finding the toy they had not seen being hidden was equal to their success at retrieving the toy they had observed being hidden. By contrast, the younger children gave no evidence that they appreciated the model–room correspondence: they seemed to draw no inference at all from their knowledge of the location of the original toy.

It should be emphasized that the 2.5-year-olds understood everything about the task *except* the crucial fact that the room and model were related and, hence, that what happened in one space told them something about the other. These children understood that there were toys hidden in the model and the room and that they were supposed to find them. They used their memory representation to retrieve the toy they had observed being hidden. They willingly searched for the other; they just failed to realize they had any way of knowing where it was. To the older children then, Retrieval 1 was a memory or reasoning game; to the younger children, it was a guessing game.

There are two main questions that need to be addressed regarding these data: (a) Why do 2.5-year-olds do so poorly in this task; that is, why do they have so much difficulty detecting the correspondence between the room and the model? (b) What is responsible for the abrupt change in performance between 2.5 and three years of age?

DISTANCING AND DUAL REPRESENTATION

Why is it so difficult for 2.5-year-old children to detect the correspondence between a scale model and a larger space? The problem may lie with the inherently dual nature of models. A scale model is, on the one hand, a highly salient, interesting three-dimensional object (or set of objects). On the other hand, a scale model is also a symbol; it represents a larger space. In the model task, the child must think about the model in both of these different ways at the same time—as the object that it is and as a symbol for something it is not. The child must achieve a dual representation of a single reality.

Representing a model as an object can block simultaneously representing it as a symbol. Getting caught up with the charm of the model as an attractive, complex, unusual toy prevents young children from realizing that it also stands for something other than itself. Thus, to understand the symbolic import of a model, children have to achieve psychological or cognitive distance (Sigel, 1970) from the three-dimensional model as object to represent it as an abstract symbol. Exploiting a model requires that one interpret it not in terms of its own concrete reality, but in terms of the reality it represents. Looking at the model, the child must think about the room.

This analysis suggests that scale models are difficult for very young children, because their attractiveness as objects makes it difficult for young children to achieve psychological distance from them, that is, to take a dual orientation. If this is correct, it follows that 2.5-year-old children should be more successful in a task in which they are given information about the location of a hidden object via a medium that does not require a dual orientation, a medium that does not make it difficult for them to achieve psychological distance.

Pictures are such a medium. Pictures are, of course, real objects as well as representations and hence have a certain "double reality" (Sigel, 1978). However, they are not as problematic as models for two reasons. First, although pictures are tangible objects, they are extremely simple and boring objects. There is very little in a plain flat surface to captivate a young child's attention. Second, even 2.5-year-old children know that the primary function of a picture is to represent something else (Burns, 1990; DeLoache & Burns, 1989). When one looks at a picture, one normally thinks only of what it depicts, not of the picture as an object itself. Thus, children do not have to suppress a strong response to a picture as an object in order to be aware of its symbolic nature.

An unusual prediction was made: 2.5-year-old children should do better at retrieving objects hidden in a room when they are given information about the location of the hidden object via pictures of the room than when the same information is conveyed via a scale model of the room. Although this prediction follows from the above line of reasoning about distancing and dual orientation, it is counterintuitive on other grounds. It flies in the face of how people normally think about two-dimensional pictures and three-dimensional objects. There is a wealth of developmental and cross-cultural research showing better cognitive performance with real objects than with pictures as stimuli (e.g., Daehler, Lonardo, & Bukatko, 1979; DeLoache, 1986; Deregowski & Serpell, cited in Cole & Scribner, 1974; Hartley, 1976; Sorce, 1980; Steinberg, 1974). Indeed, a primary contributor to this literature is Sigel, who found that younger and lower class children were much better at categorizing real objects than they were at categorizing pictures of those objects (Sigel, 1953; Sigel, Anderson, & Shapiro, 1966; Sigel & Cocking, 1977; Sigel & Olmsted, 1970). These children failed to respond on the basis of the meaning of the pictured objects.

In many situations, then, children's cognition is supported better by objects than by pictures. In the present context, however, it was predicted that pictures would be more helpful than objects.

PICTURES AND MODELS

In a study testing this prediction (DeLoache, 1987, Experiment 2), a group of 2.5-year-old children participated in two tasks, with task order counterbalanced across subjects. On one day, they experienced the standard model task already described in which they watched the experimenter hide a miniature toy in the model and then searched for its counterpart in the room. On another day, they were given a picture task in which there were four color photographs, each of which depicted one of the hiding places (items of furniture) in the room. On each trial, the experimenter pointed to one of the photographs to indicate to the child where the toy was hidden in the room: "Snoopy's hiding back [under] here." Then the child was asked to retrieve the toy from the room.

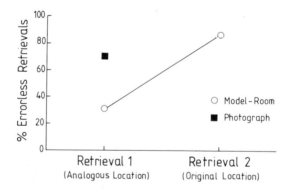

FIG. 6.2.   Percentage errorless retrievals for pictures (four color photographs) versus model. The same 2.5-year-old children participated in both tasks. From: DeLoache, J. S. (1987). Rapid change in the representational functioning of very young children. *Science, 238,* 1556–1557. Copyright 1987 AAAS. Reprinted by permission.

The results, shown in Fig. 6.2, were as predicted. The 2.5-year-olds successfully exploited the information in the pictures to retrieve the toy, achieving an errorless retrieval score of 70%. Having seen the experimenter point at the picture of the floor pillow, they usually went right to the pillow and retrieved the toy from under it. The same children performed very poorly in the model task, succeeding on only 15% of the trials. The results thus supported the dual orientation hypothesis; that is, they were consistent with the idea that a scale model is so salient and attractive as an object that 2.5-year-old children tend to respond to it only as a concrete object, and not also as an abstract symbol.

Before concluding that, as the dual orientation hypothesis claims, pictures are easier for very young children to understand than models are, it is necessary to consider alternative explanations for the superior performance of the children in the picture task. There are two clear possibilities, the first having to do with the procedure and the second with the specific stimuli.

Hiding versus Pointing

One difference between the picture and model tasks is the method by which the relevant location is communicated to the child: In the model task, a miniature toy is hidden behind an item of furniture; in the picture task, the experimenter simply points to that item. It is possible that it is more difficult to represent a hiding event involving the relation between two objects than it is to represent a simple point at a single object. Thus, the superiority of pictures over model (DeLoache, 1987) may have been due to this difference in the method of communication rather than, as claimed, the medium.

If so, then 2.5-year-olds should perform much better if the correct place in the model were simply pointed out for them. On the other hand, if their problem is that they do not detect the model–room correspondence because of the need for a dual representation, then it should not matter how the specific hiding place is communicated; performance should be poor either way. In other words, if a young child responds to the model only as an object and not as a symbol, then that child will connect neither the experimenter pointing at a picture nor her hiding an object in the model with the corresponding location in the room.

An experiment was designed to separately test the effects of medium and method (DeLoache, 1991, Experiment 1). Two conditions were replications of previous tasks. In Hide-Model, the child watched as the experimenter hid a miniature toy in the model; in Point-Picture, the experimenter pointed to the relevant location in one of the same four photographs used in the original picture study. The crucial condition was Point-Model, in which the experimenter simply pointed to the correct place in the model. Thus, if 2.5-year-olds' performance in the model task is poor due to the necessity of representing a hiding event, then performance should be good in this condition. The fourth condition of the 2×2 design was Hide-Picture, in which the experimenter hid the miniature toy behind one of the four pictures. There were eight 2.5-year-old children in each of the four conditions.

Retrieval 2 was involved in only the two Hide conditions (Hide-Model and Hide-Picture). In both cases, performance was very high (78% and 74%), indicating that the children had no difficulty remembering the hiding event they witnessed.

The results of interest in this study—the Retrieval 1 data—are shown in Fig. 6.3. In the Hide-Model and Point-Picture tasks, performance was just as expected from the previous studies—very poor with the model and very good with the pictures.

Performance in the crucial condition, Point-Model, was as predicted by the dual orientation hypothesis. It was exactly the same as in the Hide-Model condition. In other words, our young subjects had no idea where the toy was hidden in the room, regardless of whether they had observed the experimenter hiding the miniature toy in the model or simply pointing to the correct place. Thus, these results are consistent with the view that, because of the difficulty of achieving a dual representation of the model, these children never appreciated the model–room correspondence in the first place. As a consequence, it did not matter how they were given the information; they had no idea what to do with it anyway.

Further support for the dual orientation hypothesis also came from the fourth condition in this study, Hide-Picture. In this condition, the child watched as the experimenter hid the miniature dog behind one of the four pictures, saying, "This is where Snoopy is hiding in his room." These 2.5-year-olds found this condition incomprehensible; not a single child made a single successful retrieval 1. Why should this condition have been so devastating?

The reason may be that it violated, in a way that the other picture condition did not, the normal symbolic function of pictures. In this condition, the young subjects were presented with pictures, which they normally respond to as symbols and not as objects, and were to treat the pictures as objects, as hiding places, as well as symbols. In other words, they were confronted with an anomalous use of symbols. Their retrieval score of 0% suggests that they did indeed find the situation anomalous.

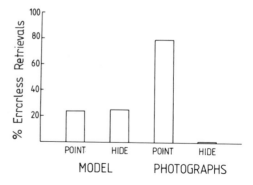

FIG. 6.3. Retrieval 1 performance as a function of medium and method of designating the location of the toy in the room. From: DeLoache, J. S. (1991). Symbolic functioning in very young children: Understanding of pictures and models. *Child Development, 62*, 736–752. Reprinted by permission of SRCD.

This result is thus the counterpart of the original model result. The standard model task (the Hide-Model condition here) is difficult, because young children are required to treat an object both as an object and as a symbol for something else. The Hide-Picture condition is difficult, because young children are required to treat a symbol both as a symbol for something else and as an object. We apparently induced our subjects to treat the pictures as objects; their high Retrieval 2 scores indicated that they understood them as hiding places. However, responding to the pictures as objects seems to have blocked interpreting them as symbols of something else.

The Hide-Picture condition of this study thus contributes two pieces to the puzzle we are trying to solve. It adds further support to the dual orientation hypothesis, and it demonstrates the inflexibility of fledgling symbol users. These 2.5-year-old children know quite a lot about pictures; indeed, they know the most crucial thing of all—that pictures are representations of something other than themselves. However, having learned to ignore the objectness of pictures and to relate to them only in terms of their representational content, they balked at the demand to treat them in both ways.

Type of Pictures

The second alternative explanation for the superiority of picture over model task reported earlier (DeLoache, 1987) has to do with the pictures used in that study. There were four individual color photographs, each of which depicted a single item of furniture in the room. It could be that the 2.5-year-old children succeeded because these pictures were so extremely simple and iconic. For one thing, showing the child a realistic photograph of a single object may be akin to naming the depicted object; pointing to the picture of the couch may be like saying, "Snoopy is hidden under the couch." If children are simply told where the toy is, they can readily retrieve it. For another thing, the extreme degree of iconicity between the color photograph and the depicted object may provide direct access to the child's mental representation of that particular object, without the child being cognizant of the overall relation between the pictures and the room.

If either or both of these possibilities is correct, then different types of pictures might not produce the same positive results with 2.5-year-olds. Accordingly, an experiment was conducted with two pictures that differed from those used in the original study (DeLoache, 1991, Experiment 2)—a wide-angle color photograph of the room and a line drawing of the room. In both of these stimuli, there was much more information than was present in the single photographs used before; both pictures depicted approximately two-thirds of the room, including all four objects used as hiding places. Thus, the amount of information they contained was more comparable to that available in the model. In addition, the line drawing was a much less realistic and less iconic stimulus than any of the color photographs.

The subjects for this study were 32 2.5-year-olds. All the children participated in one of the two picture tasks, as well as the standard model task, with task order counterbalanced across subjects.

Figure 6.4 shows the results of this study, comparing performance in the picture tasks versus the same children's performance in the model task. As is apparent, these 2.5-year-olds, like the children in the two other picture studies, did very well in the picture conditions. Their performance was substantially and significantly better than their performance in the model task.

This experiment produced two important results. The first is obvious in Fig. 6.4; it provided another replication of the original picture study (DeLoache, 1987). Replication is especially important for this phenomenon, given its counterintuitive nature. This study also extended the picture-superiority effect to a range of pictorial stimuli.

The second important result of this study is shown in Fig. 6.5—a transfer effect from the picture to the model task. This figure depicts the level of Retrieval 1 performance in the model and picture tasks as a function of task order. Performance in the model task was better for those children who received the model task in day 2, having previously participated in the picture task on day 1, than it was for those children who received the model task on day 1. Half (8 of 16) of the 2.5-year-olds who experienced the pictures first subsequently succeeded with the model (in comparison to only 2 of the 16 who received the model first).

Why did participating in the picture task enable some of the 2.5-year-old children to succeed with the model? Perhaps participating in a task in which they understood the relevant symbolic relation (the relation between a picture and what it represented) helped these children to catch on to a task with a different, otherwise incomprehensible, symbolic relation.

One question that arises immediately is whether this transfer effect is highly specific or more general. Support for a generalized effect of symbolic experience comes from a follow-up transfer study, again with 2.5-year-olds. In this study, the children participated on day 1 in a picture task involving one room. On day 2, they participated in a model task involving a different room. Significant transfer occurred; in fact, the level of performance was only slightly and nonsignificantly

FIG. 6.4. Percentage errorless retrievals for wide-angle photograph and line drawing versus model. The same 2.5-year-old children participated in both tasks. From: DeLoache, J. S. (1991). Symbolic functioning in very young children: Understanding of pictures and models. *Child Development, 62,* 736–752. Reprinted by permission of SRCD.

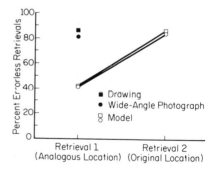

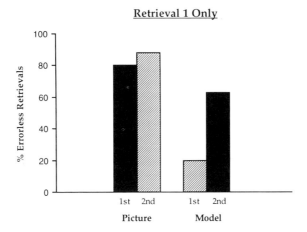

FIG. 6.5. Percentage errorless retrievals in the picture and model tasks as a function of order of task. All model data are for Retrieval 1. From: DeLoache, J. S. (1991). Symbolic functioning in very young children: Understanding of pictures and models. *Child Development, 62,* 736–752. Reprinted by permission of SRCD.

below that found in the experiment in which the picture and model represented the same room.

This transfer study provides further evidence consistent with the idea that experience with a symbolic task that does not require a dual orientation helps young children figure out a task that does require a dual orientation. More generally, the results support the idea that participation in one task involving one particular symbolic relation may have general effects on performance in subsequent tasks involving different symbolic relations. At the most general level, the discovery of picture–model transfer effects suggests that learning one symbol system may aid young children in learning others through a general heightening of symbolic awareness, an increased proclivity to notice and perhaps even to look for symbolic relations among stimuli in the environment.

TESTING THE DUAL ORIENTATION HYPOTHESIS

Thus far, the dual orientation hypothesis has been presented, and several studies that are consistent with it have been summarized. In this section, two additional experiments are presented that explicitly test predictions derived from this hypothesis. These experiments provide very strong support; although they follow logically from what has been said about dual representation, they are rather strange and counterintuitive on any other basis.

According to the dual orientation hypothesis, very young children find it very difficult to represent a scale model as an object and as a symbol at the same time.

Relating to the model concretely—as an object—makes it hard for them to simultaneously relate to it abstractly—as a symbol. This view suggests that if something could be done to decrease the salience of a model as an object, very young children should more readily apprehend its symbolic function. Conversely, if the salience of the model as an object could be increased, it should be more difficult for young children to understand its relation to what it represents.

Increasing the Salience of Model as Object

In the first of this pair of studies, an attempt was made to *increase* the salience of a scale model as an object. The specific prediction was that this would *decrease* performance in the model task. Because a performance decrement was predicted, the subjects for the study were 3-year-olds, the age group who would normally be expected to perform extremely well in this task.

The manipulation was very simple: The experimental group was given a small amount of extra experience with the model. When the children came to the laboratory, the model was sitting in the middle of the room, and they were encouraged to play with it for 5–10 min. Because this model is very attractive to young children, they happily complied. The children inspected the miniature pieces of furniture, rearranged them, played with some small dolls within the model, and generally had a good time. After the children's attention flagged or after 10 min (whichever came first), we suggested that now they would "do something different." The model was taken into its usual place in the small room next door, and the standard model task was introduced and carried out.

The prediction was that this extra experience with the model would make its objectness even more salient to these 3-year-olds and hence they would have

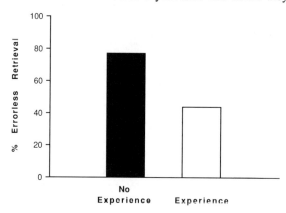

FIG. 6.6.   Retrieval 1 performance as a function of degree of experience with the model. Comparison data for the No-Experience group come from the 3.0-year-old subjects in the original model study. (DeLoache, 1991, Experiment 1).

more trouble interpreting it as a symbol. Notice that a different way of characterizing this study is that the young subjects were familiarized with the experimental materials, a manipulation that one would normally expect to improve performance in a subsequent cognitive task. Many developmental psychologists have emphasized the importance of familiarity and knowledge in young children's success in experiments (e.g., Brown & DeLoache, 1978). In this particular case, however, familiarization with the experimental materials was expected to make young children do worse.

The prediction was supported. Figure 6.6 shows the level of errorless retrievals in the model task for the 3-year-old children given the extra experience with the model, compared to a group of the same age tested in the standard task. The effect is not massive, but it is significant. Interaction with the model in a nonsymbolic context apparently made it more difficult for these children to interpret it appropriately in a symbolic context.

Decreasing the Salience of Model as Object

The second experiment in this series took the opposite tack. An effort was made to *decrease* the salience of a scale model as an object, with the prediction that doing so would *increase* young children's performance in the standard model task. Because an increase in performance was hypothesized, 2.5-year-olds were tested, the age group that would normally be expected to be extremely unsuccessful in this task.

The manipulation to decrease the objectness of the model was rather bizarre. The model was placed behind a window in a puppet theater, thus denying the children access to it. They never touched it; they never had the opportunity to interact directly with the model as an object. In addition, the experimenter never touched the model either. To designate the relevant location in the room, she would simply point to the hiding place in the model. (Recall that this is exactly the manipulation used in the Point-Model study described earlier and that the results were exactly the same as those of the standard model task in which the experimenter hides a toy in the model.)

The extremely counterintuitive nature of the predicted result must be emphasized. It is predicted that preventing very young children from interacting with the experimental materials will help them do better. Among the many demonstrations of the contrary pattern in the developmental psychology literature are some from Sigel. Many years ago, he reported a discrepancy between active and passive interaction with experimental materials. Lower socioeconomic status children who actively sorted his experimental stimuli into groups achieved better classification scores than did children who were asked to passively recognize experimenter-constructed groupings (Sigel & McBane, 1967). In the present case, however, because the stimulus has to be responded to both as an object and as a symbol, the opposite pattern was expected.

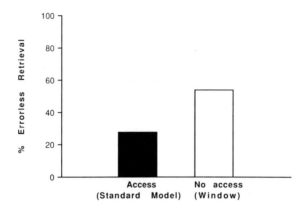

FIG. 6.7.   Retrieval 1 performance as a function of access to the model. (There was no Retrieval 2 for the No-Access condition). Comparison data for the Access (Standard Model Task) condition come from the 2.5-year-old children in the Point-Model condition of the medium by method study. (DeLoache, 1991, Experiment 1).

Figure 6.7 shows the results of this study. The prediction was supported: Performance was significantly better for those 2.5-year-olds who were denied access to the model than it was for the comparison group. The overall mean level of errorless retrievals in the window condition reflects the fact that half of the subjects did extremely well, and half did extremely poorly. In other words, the experimental manipulation resulted in half of the 2.5-year-old subjects catching on to the model–room relation.

It can be concluded that decreasing the salience of a scale model as an object does, as hypothesized, make it more accessible to young children as a symbol. The case of achieving a dual representation is related to the degree to which the two different representations conflict with one another.

These results demand to be interpreted in terms of distancing (Sigel, 1970). To achieve a dual representation of a single reality, one must have some degree of psychological distance from it. Physical manipulation of the model made it harder for these children to distance themselves cognitively from it. Putting a window in front of the model distanced children from it, both physically and psychologically. Physically separating the children from the model helped them to separate themselves cognitively from it.

THE DEVELOPMENTAL QUESTION

This research on scale models and pictures has revealed some things about the early development of symbolic functioning: (a) Representational competence, with respect to external representations, begins with representational insight.

Children must realize that a symbol is a representation of something else before they can use it. (b) With respect to scale models, this insight emerges quite abruptly, between 2.5 and 3.0 years of age in the middle-class central Illinois sample we have studied. (c) One factor that contributes to young children's difficulty with scale models is the need for a dual representation, for thinking about a single reality in two different ways at the same time. (d) Understanding the representational function of pictures precedes understanding models, presumably in large part because pictures do not require a dual representation. (e) Experience with pictures as symbols helps young children figure out that models are also symbols.

Although the studies summarized here have illuminated early development of representational functioning, they still do not provide an answer to the big question, the developmental question: How do young children come to understand the symbolic role of scale models? The developmental question is particularly compelling here, because development appears so abrupt and saltatory.

There are almost certainly numerous changes occurring in the third year of life that have an impact on how children understand models and other symbol systems. Language must be important, especially the acquisition of relational terms, words for talking and thinking about how things are the same and how they are different. Perceptual organization is probably important; children's initial organization of their perceptual experience into dimensions of similarity and sameness (e.g., same color, same relative size) may contribute to their growing sensitivity to other types of equivalence. Brain development probably underlies symbolic development as well, although it is not clear at this point what the relevant mechanisms might be.

Another candidate contributor for which there is some evidence is general symbolic experience. Data were presented earlier showing an effect of experience with pictures on performance in the model task, and it was suggested that increased experience and expertise with one symbolic system might sensitize young children to others.

Where and how do very young children gain experience with external symbols? The first external symbol system that young children in this culture typically encounter is pictures. From approximately 1 year on, middle-class American children have extensive experience with picturebooks. Picturebook reading is a favorite form of interaction between parents and their infants and toddlers. Through such everyday family interactions, young children come to understand pictures as representations; they come to understand that a picture represents or stands for something other than itself. Initially, they probably understand pictures only as generic representations; that is, the picture of a dog in an alphabet book stands for dogs in general, not any particular dog. Gradually, children learn that pictures can also possess referential specificity (DeLoache, 1989a); that is, the picture in the family photograph album represents a particular birthday party that actually occurred.

Assisting young children in learning about pictures are their parents who employ a large repertoire of what Sigel (1970) would call distancing strategies (DeLoache & DeMendoza, 1987; Ninio & Bruner, 1978). Parents ask their young children to name pictured objects ("What's that?"), to tell about them ("What does the doggie say?"), to draw inferences ("What does the doggie want?"). In other words, they lead their children to represent and respond in terms of the referential content of the pictures.

The prevalence and extent of joint picturebook reading among middle-class families may be an important influence on their children's developing representational competence. This activity may not only help young children to understand pictures and picturebooks, but it may also help them achieve representational insight with other media as well. Thus, as Sigel (1970) has argued, parental distancing strategies may be important contributors to their children's cognitive development in general and to their symbolic functioning in particular.

ACKNOWLEDGMENTS

Preparation of this manuscript was supported partially by a grant from the National Institute of Child Health and Human Development (HD-25271) and by a Hatch grant (ILLU-60-0309) from the Agricultural Experiment Station of the University of Illinois. I thank Kathy Anderson for her many extremely important contributions to this research.

REFERENCES

Brown, A. L., & DeLoache, J. S. (1978). Skills, plans and self-regulation. In R. Siegler (Ed.), *Children's thinking: What develops?* (pp. 3–35). Hillsdale, NJ: Lawrence Erlbaum Associates.
Burns, N. M. (1990). *Emergence of the understanding of pictures as symbols in very young children.* Unpublished master's thesis, University of Illinois, Urbana-Champaign.
Cole, M., & Scribner, S. (1974). *Culture and thought.* New York: Wiley.
Daehler, M. W., Lonardo, R., & Bukatko, D. (1979). Matching and equivalence judgments in very young children. *Child Development, 50,* 170–179.
DeLoache, J. S. (1985). Memory-based searching in very young children. In H. Wellman (Ed.), *The development of search ability* (pp. 151–183). Hillsdale, NJ: Lawrence Erlbaum Associates.
DeLoache, J. S. (1986). Memory in very young children: Exploitation of cues to the location of hidden object. *Cognitive Development, 1,* 123–137.
DeLoache, J. S. (1987). Rapid change in the symbolic functioning of very young children. *Science, 238,* 1556–1557.
DeLoache, J. S. (1989a). The development of representation in young children. In H. Reese (Ed.), *Advances in child development and behavior* (Vol. 22, pp. 2–39). New York: Academic Press.
DeLoache, J. S. (1989b). Young children's understanding of the correspondence between a scale model and a larger space. *Cognitive Development, 4,* 121–129.
DeLoache, J. S. (1990). Young children's understanding of scale models. In R. Fivush & J. Hudson (Eds.), *Knowing and remembering in young children.* New York: Cambridge University Press.

DeLoache, J. S. (1991). Symbolic functioning in very young children: Understanding of pictures and models. *Child Development, 62,* 736–752.

DeLoache, J. S., & Burns, N. M. (1989, November). *Pictures and models: Studies of early symbolic understanding.* Paper presented at the meeting of the Psychonomic Society, Atlanta, GA.

DeLoache, J. S., & DeMendoza, O. A. P. (1987). Joint picturebook reading of mothers and one-year-old children. *British Journal of Developmental Psychology, 5,* 111–123.

DeLoache, J. S., Kolstad, V., & Anderson, K. (1991). Physical similarity and young children's understanding of scale models. *Child Development, 62,* 111–126.

Hartley, D. G. (1976). The effects of perceptual salience on reflective-impulsive performance differences. *Developmental Psychology, 12,* 218–225.

Ninio, A., & Bruner, J. (1978). The achievement and antecedents of labelling. *Journal of Child Language, 5,* 1–15.

Sigel, I. E. (1953). Developmental trends in the abstraction ability of children. *Child Development, 24*(2), 131–144.

Sigel, I. E. (1970). The distancing hypothesis: A causal hypothesis for the acquisition of representational thought. In M. R. Jones (Ed.), *Miami Symposium on the Prediction of Behavior, 1968: Effect of early experiences* (pp. 99–118). Coral Gables, FL: University of Miami Press.

Sigel, I. E. (1978). The development of pictorial comprehension. In B. S. Randhawa & W. E. Coffman (Eds.), *Visual learning, thinking, and communication* (pp. 93–111). New York: Academic Press.

Sigel, I. E., Anderson, L. M., & Shapiro, H. (1966). Categorization behavior of lower and middle class Negro preschool children: Differences in dealing with representation of familiar objects. *Journal of Negro Education, 35,* 218–229.

Sigel, I. E., & Cocking, R. R. (1977). *Cognitive development from childhood to adolescence: A constructivist perspective.* New York: Holt, Rinehart & Winston.

Sigel, I. E., & McBane, B. (1967). Cognitive competence and level of symbolization among five-year-old children. In J. Hellmuth (Ed.), *The disadvantaged child* (Vol. 1, pp. 433–453). Seattle, WA: Special Child Publications of the Seattle Sequin School.

Sigel, I. E., & Olmsted, P. (1970). Modification of cognitive skills among lower-class black children. In J. Hellmuth (Ed.), *The disadvantaged child* (Vol. 3, pp. 300–338). New York: Brunner-Mazel.

Sorce, J. (1980). The role of operative knowledge in picture comprehension. *Journal of Genetic Psychology, 136,* 173–183.

Steinberg, B. M. (1974). Information processing in the third year: Coding, memory, transfer. *Child Development, 45,* 503–507.

7 Psychological Distance in Self-Imposed Delay of Gratification

Walter Mischel
Monica L. Rodriguez
Columbia University

A dimension of psychological distance spans from the immediacy of the moment, in which the stimulus in the here-and-now dominates, to a more remote perspective in which one is removed from the urgencies of the instant and able to consider both past and future. Conceptions of childhood in the history of Western Civilization have pervasively characterized the young child as clearly on the immediate end on such a dimension of distance. From Antiquity, to Ancient Greece, to the Enlightenment, and to the present, children are almost invariably characterized with such phrases as "helpless and unable to direct their own affairs," "unable to sit sill and prone to disorder," or "demand immediate satisfaction" (Borstelmann, 1983). Indeed, one of the main tasks of the socialization process historically has been to instigate the child's progression from the dominance of immediate stimuli and satisfactions to become, in time, able to exert volitional self-control in light of more distant considerations.

Within psychology the problem of voluntary, future-oriented delay of gratification began to be addressed with the birth of the field a century ago. In Freud's vision, the infant was seen as an impulse-driven creature, ruled by a pleasure principle, seeking immediate tension reduction here and now, and unable to wait (Freud, 1911/1959). The challenge over the years has been to understand how the child progresses from great impulsivity to overcome momentary pressures and exercise self-control for the sake of later consequences. Research by Mischel and his colleagues has pursued this problem for more than three decades. The focus of this research has been: What are the processes in the course of development that enable voluntary delay of gratification and make self-control possible? Although originally this question was not cast in terms of psychological distance, in retrospect both the research questions posed and the answers that were obtained lend themselves comfortably to such a construct and are enriched by it.

109

Sigel's psychological distance construct in many ways provides an especially compelling metaphor for understanding the nature and development of self-control processes, particularly with regard to delay of gratification. Sigel describes psychological distance as "a metaphor to denote the separation of the person from the immediate, ongoing present" (Sigel, 1982, p. 52). This separation from the urgencies of the moment seems a basic ingredient of the processes through which children, in the course of development, become able to overcome "stimulus control" and bridge delays between immediate pressures and more distant goals. A basic problem has been to understand just how cognitive representation might operate in the development of such a formidable achievement.

Understanding these important processes is important for theories of personality development and of the "self," and is equally relevant for dealing with such serious life problems as early school failure and addictive and antisocial behavior (e.g. Bandura, 1986; Bandura & Mischel, 1965; Mischel, 1966, 1968, 1986; Rutter, 1987; Stumphauser, 1972). Why do some children become able to control and regulate themselves in light of more distant future consequences, while others have trouble taking future outcomes into account? How can we understand these individual differences and their origins?

In this chapter we describe selected elements from a long-term research program on delay of gratification (see Mischel, Shoda & Rodriguez, 1989, for a summary). When Mischel and his students began to address the issue of how young children become able to sustain delay of gratification as they actually try to wait for outcomes they want, they developed a very simple method in which young children try to wait for some treats that they want and have chosen to get (e.g., Mischel, Ebbesen, & Zeiss, 1972). In this method, children are first taught a game in which the experimenter leaves the room, and is summoned immediately after the child rings a bell. Then children choose between a pair of rewards, differing in value (e.g., snacks, small toys), that through pretesting have been found to be desirable for them. The children are then told that to attain the one they prefer (e.g., two cookies) they have to wait until the experimenter returns. However, they are free to end the delay any time by ringing the bell. If they ring the bell, the experimenter will return immediately; but if they do, they will get the less preferred reward (e.g., one cookie) and forgo the other one.

Like the person waiting for an unfamiliar bus, children may have some general time expectations but do not know what the duration of the delay will turn out to be. The situation is structured to create a strong conflict between the temptation to stop the delay and take the immediately available choice (e.g., one cookie) or to continue waiting for their original choice (e.g., two cookies). After children understand the situation, they are left alone in the room until they signal. Thus, they have a continuous free choice and can resolve this conflict about whether or not to stop waiting at any time by ringing the bell which instantly brings back the adult. If they continue to wait, the adult returns spontaneously (after a maximum of 20 min).

Although a choice between waiting for two cookies or settling for one may seem artificial from an adult perspective, it is a real and engaging conflict for the children, and is as compelling as many dilemmas of life, yet is one that can be studied systematically. Shoda, Mischel, and Peake (1990) conducted a follow-up study of children who had been assessed in the delay situation when they were preschoolers at the Stanford preschool in the late 1960s. They found that those children who had waited longer in this situation at 4 years of age were rated more than 10 years later by their parents as more academically and socially competent than their peers, and as more able to cope with frustration and resist temptation. These children were seen by their parents as more verbally fluent and able to express ideas, more responsive to reason, more attentive and able to concentrate, to plan, to think ahead, and more competent and skillful. They also were rated as able to cope and deal with stress more maturely and as more self-confident. Most impressive, in certain crucial delay situations, seconds of delay time in preschool also were significantly linked to their Scholastic Aptitude Test (SAT) scores.

Finding these long-term individual differences underlines the need to clarify the psychological processes that enable the young child to achieve this type of self-control in the pursuit of desired outcomes. How does the child manage to maintain a distant or delayed goal and persevere for it, overcoming the immediate, concrete temptations and conflict of the present moment? A first question asked in the early experiments was: How does attention and thought directed at delayed rewards influence the ability to persist for their attainment? This was asked because both psychological and economic explanations of human choice attribute great power to rewards, but remarkably little is known about how the mental representation of those rewards in attention and thought affects the willingness and ability to pursue them.

In the first efforts to speculate about how thought and attention might influence voluntary delay, there were few available theoretical guides. Freud's (1911/1959) analysis of the transition from primary to secondary process suggested that during the delays of gratification that the world forces on the infant, he or she comes to construct a "hallucinatory wish-fulfilling image" of the delayed object (Rapaport, 1967, p. 315). As ego organization starts to develop, the young child substitutes hallucinatory satisfactions for the object itself (e.g., Freud, 1911/1959; Singer, 1955). It is this mental image or representation of the object of desire that presumably enables the child to "bind time" and ultimately sustain delay of gratification volitionally, bridging the delay interval by representing the goal internally.

A classic learning theory formulation is cast differently but leads to similar predictions. It emphasizes anticipatory and self-instruction responses through which the delayed rewards are made more salient: Any cues that make the delayed rewards more vivid and immediate should help the learner to anticipate some of the delayed rewarding consequences and therefore keep on going, self-administering, as it were, little "rg's" or anticipatory, fractional reinforcers that supposedly keep the rat running the long route to the distant goal (see review in Mischel, 1974).

MAKING THE REWARDS SALIENT

In essence, both views seemed to suggest that focusing attention on the delayed rewards should make it easier to sustain delay for them. Therefore, it was reasoned that if, as these views seemed to suggest, thinking about the rewards facilitates delay of gratification, then children who are exposed to them or encouraged to think about them should wait longer. To explore this, 4-year-old children were tested in several variations of the delay situation described before. The subjects were 4 years of age because it is at this age that important developments in self-control seem to unfold. The first experiments varied whether or not the reward objects in the choice were available for attention while the children were waiting (Mischel & Ebbesen, 1970).

In one condition preschoolers waited with both the immediate (less preferred) and the delayed (more preferred) rewards facing them, exposed. In a second condition, both options were also present but obscured from sight (placed under an opaque cover rather than on top of it). In two other conditions either the delayed rewards only or the immediately available one only was exposed during the delay period. The results were the opposite of those that had been initially anticipated. On average, the youngsters waited more than 11 min when none of the rewards were exposed. However, they waited only a few minutes when any of them were exposed during delay. The differences between the conditions in which the immediate reward was exposed, the delayed reward was exposed, or both rewards were exposed were not reliable, but they all led to much less delay than when the rewards were covered. Consistent with a distancing conceptualization, reward exposure, rather than invoking a "thinking" or "anticipatory" mode in the children, seemed to enhance the salience and immediacy of the desired objects, thus increasing the need for immediate satisfaction and decreasing frustration tolerance for their delay.

THE ROLE OF DISTRACTION: COGNITIVE DISTANCE

It seemed that by directing their attention and thoughts away from the rewards children might be able to wait longer for them. In distancing language, by engaging in diverting self-distractions, the child would be effectively separated from the urgencies of the moment. Informal observations of the children while waiting suggested, in fact, that delay of gratification and frustration tolerance should become easier when children distracted themselves.

To go beyond casual observation to test these expectations systematically, it was necessary to influence what the child would think about during the delay. After some poor starts, it became clear that even 3- and 4-year-old children gladly volunteered elaborate, vivid examples of the many events that made them feel happy, like finding frogs, or swinging on a swing with mommy pushing. In turn, the children were encouraged by means of suggestions to think about these fun things if they wanted to when they sat waiting alone for their preferred outcomes (Mischel et al., 1972). For example: ("while you're waiting, you can think of mommy pushing you on a swing at a birthday party if you want to"). In another condition they were cued to think about the treats: "while you're waiting, you can think about the cookies if you want to."

When they were faced with the rewards exposed to their view, many children found it difficult to wait unless they were helped to distract themselves by suggestions to think about "fun things." When the rewards were covered, no special ideation had to be suggested: waiting was easier and the children could spontaneously engage in their own distracting ideations while they simply made the time pass. However, when they were encouraged to think about the rewards when the rewards were covered, waiting was as difficult as when the rewards were exposed. In sum, how long the child delayed seems to depend on the availability of strategies that provided distraction (or "distancing") from the aversiveness of the conflict and frustration during the delay; a focus on the real rewards (or "psychological closeness") seems to hurt rather than to help the young child tolerate the delay.

DISTANCING THROUGH ABSTRACTION

Although exposure to the actual rewards, or cues to think about the rewards, reduce delay, presumably enhancing their salience or immediacy, what would happen if one made the rewards more distant, removed, or abstract? This could be done by presenting the rewards as images rather than as concrete objects. After all, it was the image or the mental representation of the objects that Freud and learning theory addressed. But how can one get at the image in the head of 4-year-old children?

In order to obtain at least some approximation of how an image of the rewards might affect delay, children were exposed to slide-presented realistic pictures of the objects, life size, rather than to the objects themselves (Mischel & Moore, 1973). Results from this study showed that, in contrast to the effects of exposing the actual rewards during the delay period, when children saw images of the rewards during the delay, it facilitated their waiting. In fact, those children who waited while exposed to lifesize and realistic images of the rewards waited significantly longer than those who viewed similar images of comparable control objects, or those who viewed slides that were blank. So attention to the actual objects reduces delay, but attention to their iconic representations—the pictures—helps delay and, most important, does so more than comparable images of objects that are *not* the rewards.

The next experiments explored more directly whether the effects obtained were really due to differences in mental representation. Children were taught to transform "in their heads" the stimuli present during delay, that is, the real reward objects, or pictures of them. For example, when looking at the real objects it was suggested to the children before the delay began: "if you want to when you want to you can pretend they (the pretzels) are not real, but just pictures, just put a frame around them in your head, like in a picture." In another condition, they saw the picture of the rewards but were cued to think about the objects as if they were real: "in your head, you can make believe they're really there in front of you, just make believe they're there."

The results indicated that by thinking about the rewards as real it became more difficult to delay gratification, whereas by thinking about them as pictures it became easier to delay gratification regardless of what was really in front of the child. For example, children facing pictures delayed almost 18 min, but when they pretended that the real rewards, rather than the pictures, were in front of them they waited less than 6 min. Even when children faced the real rewards they could wait almost 18 min by imagining that they were pictures. How the children reframed or represented the rewards mentally in their heads was the more powerful determinant of delay of gratification: The impact of the actual stimulus that they were facing depended on how they thought of it.

This pattern of results appears to reflect two different aspects of how stimuli may be represented and, in turn, may result in opposite effects on self-control. Stimuli can be represented in the mind either in an arousing (immediate) or in a more abstract (distant) manner. In an immediate representation, the focus is on the salient, "hot" aspects of the reward objects, whereas in a more distant representation, the focus is on the abstract, informative, "cool" aspects of the reward objects. Clearly these distinctions seem to have at least a family resemblance to what Sigel (cf. 1982) might describe in the language of psychological distance, from the close-up, immediate three-dimensional to the more remote or distant pictorial representation. Regardless of the particular terms, these mental transformations seem to have predictable consequences for important aspects of self-regulation on some type of distance dimensions.

As a next step it was suggested to some children that they could focus their thoughts on the arousing qualities of the rewards (Mischel & Baker, 1975). For example, for children waiting for pretzels, the suggested focus was on the pretzels' crunchy, salty taste. Other children were encouraged to focus on the more abstract qualities of the reward objects and their associations (by thinking about pretzel sticks, for example, as long, thin brown logs). The same type of suggestions for how they could think while waiting, but directed at comparable objects that were not the rewards in the situation, were given to two other groups. For example, children in one of these control groups, when waiting for pretzels, were encouraged to focus on the arousing qualities of marshmallows (their chewy sweet taste). Those in the other group were cued to focus on their nonarousing features and associations, for example, by thinking about the marshmallows as round and puffy like clouds.

Children waited an average of more than 13 min when encouraged to focus on the abstract or more psychologically distant qualities of the rewards in the choice situation. In contrast, they waited less than 5 min when the same type of thoughts were directed at comparable objects that were not the rewards. This suggests that the nonarousing, more abstract or "distant" representation of the actual reward objects provides more than just distraction. In order to help delay, the children's abstract representation has to be focused on the rewards in the choice they are making.

The average delay time was longest (almost 17 min) when arousing thoughts were also suggested about objects that were not the rewards in the choice but that were otherwise similar. This occurred, for example, when children waiting for marshmallows had been cued to think about the salty, crunchy taste of pretzels. Thus, while arousing thoughts about the rewards made waiting difficult, arousing thoughts focused on desirable outcomes that are simply unavailable in the context may provide interesting distraction rather than aversive frustration. This type of arousing or hot thought about outcomes that are unavailable or irrelevant to the immediate situation actually may be an ingredient that makes fantasies and daydreams compelling.

The results at this juncture led to revising the original hypothesis that attention to the delayed rewards will enable the child to wait longer. We know now that when the young child is exposed to the rewards in this type of dilemma delay is *more* difficult; in contrast, attention to pictures of the rewards makes waiting easier. This paradox is resolved by recognizing that the key determinant is *how* the child thinks about and represents the rewards mentally. When 4-year-old children think about the rewards facing them they naturally focus on their arousing, hot features, which makes delay harder. To think about a pretzel for the 4-year-old is to think about how crunchy and salty it is and to want it. Looking at the pictures of the rewards helps 4-year-old children to represent them mentally with a less arousing, more abstract focus. But when they see the real rewards, or think about the pictures of them as if they were real, or think about the rewards spontaneously, the effect is arousing—that is, motivating—and it becomes difficult to continue to delay. It is the internal representations that can predictably reverse the impact or "pull" of the external stimuli: The abstract, cool or distant focus helps dramatically; the arousing, hot or close-up focus on the realness of the objects impedes delay almost triggering the action, making it hard for the children to resist ringing the bell. By shifting the "psychological distance," the same children who ring the bell in 60 sec might wait until they get their chosen goal. The key determinant seems to be how children self-regulate this distance. Mental reframing of the objects as "pictures" or as "real" can completely reverse the impact of the actual exposure of the objects themselves.

In sum, the mechanisms in delay of gratification discussed so far, while discovered independently and originally guided by different hypotheses, also fit Sigel's distancing construct. Sigel sees representational thinking as the mental product of the operational demands parents make to their children through the use of distancing strategies. One of the strategies he describes (Sigel, 1982) is transformation: that is, the changing in nature, function, and appearance of instances. His views here certainly seem consistent with the findings from Mischel and his colleagues about the kinds of mental transformations that can predictably reverse the impact or "pull" of the external stimuli. Using a psychological distance interpretation, ideation and representation that focus on the realness of the rewards, or their arousing properties, reduces the psychological distance between child and the desired object, thereby making continued delay even more difficult. Conversely, strategies that increase the psychological distance and separate the child from the urgencies of the moment and the pull of the stimulus, such as a reframing of the three-dimensional object into a two-dimensional representation or focus on abstract features of the object, help the young 4-year-old to persist. Sometimes distance not only makes the heart grow fond: It also can help one attain the object of desire.

DEVELOPMENT OF THE CHILD'S UNDERSTANDING OF STRATEGIES FOR DISTANCING

Distancing strategies of course are not merely experimental manipulations and insights revealed to psychologists. These insights and strategies also become available to the child in the course of development. The nature of this kind of development was explored in studies of how children's knowledge and understanding of self-control (or distancing) strategies progresses over time (Mischel & Mischel, 1983). For this goal, children from age 3 to 13 years were encouraged to rearrange self-control situations in ways that make them easier. In these studies, for example, the children can either cover or expose the objects while they are waiting for them. What would help more? The children also were asked to indicate what kinds of actions and thoughts would make it easier.

In the middle-class sample studied, this type of insight develops in a sequence that strikingly parallels the findings in the experiments summarized before. For example, many 4-year-olds prefer the least effective strategies; they believe that exposing the rewards during the delay period and thinking about them would make waiting easier. Their reasons are that having the treats in front of their eyes would make them "feel good" or they "just want to see it." But by exposing the rewards they make self-control exceedingly difficult for themselves, and defeat their own efforts to wait, often surprising themselves when they find they are ringing the bell.

By about 5 years of age, the majority of the middle-class children that were studied preferred to obscure the rewards and consistently rejected arousing thoughts about them as a strategy for self-control. At this age they try to distract themselves ("just sing a song"), as they realize that by thinking about the arousing attributes of the rewards the temptation to stop waiting increases. They now seem to understand the principle of "Satan get thee behind me."

At the same time, age 5 to 6, they also come to see the value of focusing on the contingency and reiterating it ("If I wait, I can get the two marshmallows but if I ring I'll get just one"). And they advise themselves, "I'll say, 'No, do not ring the bell'. . . If I ring the bell and the teacher comes in, I'll get just that one"). Many children, however, do not seem to recognize the value of abstract rather than arousing thoughts until around the sixth grade.

Results of this type have now been extended and replicated in other studies (e.g., Yates, Yates, & Beasley, 1987) and are convergent with findings in cognitive and developmental psychology in contexts such as the learning, remembering, and understanding required for the effective training of such skills such as reading and memory (e.g., Brown, Bransford, Ferrara, & Campione, 1983; Brown & Deloache, 19178; DeLoache, Cassidy, & Brown, 1985; Wellman, 1985). The conceptual and empirical analyses of how young children can be helped to generate distancing strategies spontaneously and to develop better "executive skills" such as planning, checking, and self-monitoring certainly constitute a continuing research challenge. A necessary preliminary step toward this goal in our work was to examine more systematically the links between some of the components of the self-regulatory process that have been identified in the experimental analysis of the delay of gratification process. We therefore have been examining how these self-regulatory components interrelate and whether they actually can predict relevant aspects of the social behavior of children with social adjustment difficulties, for whom self-control is assumed to be so characteristically difficult.

IMPLICATIONS FOR CHILDREN AT RISK

To illustrate briefly, we recently extended our methods to a population of older children ages 6–13 years, in a summer camp residential treatment facility (Rodriguez, Mischel, & Shoda, 1989). In this setting, most children had a variety of social adjustment difficulties. These problems ranged from uncontrolled aggressiveness to extreme social withdrawal, often displayed by the same child. Most came from Boston's inner city areas. The youngsters also were considered at high risk for serious problems in the future. The children participate in a highly structured daily program that consists of a wide range of situations: art, athletics, canoeing, clay, crafts, fishing, movement, nature, rod and reel, swim, theater, think city, and woodworking. One of the activities incorporated into their program during the summer was the delay of gratification activity or "M&M" time. As noted earlier, our interest in extending this paradigm to a population of older subjects with social-adjustment problems was to examine how the processes identified experimentally operate as individual differences variables, and to identify the different competencies associated with such variables as well as their links to the delay of gratification construct.

Some of the modifications of the work with 4-year-old children, introduced into the work with older children, included an extension of the maximum waiting time to 25 min and the use of a large pile of M&M's as the large reward. Although in the earlier experiments attention to rewards has been manipulated deliberately, the links between spontaneous attention deployment during delay and delay behavior were not investigated. Therefore, in this study we recorded the older children's attention deployment through a one-way mirror by continuously scoring behaviors directed toward the rewards, the bell, or elsewhere, that is, to any distractions. We assessed children's knowledge and understanding of the delay rules at the end of the delay period by asking them to evaluate which of these two sentences would make waiting easier: Saying to themselves: "The M&M's taste yummy and chewy," or "The M&M's are round like buttons."

Because verbal intelligence is likely to have a role in rule knowledge, delay of gratification and attention deployment, we also examined its relation to these components, using the Peabody Picture Vocabulary Test as our measure of verbal competence. Some of the main results are illustrated in Fig. 7.1. This figure represents two multiple regression equations: The regression of age, rule knowledge, verbal intellectual ability and attention deployment on waiting time, and the regression equation of age, rule knowledge, and verbal intellectual ability on attention deployment.

As inspection of the figure suggests, moment-to-moment "attention deployment," as well as the child's "knowledge of self-control," both seem to be crucial ingredients for helping children effectively "distance" themselves from the immediate pressures and temptations of the present moment while holding on to desired but delayed goals. The significant path from rule knowledge to delay behavior indicates that, in fact, children delayed longer if they knew more about effective delay strategies. (Specifically, children delayed longer if they knew that an abstract rather than arousing representation of the rewards would make waiting easier.)

Likewise, the path from attention deployment to delay behavior was also significant. It indicates that those children who effectively distracted themselves from the tempting elements of the delay situation waited longer. Note that both rule knowledge and attention deployment uniquely contribute to explain the

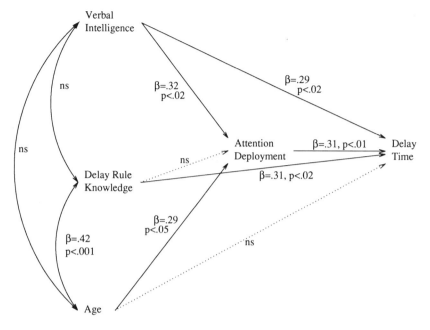

FIG. 7.1.   Path diagram illustration of the relationships between age, verbal intelligence, delay rule knowledge, attention deployment, and delay time. Reproduced from Rodriguez et al. (1989).

delay behavior variance. That is, the effects of rule knowledge and attention deployment on delay behavior are significant even when statistically controlling for the effects of verbal/intellectual ability and age.

We also have found that both children's knowledge of distancing or self-control strategies and execution of such strategies seem to be reliably related to different aspects of their social adaptation and coping in their everyday lives during the summer (Rodriguez, Shoda, Mischel, & Wright, 1989). Youngsters with impulsivity-related difficulties who knew effective strategies for self-control also were the ones more likely to exert self-control: They complied significantly more with limits and were significantly more prosocial and adaptive in their everyday behavior observed during the summer. In contrast, children who used ineffective attention deployment strategies, or, in other words, had difficulty with the "enactment" of self-control, also were the ones with enactment difficulties in their everyday lives at the action level: They were significantly more verbally and physically aggressive throughout the summer.

It seems to us encouraging that the same psychological processes that allow effective delay as identified in the earlier experiments with preschool middle-class children also seem to apply to older youngsters in this high-risk population and can be measured in similar ways. These results therefore may have direct relevance for the design of training or intervention programs aimed at enhancing self-regulatory skills. They begin to identify alternative types of distancing strategies, as it were, that could be deliberately modeled and encouraged. Another challenge now is to examine how self-regulatory competencies evolve and interact with risk factors to affect developmental outcomes over time. In this direction, we have begun a study of the developmental course of self-regulatory competencies, concurrently searching for effective ways in which delay of gratification skills and strategies might be taught (Rodriguez & Mischel, 1992).

Finally, it should be plain that too much delay, like too much distance, is not a virtue. Excessive distance can be as self-defeating as excessive responsiveness to the urgencies of the immediate situation. The achievement of an appropriate balance with regard to this dimension may be a lifelong challenge for which there is no easy prescription. The ability to delay, however, when one wants or needs to do so, like the ability to attain psychological distance, seems basic for a life that can consider the past and future as well as the moment itself.

ACKNOWLEDGMENTS

Preparation of this chapter was supported by grant MH 45994 from the National Institute of Mental Health. This chapter draws extensively on materials previously in Mischel and Mischel (1983), Mischel, Shoda, and Rodriguez (1989), Rodriguez, Mischel & Shoda (1989), and on a Columbia University Lecture by Walter Mischel in November 1989.

REFERENCES

Bandura, A. (1986). *Social foundations of thought and action: A social-cognitive theory.* Englewood Cliffs, NJ: Prentice-Hall.

Bandura, A., & Mischel, W. (1965). Modification of self-imposed delay of reward through exposure to live and symbolic models. *Journal of Personality and Social Psychology, 2,* 698–705.

Borstelmann, L. J. (1983). Children before psychology. In P. H. Mussen & W. Kessen (Eds.), *Handbook of child psychology: Vol 1: History, theory, and methods* (4th ed., pp. 3–40). New York: Wiley.

Brown, A. L., Bransford, J. D., Ferrara, R. A., & Campione, J. C. (1983). Learning, remembering, and understanding. In P. H. Mussen (Ed.), *Handbook of Child Psychology. Vol. III: Cognitive Development* (J. H. Flavell and E. M. Markman, Volume Eds.). New York: John Wiley & Sons.

Brown, A. L., & DeLoache, J. S. (1978). Skills, plans, and self-regulation. In R. S. Siegler (Ed.), *Children's thinking: What develops?* Hillsdale, NJ: Lawrence Erlbaum Associates.

DeLoache, J. S., Cassidy, D. J., & Brown, A. L. (1985). Precursors of mnemonic strategies in very young children's memory. *Child Development, 56,* 125–137.

Freud, S. (1959). Formulations regarding the two principles of mental functioning. *Collected Papers, Vol. IV.* New York: Basic Books. (Original work published 1911)

Mischel, W. (1966). Theory and research on the antecedents of self-imposed delay of rewards. In

B. A. Maher (Ed.), *Progress in experimental personality research* (Vol. 3, pp. 85–132). New York: Academic Press.

Mischel, W. (1968). *Personality and assessment.* New York: Wiley.

Mischel, W. (1974). Processes in delay of gratification. In L. Berkowitz (Ed.), Advances in experimental social psychology, Vol. 7. New York: Academic Press.

Mischel, W. (1986). *Introduction to personality: A new look.* New York: Holt, Rinehart & Winston.

Mischel, W., & Baker, N. (1975). Cognitive appraisals and transformations in delay behavior. *Journal of Personality and Social Psychology, 31,* 254–261.

Mischel, W., & Ebbesen, E. B. (1970). Attention in delay of gratification. *Journal of Personality and Social Psychology, 16,* 329–337.

Mischel, W., Ebbesen, E. B., & Zeiss, A. R. (1972). Cognitive and attentional mechanisms in delay of gratification. *Journal of Personality and Social Psychology, 21,* 204–218.

Mischel, H. N., & Mischel, W. (1983). Development of children's knowledge of self-control strategies. *Child Development, 54,* 603–619.

Mischel, W., & Moore, B. (1973). Effects of attention to symbolically-presented rewards upon self-control. *Journal of Personality and Social Psychology, 28,* 172–179.

Mischel, W., Shoda, Y., & Rodriguez, M. L. (1989). Delay of gratification in children. *Science, 244,* 933–938.

Rapaport, D. (1967). On the psychoanalytic theory of thinking. In M. M. Gill (Ed.), *The collected papers of David Rapaport.* New York: Basic Books.

Rodriguez, M. L., Mischel, W., & Shoda, Y. (1989). Cognitive person variables in the delay of gratification of older children at-risk. *Journal of Personality and Social Psychology, 57,* 358–367.

Rodriguez, M. L., Shoda, Y., Mischel, W., & Wright, J. (1989, January). *Delay of gratification and children's social behavior in natural settings.* Paper presented at the meeting of the Eastern Psychological Association, Boston.

Rodriguez, M. L., & Mischel, W. (1992, July). *Self-regulatory competencies in children at risk.* Paper presented at the XXV International Congress of Psychology, Brussels.

Rutter, M. (1987). Psychosocial resilience and protective mechanisms. *American Journal of Orthopsychiatry, 57,* 316–331.

Shoda, Y., Mischel, W., & Peake, P. K. (1990). Predicting adolescent cognitive and self-regulatory competencies from preschool delay of gratification: Identifying diagnostic conditions. *Developmental Psychology, 26,* 978–986.

Sigel, I. E. (1982). The relationship between parental distancing strategies and the child's cognitive behavior. In L. M. Laosa & I. E. Sigel (Eds.), *Families as learning environments for children* (pp. 47–86). New York: Plenum.

Singer, J. L. (1955). Delayed gratification and ego development: Implications for clinical and experimental research. *Journal of Consulting Psychology, 19,* 259–266.

Stumphauzer, J. S. (1972). Increased delay of gratification in young prison inmates through imitation of high delay peer models. *Journal of Personality and Social Psychology, 21,* 10–17.

Wellman, H. M. (Ed.). (1985). *Children's searching: The development of search skills and spatial representation.* Hillsdale, NJ: Lawrence Erlbaum Associates.

8 Structural Changes in Children's Understanding of Family Roles and Divorce

Malcolm W. Watson
Brandeis University

Kurt W. Fischer
Harvard University

During interviews with children concerning their understanding of family relationships, one first-grade boy was able to talk about how his parents were divorced and how they no longer lived together (Watson & Amgott-Kwan, 1984). His conversation seemed to indicate that he understood that being divorced meant his parents were no longer married. However, when the interviewer asked him whether his father was still his father even though he did not live at home, the boy looked concerned and finally answered that his parents were actually still married because his father was still his father. He concluded that the divorce meant that they lived in two different houses even though his parents were still married and they were all one family.

This anecdote illustrates confusions that children may have as they attempt to organize and represent social relationships in the face of discrepancies and dilemmas thrown at them by real-life conflicts. This boy seemed to have a partial understanding of marriage and spousal role relationships and was trying to grapple with the changes that were happening in his family (and had no doubt been discussed with him). He also had some sense of an understanding of parent–child role relationships, but when the two sets of relationships were juxtaposed, he showed that his understanding did not include a clear differentiation of spousal roles from parental roles and a clear definition of marriage. When he thought about the fact that his parents were no longer married and what this change would do to the role of the noncustodial parent—the father—this was more than he could handle. He resolved his dilemma by creating a new scenario in which the parents were still married, and thus the father–son relationship could remain intact. Clearly, he did not separate spousal and parental roles.

The dilemma could have been resolved in other ways. The child might have concluded that the father was no longer his father because he no longer lived at home and was not married to his mother. Or he might have concluded that ending a marriage in divorce does not destroy the parent–child relationship, and so his father would go on being his father. Indeed, different children come to all these conclusions as they deal with the separation and divorce of their parents.

As shown in this example, a major confusion seems to arise from children's lack of skill in recognizing the joint independence and simultaneity of multiple role relationships for the same person—that a person can be both a father to his child and a husband to his wife, as well as other things, all at the same time (Watson, 1984). Each role influences the other roles and is coordinated with them, but they are not identical.

These confusions do not arise in an emotional vacuum but are permeated with feelings. In the example, the child was not a detached bystander, objectively attempting to solve a mental puzzle. Instead, he was truly concerned, confused, and intensely emotional as he talked about his father. The problem in social role relationships was of prime importance to the boy. The strong emotions may have focused his attention on the problem at the same time that they distorted his judgment and made him less adept at resolving the dilemma in an accurate manner (see Fischer, Shaver, & Carnochan, 1990; Sigel, 1984). Although all normal children would be expected eventually to consider and represent the social role relationships in which they are enmeshed, it seems that divorce in a family is a highly emotional family conflict that pushes children to come to grips with the way their social world is organized. This family conflict seems to force a reorganization of children's social systems in that it exposes them to differences between their living situation and the situations of their friends, which they observe. It thus promotes comparisons and judgments about differences.

The objective of this chapter is to consider how highly emotional family conflicts—in particular, separation and divorce—provide discrepancies and dilemmas for children, who then have to come to grips with the changing family role relationships surrounding them. We think that children typically develop through a hierarchical sequence of increasingly sophisticated skills in representing and acting out role relationships. At the same time, highly emotional and personal family conflicts heighten role discrepancies that push children to reorganize the structure of their skills. This development involves issues forced on the child by the parents' divorce (Wallerstein & Kelly, 1980), the process of distancing brought on by the family environment (Sigel & Cocking, 1977), normal structural changes in social-cognitive understanding (Fischer, 1980), and the influence of emotions in organizing and motivating change (Fischer et al., 1990). Several studies carried out in our laboratories investigated the relation between understanding family roles, children's emotions, and divorce.

THE DILEMMA OF DIVORCE

There has, of course, been much research on the effects of divorce on children's development and adjustment (e.g., Hetherington, 1979; Hetherington, Stanley-Hagan, & Anderson, 1989; Kurdek, Blisk, & Siesky, 1981; MacKinnon, 1989; Wallerstein & Kelly, 1980). Most of this research has focused on the various factors surrounding the divorce, including children's age, their adjustment to the change, and their eventual psychological outcome. There has been less focus on children's understanding of divorce at the time of the crisis or the way the divorce influences children's social-cognitive understanding (for exceptions, see research papers from our laboratories by Denham, 1982; Purcell, 1983; and Watson & Reimer, 1990; plus Hilbers, 1987; Pickar, 1982; Warshak & Santrock, 1983). Research on children's developing understanding of divorce and the effects of divorce on their understanding can provide insight into the processes of social and cognitive development, specifically the understanding of the role of relationships in the family environment.

Many studies indicate that children face at least four major dilemmas or issues when their parents divorce. First, they must deal with the actual loss of contact with someone to whom they are attached—usually the father. Second, they must deal with the fear of possible further loss of contact with both parents and the lack of security brought on when a parent leaves the home. Third, they must deal with feelings of responsibility and guilt for personally causing the divorce or at least exacerbating the marital conflict. And fourth, they must deal with real-life discrepancies to their representation of their parents as good, loving, and trustworthy people.

If something has gone awry in the family, children, like adults, will attempt to understand the situation and find a cause. It seems that many young children blame themselves for the separation, while older children more often blame the parents (see Wallerstein & Kelly, 1980). But blaming the parents leads to the conclusion that the parents are not adequately loving or trustworthy and may not always be relied on. Thus, all the issues noted above are intertwined. For example, either the parents are guilty for the conflict, or the child is guilty, or both are guilty. None of these alternatives is particularly easy for a child to deal with.

We contend that the level of children's structuring of family role relationships will in part determine how they resolve these dilemmas, just as the crises will likely force the children to restructure their level of understanding.

THE CONCEPT OF DISTANCING

The concept of distancing, as formulated by Sigel and his colleagues (see Sigel, 1984, 1986; Sigel & Cocking, 1977), contains two aspects that help explain structural changes in role understanding and the effect of divorce on children. First, distancing is a process whereby children are able to establish a psychological separation between themselves and an event thus allowing them to consider the event without being involved with it in the present environment. In other words, children can represent a past and a future, as well as hypothetical situations, when they have distanced themselves from the immediate here and now. In addition, children can stand back and use metacognitive skills in monitoring their own processing (Flavell, 1979) and can use a dual coding capacity (Fischer, 1980; Flavell, Green, & Flavell, 1986) and decentration skills (Piaget, 1962) in order to see and compare things from two or more perspectives.

With respect to children's understanding of family role relationships, distancing can be thought of as the process through which children step back from their personal roles to see the roles as they exist for other people as well as themselves. Whenever children consider the general nature of role relationships, particularly the ability of people to occupy multiple roles simultaneously, they have distanced themselves from their immediate relationships, which usually carry intense emotions that can affect their behavior and understanding. The distancing process helps children to disentangle themselves from role relationships so that they can assess the general nature of roles.

For children to understand the changes brought on by divorce and to deal with their intense emotions about these changes, they need to develop some psychological distance from their family role relationships. In the example provided at the beginning of this chapter, the boy would need to distance himself from the dilemma in his family so as to gain an accurate understanding of what was lost and what remained in his relationship to his father, as well as what aspects changed but were not lost.

Second, distancing concerns the actions of people close to children that force the children to deal with discrepancies to their current perception of the world. In some cases, these distancing behaviors are the challenges and the scaffolding that parents provide to help their children reorganize their thinking (Bruner, 1975; Vygotsky, 1978; Wertsch, 1984). In addition, parents also provide unintended discrepancies and challenges that come from marital discord and divorce. In the anecdote at the beginning of the chapter, the father's leaving caused a discrepancy in the child's understanding of spousal and parental roles as inseparable, and the child could not ignore this discrepancy because it was so emotional and important to him.

Divorce in a family pushes for a separation of spousal and parental roles, so that any child who has not already differentiated them will be forced to take a fresh look at how the roles are different and how they are related. Indeed, roles may be especially important to children when there is conflict between the roles or the chance of losing an important role relationship (see Pickar, 1982, for typical confusions for children). For example, we have heard children express a concern that the parent role will not continue when one of their parents gets a new job or enters a new role (e.g., becomes a doctor, works as a teacher) or when the children enter a new role (e.g., think about getting married or going to college): "Mommie, when you become a doctor, will you still be my mother?" or

"When I get married, will you still be my mother?" (Watson & Amgott-Kwan, 1983; Watson & Fischer, 1980). These concerns seem to appear precisely when the role relationships are seen as in danger of being lost. Highly emotional and personal discrepancies seem to push for reorganization of role understanding.

DEVELOPMENT OF FAMILY ROLE CONCEPTS

In the studies to be reported, skill theory (Fischer, 1980) was used to analyze and predict children's understanding of role relationships. Skill theory specifies how the organization of skills changes with development. A skill is defined as a structure for acting or thinking or feeling. A person can be skilled in throwing a ball, writing poetry, carrying out mathematical operations, expressing love, or controlling fear. In addition, no skill can be described without also specifying the particular context and task in which the skill is carried out. Thus, it is meaningless to talk about general stages of skills that are independent of context. There is evidence, however, for a broadly based developmental pattern of coordination and differentiation common to all skills, even though rate of development and specifics of sequences vary depending on skill domain, context, task, and the person's state. This pattern is described through a sequence of developmental levels of skill control systems.

With skills as the basic units of analysis, there are several constructive processes that allow children to restructure their skills to gain control over increasingly varied contexts, tasks, and states (Fischer & Farrar, 1987). For instance, through the transformation of compounding, a skill at a given level is made more complex through the addition of a component similar to the ones already present, without any reorganization to form a higher developmental level. Through the transformation of intercoordination, two skills are reorganized to form a new unit at a higher structural level. These intercoordinations move a skill from one level of organization to the next, which is more complex, more coordinated, and more differentiated. The skill structure cycles through four levels of intercoordination, called a tier; then a radically new type of skill structure emerges, resulting in the beginning of a new tier. Skill theory specifies that people develop through four tiers: reflexes (generally in neonates), sensorimotor actions (generally in infants), representations (generally in preschoolers and school-age children), and abstractions (generally in older children, adolescents, and adults). As noted, these skills can involve action, thought, or emotion, and typically they involve all of these aspects of behavior in combination (Fischer et al., 1990).

Developmental Sequence

Table 8.1 depicts a sequence of skill levels in children's understanding of social roles in the family. At about 2 years of age, children's skill in using social roles begins with *independent agents,* people who carry out single actions that may fit

TABLE 8.1
Developmental Sequence for Understanding Family Roles

Level and Step	Roles	Skills	Examples of Behaviors
Level Rp1: Single Representations			
1	Independent Agents: A child acts as if an agent can perform one or more behaviors, not necessarily fitting a social role.	[agent]	Child describes a doll's actions or acts them out.
2	Family Behavioral Roles: An agent performs several behaviors fitting a single role category.	[mother] [father] [child]	Child describes a mother (or father or child) in terms of his or her typical behaviors or acts them out.
Level Rp2: Representational Mappings			
3	Family Social Roles: One agent behaving according to one role relates to a second agent behaving according to a complementary role, that is, one role is mapped onto another role.	[mother—child] [father—child] [mother—father]	Child describes or acts out the role of mother (or father or child) in terms of having and taking care of children.
4	Family Social Role with Three Agents: One agent in one role relates simultaneously to two other agents in complementary roles.	[child / \ mother—father]	Child describes or acts out the roles of mother, father, and child all together.

Level Rp3: Representational Systems

5   Family Role Intersection:
Two agent-complement role relations are intercoordinated so that one agent can be in two roles simultaneously and relate to both complementary roles.

$$\begin{array}{ccc} \text{wife} & \longrightarrow & \text{husband} \\ & & \uparrow \downarrow \\ \text{mother} & & \text{father} \end{array}$$

Child describes or shows how a man can be both a father and a husband simultaneously with a mother who is also his wife.

6   Family Role Intersection with 3 Agents:
Three agent-complement role relations are compounded so that one agent can be in several roles simultaneously and relate to the complementary roles.

$$\begin{array}{ccc} \text{wife} & \longrightarrow & \text{husband} \\ & & \uparrow \downarrow \\ \text{mother} & & \text{father} \\ & \searrow \;\; \nearrow & \\ & \text{child} & \end{array}$$

Child describes or shows the same role intersections as in step 5 but with the child added to the interaction.

Level Rp4/A1: Single Abstractions

7   Role Network:
At least two role intersections are intercoordinated and compared to form a definition of a complex role system or network.

$$\begin{array}{ccc} \text{wife} & \longrightarrow & \text{husband} \\ \text{mother} & & \text{father} \\ \text{wife} & \Longleftrightarrow & \text{husband} \\ \text{grandmother} & & \text{grandfather} \end{array}$$

which is the same as the single abstraction:
[Nuclear Family]

Child compares family role relationships across two generations and forms a concept of a traditional family in terms of intersecting parental and spouse roles.

129

social roles (Watson & Fischer, 1977). By 3 years, children build from this initial representation of agents by compounding together various actions fitting a role to form a *behavioral role*. This first role is based on what people in a particular category do or say or how they look. For example, a mother role is a category of people whom children define as having the following characteristics, among others: They are women, cook meals, and play with children. The specific behaviors or characteristics that any one child uses in defining a mother role are not so important as the general organization: Mothers are people who do certain things and look a certain way.

The next major transformation occurs when children of about 4 years inter-coordinate one behavioral role with another, such that one role is defined and determined by the complementary role. This structural level is labeled a *social role* to differentiate it from the earlier behavioral role and to stress the new aspect that is added—the social relationship. At this level, a mother role may be conceptualized as a category of people whose actions are closely tied to the complementary role of child. A mother has a child and must take care of her child and respond to her child. Of course, the child role can also be defined in terms of a complementary role of mother.

At the next level, children of about 6 years and older can intercoordinate one social role with another to form what is labeled a *role intersection*. For instance, the complementary role relationship of mother and child can be combined with the complementary role relationship of wife and husband. Thus, one person can take part in this complex role relationship as both a mother to her child and a wife to her husband. The child can now understand how one person can occupy multiple role relationships simultaneously, how social roles are differentiated, and also how one social role influences another when they are part of an intersection. In everyday life, roles may never be completely simultaneous or completely separate. Nevertheless, role intersections differentiate two role relationships and indicate how one role continues to exist when a person happens to be functioning in the other role. By functioning in the wife role, for example, a person need not lose her mother role.

At yet a higher level, children of 9 or 10 years can intercoordinate one role intersection with another to form a *role network*. For instance, the child can combine the role intersection for one generation with that for another generation to understand relationships across generations in extended families, such as how one person can be mother and wife in one nuclear family and grandmother or daughter in another nuclear family.

In addition, intermediate steps occur as transitions between these major levels. In our research, the steps assessed were based on the child's compounding of new skill components to make role understanding at a given level more varied and complex. For instance, in the family the social role of mother may have two, rather than just one, complementary roles (e.g., mother goes with child and father).

Several studies provide evidence that children develop through this hierarchical sequence in the same order, even when different concrete family and occupational roles are used in assessments. Scalogram analyses in a series of studies showed that virtually all children tested fit the predicted task profiles for this sequence (Watson & Amgott-Kwan, 1983, 1984; Watson & Fischer, 1980). In general, 3- and 4-year-olds understood behavioral roles, 4- and 5-year-olds understood social roles, 6- to 8-year-olds understood role intersections, and some 9- and 10-year-olds understood role networks. Of course, there are more abstract roles that do not follow this sequence, such as those of labor negotiator or matriarch.

Related to the issue of divorce, Table 8.2 shows a sequence of role understanding in families of divorce, where the parental role is maintained but the

TABLE 8.2
Developmental Sequence for Understanding Divorced Family Roles

Step	Roles	Skills
3	Family Roles: Parental Paternal Maternal	[mother—father] [father—child] [mother—child]
4	Family Role with Three Agents	child ╱ ╲ mother—father
5	Divorce Role Intersections: Parental	divorced wife ⟷ divorced husband mother father
	Paternal	divorced child ⟷ divorced husband still a child father
	Maternal	divorced child ⟷ divorced wife still a child mother
6	Divorce Role Intersection with Three Agents	divorced wife ⟷ divorced husband mother father ↘ ↙ divorced child still a child
7	Coordinated Comparison of Family Roles before and after Divorce: Parental[a]	married wife ⟷ married husband mother father ⇕ divorced wife ⟷ divorced husband mother father

[a]There is also a similar step 7 skill for coordinating paternal/child and maternal/child systems (as in steps 5 Paternal and Maternal) into a single skill.

spousal role is ended. In two separate studies of 5- to 9-year-olds from both intact and divorced families, scalogram analyses showed that virtually all children fit the predicted profiles for this sequence (Denham, 1982; Purcell, 1983). The understanding of divorced role intersections, where spousal and parental roles were clearly differentiated and coordinated, varied widely across children, first developing as early as 6 years but often not appearing even by 9 years.

Developmental Range

The developmental sequences for family roles have been described as if children's role understanding is only at one step on the scale; however, children's understanding typically varies across a wide range of steps (Fischer, Hand, Watson, Van Parys, & Tucker, 1984). The highest, most complex level of children's understanding is called their *optimal level,* which occurs when children are assessed in highly supportive contexts, where explicit cues to key components of a task are provided to support children's understanding. In some of the family-role studies, for example, children were shown a story that embodied one of the steps in Table 8.1 or 8.2 and then asked to explain or act out the story themselves (e.g., Denham, 1982; Watson & Fischer, 1980). This modeled story primed the children's understanding of the key components at a given step. The children than had to explain or act out the story on their own, without any direct assistance from the examiner, but the priming did help them to produce a high-level story.

In contrast, children's *functional level* of understanding occurs when children are performing without contextual support; it is the upper limit of their spontaneous understanding; it is typically lower than their optimal level; and it shows high variability across children at a given age. In some of the family-role studies, functional level was assessed by asking children to make up their own stories about roles in a family, or specifically in a divorced family (e.g., Denham, 1982; Purcell, 1983). There were no immediate models or prompts given to support high-level understanding. The stories that children told varied across a number of the steps identified in Tables 8.1 or 8.2. One typical pattern for divorced family roles (Table 8.3) was for 8-year-olds to show a functional-level understanding at step 3 or 4 and an optimal-level understanding at step 5 or 6. In this way, the same child demonstrated an understanding of the intersection of spousal and parental roles under optimal conditions but showed a much more primitive understanding under spontaneous conditions.

Children typically show evidence for such clear differences between their optimal and functional levels of understanding. This developmental range reflects the psychological distance between what children can understand with no help from the context and what they can understand with social priming of key components of a task. Both optimal and functional levels are upper limits on children's understanding, but the limits vary as a function of contextual support.

TABLE 8.3
Developmental Range
of an 8-Year-Old

Level	Step	
RpI	1	
	2	
RpII	3	Functional level (low support)
	4	
RpIII	5	Optimal level (high support)
	6	
RpIV	7	

As such, children cannot be said to have a single competence for understanding family roles, even within a narrow domain, such as understanding of roles in a divorced family (Fischer, Bullock, Rotenberg, & Raya, in press). Instead, the limit of their understanding varies with contextual support, as well as with other contextual and organismic factors. In fact, their behavior typically will not be stable at one developmental step but will vary. People show many skills at levels lower than the highest or most complex of which they are capable.

Constructive Process

In the process of restructuring role understanding, as required by a change such as divorce, children reconsider and reevaluate the attributes of categories of people, as well as those of social relationships. With the normal developmental sequence, the child first expands roles beyond sensorimotor components to behavioral roles and can thus step back from (or beyond) the personal actions of roles. He or she then expands roles beyond behavioral roles to social-role relationships and can step back from specific behaviors or characteristics. Next he or she expands roles beyond specific relationships to look at broader networks of relationships, which may be less likely to be tied to the specific roles that he or she inhabits.

What makes this flexibility in handling roles possible is the construction of multipart skills, the availability of lower level skills when children are capable of higher levels, and the ability to step back from personal relationships and treat roles in a more objective manner. Thus, the construction process of skill development seems to be in part an explanation for the process of distancing—being able to evaluate general role relationships. In effect, distancing allows the child to see two complementary aspects of roles: A given role is greater than the individual members, and a given individual is greater than an individual role he or she inhabits.

EMOTIONS AS ORGANIZERS OF CHANGE

As already noted, skills control not only actions and thoughts but also emotions (Fischer et al., 1990). According to skill theory, these various factors interact in influencing the rates and pathways of development. As children come to control increasingly complex skills, they use these skills to appraise situations in new ways. As a result they feel new emotions (e.g., moving from sadness to grief, guilt, and loneliness), relate their emotions to other actions and events (e.g., coming to realize they are feeling angry because of a particular person, such as their father), and develop more self-control over their emotions (e.g., turning overt anger into a more subdued and covert contempt).

At the same time, the emotions experienced in any given context also organize children's behavior. An emotion can facilitate the restructuring of skills in that context, or it can lead to a narrowing of approach so that children cannot step back and gain distance from the context. Emotional reactions to divorce can have either a facilitative or an inhibiting effect on understanding of family relationships. The person may or may not be conscious of the influence of emotions.

Emotional development, like role concept development, is context dependent. Thus, a child will develop different levels of feelings and attachments for different individuals in different situations. This emotional variation may in turn affect the role-level understanding the child develops for any given relationship. A child who has experienced neglect or abuse in his or her family may not structure parent–child role relationships at the same level or in the same way that he or she structures other role relationships, such as those of teacher/student or doctor/patient. A child who has experienced the divorce of his or her parents may develop sophisticated structures for understanding and differentiating spousal and parental roles in his or her family. Or because of the strong emotions accompanying the loss of a parent from the home, he or she may distort his or her understanding of family role relationships and of his or her parents in those relationships.

In summary, strong emotions can focus children's attention on a situation such as divorce and lead children to restructure their understanding of family roles. For example, losing a father from the home can make a boy sensitive to what he can expect from both his parents and what he can do to keep his father in his life. Or high emotions may increase the difficulty of the task. Anger, for instance, can lead a child to see his father as all bad instead of seeing him as having both positive and negative qualities. Fear can lead a child to avoid thinking about the consequences of divorce and the limitations of the parents and this means that they do not develop an age-appropriate, realistic view of them. For children grappling with their relationships to their parents following a divorce, emotions can both facilitate understanding and interfere with it.

ROLE CONCEPT DEVELOPMENT AND
UNDERSTANDING THE CAUSES OF DIVORCE

Three studies in our laboratories related children's level of family role under-standing for either intact or divorced families to other aspects of their behavior and family situation. Two of the studies suggest how divorce and the attendant emotions relate to children's level of understanding of role relationships.

In a study of 47 kindergarten and third-grade children from divorced and intact families, Purcell (1983) found that although divorce did not affect the more structured, optimal level, it did affect the more spontaneous, functional level of kindergarten children's understanding of divorce roles. That is, for kindergarten children from divorced families, the highest level of understanding in sponta-neous stories was typically at step 3 or 4, but for kindergartners from intact families it was typically one step higher. However, divorce status did not relate to the functional level of first graders. It appeared that conflict brought on by the divorce situation acted as a propellant for the development of role understanding in kindergarten children, who were at a period of transition between levels and because of this reorganization in their thinking were more susceptible to such conflict.

Children's emotions in their stories also related to the effects of divorce. Children of both ages from divorced families depicted more emotional themes in a story-completion task than children from intact families. Children who showed more positive emotions in connection with divorce had higher levels of role understanding.

A study of 10 third- and fourth-grade boys, all from divorced families, sug-gests one explanation for the absence of a relation between divorce and role understanding in the older children. Denham (1982) studied the relation of role understanding in divorced families to feelings about parents. Role understanding was assessed with the high-support condition of the divorce role sequence in Table 8.2. Perceptions of parents were assessed on the Parental Satisfaction Scale, adapted from the Perceived Competence Scales of Harter and Pike (1984). In this task, children were asked to indicate how happy they were with various aspects of their parents' behavior toward them.

The children also participated in a 6-week intervention condition designed to help them both to talk and learn about relationship problems. For 1 hr each week, half of them focused on the problems of divorced families, while the other half (a control group) focused on problems between friends. In each group, the boys were given experience dealing with the complexities of role relationships and discrepancies and changes in these roles, especially as a result of divorce or shifts in friendships, respectively. The groups also focused on understanding people's emotions in the face of such changes—parents and children, or friends. This intervention thus pushed children to distance (Sigel, 1984, 1986) by considering people's role relationships, emotions, and perspectives in divorced families or changing friendships.

Although the intervention did not produce a change in the mean level of role understanding, it did change the relation between the children's understanding and their feelings about their parents. Before the intervention, there were no reliable correlations between children's role understanding and their evaluation of their parents; correlations were positive, modest in size, and not statistically significant. Following the intervention, the correlations shifted dramatically: Children's role understanding showed strong negative correlations with their evaluations of their parents. Boys with lower levels of role understanding gave exceedingly positive evaluations of their parents, but those with higher levels of role understanding had more moderate, realistic evaluations of their parents. All the boys with exceedingly positive parental evaluations failed to understand intersections of parental and spousal roles (step 5 and beyond), and all the boys with more moderate parental evaluations understood some of these intersections (passing at least one task at step 5 and beyond). This effect was strong and reliable for the group that had focused on divorce in the intervention. For the group that focused on friendship, the pattern was similar, but the correlations were not as large and were not statistically reliable.

It seems that the distancing involved in the intervention led some of the children to recognize that their parents were not all good or all bad. In fact, after the intervention focusing on divorce, the children who understood role intersections gave lower evaluations of their parents' behavior than they had before the intervention. In contrast, the children who did not understand role intersections before the intervention gave higher evaluations of their parents' behavior.

One plausible interpretation is that emotions caused some of the boys to be defensively positive about their parents, allowing them to think about their parents' faults and mistakes, including the divorce. They therefore said that their parents were nearly perfect. These were the children who were unable to understand the intersections of spousal and parental roles in divorce. The boys who were open to understanding their parents as not being perfect were better able to deal with the separation of roles in divorce.

In summary, children who could understand the nature of role intersections were more likely to develop a realistic understanding that divorce is caused by the parents. Furthermore, use of an intervention that involved focusing the boys on the discrepancies associated with divorce relationships appeared to facilitate a different level of understanding of these relationships.

A third study (Watson and Reimer, 1990) investigated the relation between family-role understanding and recognition of parents' contributions to the divorce by focusing on children's understanding of normal family roles as depicted in Table 1 (not the understanding of divorce roles). The children in this study ranged from 3 to 9 years of age. They were from divorced families and living with their mothers. Findings from this study indicated that recognition of parents' contributions to the divorce increased dramatically as role understanding improved. Of those children who understood at the level of behavioral roles (step 2), only 20% could discuss causes for the divorce related to the parents' behaviors. At the level of social roles (step 3 or 4), 40% gave parent-related causes. At the level of role intersections (step 5 or 6), 75% gave parent-related causes. Despite differences in the specific family roles studied—divorce roles or conventional family roles—both the intervention study and this study suggest that children's ability or willingness to criticize the parents, such as blaming them for the divorce, increased with role understanding, especially the understanding of role intersections.

These findings suggest that when children are able to differentiate the spousal and parental roles, they can step back and see their parents realistically, as neither all good nor all bad. Their ability to distance themselves from the causes of the divorce seems to provide them with a way out of the dilemmas of divorce—losing a parent, seeing one or both parents as bad because of the divorce, or possibly being to blame themselves for the parent's leaving. With the distance of the higher-level understanding, they are more likely to reach constructive conclusions: Their parents are responsible for the divorce, their parents are not all bad just because they did some things wrong, and their relationships with both parents can continue even though the spousal relationship has ended and one parent has left the home.

In a similar vein, several investigators have noted that preschool children have a difficult time understanding that a person may feel two or more emotions (e.g., both happy and sad) at the same time or that a person may be both good and bad (Hand, 1982; Harter and Buddin, 1987), although they can deal with such combinations in very limited ways (Fischer et al., 1990). Ready understanding of the intersection of emotions seems to begin at 6 or 7 years, like understanding role intersections. Perhaps younger children cannot bring themselves to blame their parents when this blame results in seeing their parents as all bad. Consistent with this argument and the findings of the three studies, Wallerstein and Kelly (1980) also reported that preschoolers were more likely to blame themselves for their parents' divorce and to fear a parent's leaving them, while older children were more likely to show anger at the parents for the divorce.

Despite the adaptive developmental shift in the understanding of divorce that seems to be linked to understanding role intersections, strong emotions can still hinder children's perception of reality and even make children defensive. Older children of divorce in the Watson and Reimer study continued to show a belief in the possible reconciliation of their divorced parents (see also Warshak & Santrock, 1983). In such an emotionally charged context, these children's perceptions continued to be distorted in the direction of their strongest desires, despite the realities of the divorce situation.

In the studies reported here, it appears that divorce does not have a single, across-the-board effect on children's basic level of understanding family roles.

Its effects on role understanding—and on much else, we suspect—can be understood only by considering the child's emotional reactions to the family situation.

CONCLUSIONS

Children seem to face four major issues when their parents divorce, and advanced family-role understanding seems to correlate with children's coping with three of the four. First, children often feel responsibility and guilt for the divorce, and understanding role intersections may help them to realize that they are not to blame. Second, with regard to their parents' limitations and mistakes, understanding role intersections and multiple emotions may facilitate saying, in effect, "My parents blew it! They did some things wrong, but they are still good in many ways, they are still my parents, and they still love me." Third, with regard to fear of losing parents, role intersections help children to realize that parent–child roles continue despite the dissolution of spousal roles: Their parents will still be their parents. The one issue where role understanding probably cannot help is when the divorce leads to loss of contact or reduced contact with one parent; the contact may decrease even though the missing parent will always remain the child's actual parent.

These two correlated domains of crisis and development (skill in understanding family roles and skill in dealing with divorce) provide examples of the constructive process of skill development, which includes the children's distancing of themselves from the personal roles and circumstances in which they are enmeshed as they construct more general and abstracted family role understanding. In addition, highly emotional contexts such as divorce seem to force children to face discrepancies in their understanding of role relationships, which are resolved through restructuring their understanding. The higher level of understanding seems in turn to help children to regulate their emotions. For some children, however, emotions appear to interfere with understanding, and the reciprocal advances in understanding and emotion regulation do not occur.

In summary, it is important to recognize that the relation between role understanding and emotions is bidirectional. Emotions affect understanding just as understanding affects emotions. In further research, ideally including longitudinal studies, researchers need to determine the sequence of effects from a given developmental level of role understanding to a given emotional reaction, and vice versa. Questions for the future include: When do children show stronger or more disruptive emotions related to the conflicts of divorce, and particularly, do these emotions occur at specific levels of role understanding? Under what conditions do strong emotions lead children to be defensive, and under what conditions do these emotions lead instead to the reorganization of understanding? Perhaps a path of influence can be traced that shows a subtle but precise sequentiality of development rather than just overall reciprocal influences between these domains.

ACKNOWLEDGMENTS

The authors thank Gayle Denham, Helen Hand, Kathleen Purcell, and Wendy Reimer, who contributed ideas and research reviewed in this chapter. Some of the work was supported by grants from the Carnegie Corporation of New York and Harvard University. The statements made and views expressed are solely the responsibility of the authors.

REFERENCES

Bruner, J. S. (1975). From communication to language: A psychological perspective. *Cognition 3*, 255–287.

Denham, G. (1982). *Children's understanding of divorce*. Unpublished senior thesis, University of Denver, Denver, CO.

Fischer, K. W. (1980). A theory of cognitive development: The control and construction of hierarchies of skills. *Psychological Review, 87*, 477–531.

Fischer, K. W., Bullock, D. H., Rotenberg, E. J., & Raya, P. (in press). The dynamics of competence: How context contributes directly to skill. In R. Wozniak & K. Fischer (Eds.), *Development in context: Acting and thinking in specific environments*. Hillsdale, NJ: Lawrence Erlbaum Associates.

Fischer, K. W., & Farrar, M. J. (1987). Generalizations about generalization: How a theory of skill development explains both generality and specificity. *International Journal of Psychology, 22*, 643–677.

Fischer, K. W., Hand, H. H., Watson, M. W., Van Parys, M., & Tucker, J. (1984). Putting the child into socialization: The development of social categories in preschool children. In L. Katz (Ed.), *Current topics in early childhood education* (Vol. 5, pp. 27–72). Norwood, NJ: Ablex.

Fischer, K. W., Shaver, P., & Carnochan, P. (1990). How emotions develop and how they organize development. *Cognition and Emotion, 4*, 81–127.

Flavell, J. H. (1979). Metacognition and cognitive monitoring: A new area of cognitive-developmental inquiry. *American Psychologist, 34*, 906–911.

Flavell, J. H., Green, F. L., & Flavell, E. R. (1986). Development of knowledge about the appearance-reality distinction. *Monographs of the Society for Research in Child Development, 51* (1, serial no. 212).

Hand, H. H. (1982). The development of concepts of social interaction: Children's understanding of nice and mean (Unpublished doctoral dissertation, University of Denver, 1981). *Dissertation Abstracts International, 42*(11), 4578B. (University Microfilms No. DA8209747)

Harter, S., & Pike, R. (1984). The pictorial scale of perceived competence and social acceptance for young children. *Child Development, 55*, 1960–1982.

Harter, S., & Buddin, B. (1987). Children's understanding of the simultaneity of two emotions: A five-stage developmental sequence. *Developmental Psychology, 23*, 388–399.

Hetherington, E. M. (1979). Divorce: A child's perspective. *American Psychologist, 34*, 851–858.

Hetherington, E. M., Stanley-Hagan, M., & Anderson, E. R. (1989). Marital transitions: A child's perspective. *American Psychologist, 44*, 303–312.

Hilbers, J. (1987). *Children's understanding of families, family-role concepts and divorce*. Unpublished thesis, University of Western Australia, Nedlands, Western Australia.

Kurdek, L. A., Blisk, D., & Siesky, A. E. (1981). Correlates of children's long-term adjustment to their parents' divorce. *Developmental Psychology, 17*, 565–579.

MacKinnon, C. (1989). An observational investigation of sibling interactions in married and divorced families. *Developmental Psychology, 25*, 36–44.

Piaget, J. (1962). *Play, dreams and imitation in childhood* (C. Gattegno & F. M. Hodgson, Trans.). New York: Norton.

Pickar, J. L. (1982). *Children's understanding of marriage.* Unpublished mater's thesis, University of Michigan, Ann Arbor.

Purcell, K. A. (1983). *Children of divorce: The relationship between cognitive level and children's socio-emotional reactions to divorce.* Unpublished master's thesis, University of Denver, Denver, CO.

Sigel, I. E. (1984). A constructivist perspective for teaching thinking. *Educational Leadership, 42,* 18–21.

Sigel, I. E. (1986). Early social experience and the development of representational competence. In W. Fowler (Ed.), *Early experience and the development of competence. New directions for child development. No. 32* (pp. 49–65). San Francisco: Jossey-Bass.

Sigel, I. E., & Cocking, R. R. (1977). Cognition and communication: A dialectic paradigm for development. In M. Lewis & L. A. Rosenblum (Eds.), *Interaction, conversation, and the development of language: The origins of behavior* (Vol. V, pp. 207–226). New York: Wiley.

Vygotsky, L. (1978). *Mind in society: The development of higher psychological processes* (M. Cole, V. John-Steiner, S. Scribner, & Ellen Souberman, Trans.). Cambridge, MA: Harvard University Press.

Wallerstein, J. S., & Kelly, J. B. (1980). *Surviving the break-up: How children actually cope with divorce.* New York: Basic Books.

Warshak, R. A., & Santrock, J. W. (1983). The impact of divorce in father-custody and mother-custody homes: The child's perspective. In L. A. Kurdek (Ed.), *Children and divorce. New directions for child development. No. 19* (pp. 29–46). San Francisco: Jossey-Bass.

Watson, M. W. (1984). Development of social role understanding. *Developmental Review, 4,* 192–213.

Watson, M. W., & Amgott-Kwan, T. (1983). Transitions in children's understanding of parental roles. *Developmental Psychology, 19,* 659–666.

Watson, M. W., & Amgott-Kwan, T. (1984). Development of family-role concepts in school-age children. *Developmental Psychology, 20,* 953–959.

Watson, M. W., & Fischer, K. W. (1977). A developmental sequence of agent use in late infancy. *Child Development, 48,* 828–836.

Watson, M. W., & Fischer, K. W. (1980). Development of social roles in elicited and spontaneous behavior during the preschool years. *Developmental Psychology, 16,* 483–494.

Watson, M. W., & Reimer, W. K. (1990, March). *The relation between children's concepts of family roles and their understanding of divorce.* Paper presented at the Conference for Human Development, Richmond, VA.

Wertsch, J. V. (1984). The zone of proximal development: Some conceptual issues. In J. V. Wertsch & B. Rogoff (Eds.), *Children's learning in the "zone of proximal development." New Directions for Child Development, No. 23* (pp. 7–18). San Francisco: Jossey-Bass.

9 The Centrality of a Distancing Model for the Development of Representational Competence

Irving E. Sigel
Educational Testing Service

In a recent paper, Chapman (1988) argued that developmental progress must be described in terms of contexts. Because contexts can differ widely, developmental progress presumably may not follow a shared or fixed predetermined route, but may traverse different courses. One implication of this assertion is that assessment of developmental progress can only be made after the fact, that is, assessing the individual relative to where he or she has been with respect to a particular developmental status as exemplified perhaps in the child's understanding of a particular set of concepts. The metric for such an assessment, according to Chapman, is developmental distance, that is, the difference in performance level between the present and some time in the past, the distance between two points in time. Such an approach to study development precludes prospective prediction. Chapman also holds that the conditions and mechanisms that propel the organism in a "progressive" direction toward a goal are largely an open question. Chapman's assertions and concerns raise some important theoretical questions about research in human development. One of the implications of Chapman's assertions is the foreclosure of systematic and predictive approaches to development.

The distancing model presented in this chapter addresses some of the concerns voiced by Chapman, proposing some solutions by providing basic constructs that, when operationalized, allow for prospective predictions, particularly with respect to the development of representational competence. The model is context relevant, developmental in scope, and represents a dynamic interactive system that depicts the processes and mechanisms involved in the development of representational competence. The conditions and the mechanisms that propel the organism in a progressive direction, to paraphrase Chapman, are specified. The model is prospective with distancing as a core construct, and hence it is referred to as the *distancing model*. While distancing is a metric for Chapman, the term as used here refers to a class of cognitive demands that serve to activate a separation of self cognitively from the here and now as well as the future or the past. Distancing is expressed in actions, and hence the behaviors subsumed under the construct are referred to as *distancing acts*.

In this chapter the details of the distancing model are presented and examples demonstrate how the model describes a progressive developmental trajectory leading to clear goals, the most important being representational competence. *Representational competence* refers to the individual's awareness and understanding that an instance can be represented in various forms and still retain its essential meaning. Such competence is basic to effective symbolic thinking and reasoning. A developmental feedback route is described showing the organism's path toward representational competence. En route, the individual has experiences in which knowledge is acquired. Becoming competent in representational understanding allows for enrichment and for movement toward more complex cognitive organizations and skills. It is for this reason that the model is conceptualized as a central explanation for the development of representational competence. Finally, the model can be characterized as transcendental and process based, thus maximizing its applicability to a variety of contexts.

THE DISTANCING MODEL

The formal definition of distancing denotes: Behaviors or events that separate the child [individual] cognitively from the immediate behavioral environment.

The behaviors or events in question are those that require the child [individual] to attend to or react in terms of the nonpresent (future or past) or the nonpalpable (abstract language). (Sigel, 1970, pp. 111–112)

Distancing acts (previously referred to as strategies) comprise a class of social interactions that may be expressed in cognitive demands, directly as in verbal statements or questions or indirectly as in environmental manipulation of the environment or of the context. The individual employing such acts may direct attention to another, who, in order to respond, must separate him- or herself mentally from the ongoing here and now, and project him- or herself to some other temporal plane (past or future or the nonpalpable present), in turn transforming the received communication into some symbol or sign system. Cognitive demands may also be self-directed by placing demands on one's self. For example, when one is solving a problem alone, some of the self-directed strategies may function similarly to the social situation.

Distancing acts as types of instrumental behaviors generate discrepancies between the ongoing behaviors of the participants in the interaction. For example, an adult may ask the child to consider an alternative strategy while the child is engaged in a problem-solving task, or the individual working alone may instruct him- or herself to stop and reflect on what is going on. In each case, there is a cognitive demand that creates a discrepancy between the ongoing and the anticipated or requested behavior.

The discrepancy that emerges as a function of the distancing activities is thought to create an inner tension, which in turn sets cognitive activity in motion, thereby activating mental transformation, which ultimately influences the individual's representational system. Changes in the representational system provide learning experiences, which form the basis for subsequent awareness and understanding that experiences are transformed into representations. Although these transformations may appear automatic, the individual still has to come to understand that the transformation does not necessarily change the essential meaning of the experience.

The Relationship Between Representational Thinking and Knowledge

Presumably, all knowledge is in the form of mental representations such as words, pictures, graphics, and notational systems. It follows that competence to understand the representational rule, to understand as well that signs and symbols are representations of experience (including specific knowledge systems), and to be able to work with symbols and their transformations are central to cognitive functioning. The competence to understand and to perform such cognitive acts is thought to be a product of the child's cultural-socialization experience, initially in the family, followed by experience with other individuals, groups, and institutions. In sum, the central argument is that distancing acts[1] are critical and necessary, but not sufficient, for the development of representational competence. The model is one of reciprocal interaction and hence of mutual influence.

Distancing in this context is in the genre of objectification, of separation, of moving away from a situation or a condition.[2] Irrespective of the context in which it is used, the meaning of distancing is similar, namely, the interposing of physical and/or psychological space between the person and the event. Distancing is also transcendental in nature and can be described as internal movement away from one situation or state to another.

---

[1]In previous publications I used the term *distancing strategies*. I now prefer the terms *distancing acts* because strategies implies a logistic purposeful strategy and the evidence suggests this is not necessarily the case. In view of the use of the term *strategy* in the past, in this chapter I use the terms interchangeably. Further nonanimate stimuli can function as a distancing experience, and I am not ready to attribute consciousness to the inanimate.

[2]See Werner and Kaplan (1963) for an extensive discussion of distancing as applied to the development of symbols.

The distancing concept closest to the one I employ is described by Werner and Kaplan (1963) as follows:

> For the designation of the process of differentiation in the domains of object formation and symbolization, we shall employ the concept of distancing or polarization . . . in the course of development there is a progressive *distancing* or *polarization* between person and object of reference, between person and symbolic vehicle, between symbolic vehicle and object, and between the persons in the communication situation. (p. 42)

In contrast to Werner and Kaplan, distancing is here conceptualized as an action on the part of an addressor (or to borrow Werner and Kaplan's term [1963], directed to an addressee.) In the Werner and Kaplan conceptualization, distancing occurs in the mental activity of the addressed as a precursor to achieve understanding of signs and symbols.

In my model, distancing encompasses two steps: the cognitive demands in the distancing act (the function of distancing), and the mental activity set in motion by the distancing act. Thus distancing forms a unit, including the action of the

TABLE 9.1
Types of Distancing Acts Categorized by Levels

High-Level Distancing	Medium-Level Distancing	Low-Level Distancing
Evaluate consequence	Sequence	Label
Evaluate competence	Reproduce	Produce information
Evaluate affect	Describe similarities	Describe, define
Evaluate effort and/or performance	Describe differences	Describe—interpretation
Evaluate necessary and/or sufficient	Infer similarities	Demonstrate
Infer cause–effect	Infer differences	Observe
Infer affect	Symmetrical classifying	
Generalize	Asymmetrical classifying	
Transform	Enumerating	
Plan	Synthesizing within classifying	
Confirmation of a plan		
Conclude		
Propose alternatives		
Resolve conflict		

Note: From "Parents as Teachers of Their Children: A Distancing Behavior Model" by I. E. Sigel and A. McGillicuddy-DeLisi, 1984, in *The development of oral and written language in social contexts* (p. 77), A. D. Pellegrini and T. D. Yawkey (Eds.), Norwood, NJ: Ablex. Copyright 1984 by Ablex Publishing Corporation. Adapted by permission.

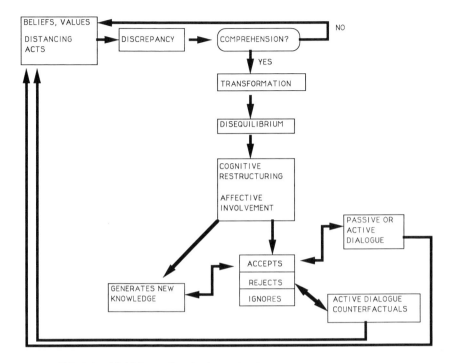

FIG. 9.1.   Multidimensional schematic of social interaction distancing cycle.

addressor and the addressee's response—initially an internal separation from the here and now, followed by and a transformation into some symbol or sign system. (See Table 9.1 for a list of distancing acts.)

The results of the distancing research described in this chapter show that parental use of distancing acts do relate to the representational competence of their children. Figure 9.1 is a representation of the distancing model depicting the interaction process in a dyadic context.

Distancing as Social Acts

Underlying distancing theory is an assumption that any change in mental state, cognitive or affective, has its roots in some external or internal stimulation that creates a discrepancy (Sigel & Cocking, 1977). The individual is generally in a cognitively steady dynamic state, ready to respond to an external stimulus or to initiate action. Responsivity and subsequent activity are defined by the source and context of the stimulus (stimuli).

An external source of discrepancy, for example, can be a parent's asking a child to solve a problem by posing a question that creates a discrepancy. Resolution of the discrepancy may require formation of a hypothesis. If the child accepts the demand, a set of mental operations particular to answering that demand is activated, for example, by recalling some previous knowledge. An example of an internal discrepancy, in contrast, is based on the child's capacity to observe the unexpected discrepancies or novelty. Both external and internal discrepancies activate the child to use relevant mental representational processes.

The decision to respond to the discrepancy and how the response should be framed are personal individual choices. The important point is that all distancing acts contain the "cognitive demand" dimension, but they vary in what mental operations are targeted.

The hypothesis guiding the conception of the distancing model, then, is that the frequency of distancing acts that a child experiences will influence the developing level of representational competence, and the quality of those distancing experiences will account to a significant degree for the variation in representational competencies a child will acquire. Thus, variations in representational competence are attributed to the child's distancing experiences, the ongoing thought processes, and problem-solving skills. For example, think of two children, each one coming from homes where parents frequently use distancing strategies, but where one set of parents uses a high frequency of low-level strategies and the other high-level strategies. Such differences in the distancing environments of the children should lead to competence differences.

The readiness and quality of the child's reaction to external or internal distancing stimulation depends on that child's receptivity to the message, which in turn depends on various cognitive, emotional, and social factors, not to mention the developmental maturity of each of these factors. For example: Does the child understand the language of the message? Does the child have the knowledge or the skill to meet the cognitive demands of the message? Is the child emotionally able to respond? Receptivity of the message or the response to the distancing act is also determined by a response threshold, that is, the readiness to recognize simultaneously what the cognitive demand is and how to respond to it. The dynamics of the distancing act response relationship form a fundamental core of the model.

While the distancing model has general applicability to interpersonal interactions, the interactions of interest in this chapter are those that occur in the family context, because to understand the course of the development of representational competence it is necessary to begin with the primary socialization context in which the child engages in distancing experiences. This process is referred to as the *socialization of cognition*. The child's distancing experiences are hypothesized as the primary influence in the development of his or her ongoing and long-term representational competence.

Distancing acts are not considered to be random behaviors, but rather are the behavioral expressions of values and beliefs, and as such reflect the intentions and expectations of parents for their child's social and intellectual development (McGillicuddy-DeLisi, 1982a, 1982b; Sigel, 1985, 1986; Sigel, Stinson, &

Flaugher, in press; Stinson, 1989). Incorporating beliefs and values in the distancing model reflects the sociocultural context from which distancing acts evolve (McGillicuddy-DeLisi, 1982a).

RESEARCH ON THE DISTANCING MODEL

The distancing construct was initially formulated as a hypothesis (Sigel, 1970, 1990). This hypothesis was generated from observations of young, underprivileged children's difficulties in classifying photographs. Even more surprising was the finding that children could name the item in the photograph, but the knowledge of the name did not change the way the children classified the object. This difficulty was interpreted as reflecting children's understanding that photographs are representations of objects whose meaning was not altered just because the three-dimensional object was depicted in a photograph. Privileged children, on the other hand, used appropriate categories, irrespective of the type of stimulus they were working with. For them, the object of knowledge was similar, whether it was a picture or its three-dimensional counterpart, since the picture and object referred to each other. It appeared that the cognitive requirement to understand the meaning of pictures as an indicator of representational competence, that is, the understanding that objects can be represented in forms other than their ostensive selves, was understood by the privileged children. Further, this competence was labeled *conservation of meaning*—that is, in spite of change in appearance and in dimensionality, a picture and its three-dimensional referent had the same meaning.

The finding of differences between these two social class groups in their ability to classify pictures suggested that there might be some social factor that would account for the obtained difference (Sigel, Anderson, & Shapiro, 1966; Sigel & McBane, 1967). The family as the primary source of socialization was thought to account for differences in children's performance. However, what aspects of family functioning affected the development of the children's representational competence were less clear (Sigel, 1990; Sigel & Olmsted, 1970a, 1970b).

A survey of parent practices relative to intellectual development in the home was undertaken. Parents of underprivileged children were interviewed to determine how they interacted with their children around reading, planning, and dialogue discussions. Based on the Piagetian notion (1954) that children's representational understanding derived from social experience, it was expected that the family, whether consciously or not, could be considered to be providing opportunities for children to learn to plan, reconstruct, and report previous experiences, along with encouraging them to think in terms of representation of their experiences. Findings from this investigation indicated that these low-income parents engaged their children in limited dialogues. Their interactions were primarily around matters of discipline with particular emphasis on safety (Sigel, 1973). Distancing acts were minimal, even when they focused on safety issues. The strategies were authoritarian in nature, with little explanation of the rationale for the demands. Middle-class parents, on the other hand, were found to engage their children in fantasy play, read to them, have discussions with them, and stimulate their intellectual development.

Based on these findings, a series of studies to test the distancing hypothesis was undertaken with children from impoverished backgrounds in an effort to understand pictures as representations, a presumed prerequisite for reading comprehension (Sigel, 1971; Sigel & McBane, 1967). The techniques employed in this research involved strategies that required children to decenter, to think of alternative ways of presenting things, to describe objects, to list attributes, etc. (Sigel, 1984; Sigel & Olmsted, 1970a, 1970b). These strategies were found to help the children understand that the pictures had meaning similar to their referential objects. A more effective strategy involved separate presentations of pictures and objects, following which children were asked to discuss them and to make connections between them. The least effective strategy for these children was simultaneous presentation of the picture and the object. In this condition the children appeared to be confused when they saw the two objects together. When one of the items was absent, the child had to rely on an internal image and seemed to be less confused. This finding was taken as support for the argument that the cognitive activity involved was representational competence, that is, understanding of the representational rule.

On the basis of these findings, a distancing model was developed that focused on distancing acts as instrumental behaviors fostering developmental progress. The point was that if it could be shown that the model worked with children from privileged homes as well as it did with children from underprivileged homes, then it would support the notion that the model is generally applicable. In order to test the distancing hypothesis, two preschool intervention studies (Cocking & Copple, 1979; Copple, Sigel, & Saunders, 1979/1984; Sigel, Secrist, & Forman, 1973) and three family studies, (McGillicuddy-DeLisi, 1982a, 1982b; McGillicuddy-DeLisi & Sigel, 1982; Sigel, 1982; Sigel & McGillicuddy-DeLisi, 1984; Sigel, McGillicuddy-DeLisi, Flaugher, & Rock, 1983; Sigel, McGillicuddy-DeLisi, & Johnson, 1980; Sigel, Stinson, & Flaugher, in press; Sigel, Stinson, & Kim, in press; Stinson, 1989) were carried out. One of them reported longitudinal findings (Sigel, Stinson, & Kim, in press) at two time points with a 5-year hiatus in between. The overall findings from these studies can be summarized as follow:

1. Parents' distancing strategies can be identified and assessed (Sigel et al., 1980).

2. The distancing acts were significantly associated with children's representational performance. In fact, the strongest set of relationships was the negative

relationship between low-level distancing and representational competence. Thus, we concluded that "low-level distancing strategies do seem to function as depressors of representational performance, as least as measured by anticipatory imagery, memory, seriation and general mental ability" (Sigel, Stinson, & Flaugher, in press).

3. Parental strategies that were didactic and controlling were associated with low-level performance on representational tasks. (Sigel, 1982).

4. Parental teaching strategies varied depending on the intellectual level of the child. Parents were more likely to use high-level strategies if the children were bright. The reverse was also the case—parents used low-level strategies with children who had lower mental ability, but scored within the normal range (Sigel et al., 1983).

5. Children who did well on Piagetian tasks came from homes where parents used high-level distancing strategies. In addition, the children's school performance in mathematics achievement was related (Sigel, Stinson, & Flaugher, 1991) to parental use of distancing strategies.

6. It would seem that parents' expressions of approval, such as positive verbal feedback while sharing a book-reading experience with their young children, may have facilitated the internalization processes underlying early linguistic competence and subsequent levels of reading achievement observed in these children 5 years later (Pellegrini, Brody, & Sigel, 1985; Sigel, Stinson, & Flaugher, in press).

Based on these findings, it appears that the distancing model is capable of predicting in the short and long run to representational competence as assessed directly at the preschool level, and with academic achievement tasks as proxies for representational knowledge at the elementary school level.

The Distancing Model as Filling in the "Gaps"

At present, there is no way to account for cognitive change in the children other than to assert that an experimental intervention did in fact lead to change. Without such specifications we are left with a gap between the abstract level of the theory asserting the nature of the stage or level of the child and the observed change without identifying the mediators of that change. For example, in the training studies on conservation from a Piagetian perspective, investigators employed intervention strategies but did not conceptualize the function these strategies play in effecting the change. Inspection of training studies revealed that many of the intervention strategies used fit the present definition of distancing (Johnson & Hooper, 1982; Sigel, Roeper, & Hooper, 1966). Yet none of these studies clarified the function of the interventions.

The same can be said for work done within a Vygotskian framework. Vygotsky, as quoted in Wertsch (1985), wrote, "*Instruction is good only when it proceeds ahead of development.* Then it awakens and rouses to life an entire set of functions which are in the stage of maturing, which lie in the zone of proximal development" (p. 71). Using the Vygotskian idea that "instruction creates the zone of proximal development," Brown and Ferrara (1985) reported a number of studies working within the zone of proximal development (Vygotsky, 1962). The strategies that are used can be coded as distancing strategies and the entire procedure is comparable to the distancing model, for example, "paraphrasing the main idea, questioning any ambiguities, predicting the possible questions . . . and hypothesizing about the content of the remaining passage segments" (p. 300).

Typically, training studies use intervention strategies that serve to create psychological distance. The outcomes in each of these interventions have been assessed in terms of some type of mental representation (Farah & Kosslyn, 1982). Considering the intervention outcomes in a distancing framework provides evidence that distancing acts effect change in children's representational competence, but the change cannot be attributed to a particular theoretical framework. The reason for this assertion is that the intervention strategies are not intimately linked to theory. It may be argued that the theories share common features on a process or operational level and the differences in basic assumptions are not conceptually or operationally linked to the specific praxis in the intervention context.

To be sure, the distancing model could be used to analyze in detail each of the developmental theories to tighten up the relationship between theories (e.g., Piaget, Vygotsky). Relating intervention strategies to cognitive change in these intervention experiments requires a categorization of the intervention techniques and testing their effectiveness for change. Such a research effort requires an experimental model that includes the mediational strategies (training techniques) in the conceptual equation. An example of how existing studies might be analyzed to test the relationship between teaching strategies and cognitive outcome is to use the distancing categories and apply them to the training studies.

These distancing acts could serve, for example, as instructions within Vygotsky's zone of proximal development. Here particular distancing acts can be evaluated to determine which, if any, move the child along. Since all distancing acts vary in form and function, there is an opportunity to evaluate their relevance. In this way instructional models can be developed within the larger Vygotskian context. The same can be said for applying the distancing model to Werner and Kaplan (1963). Again, particular distancing acts can be identified that will enhance differentiation and subsequent integration as well as further hierarchic integration. Other strategies may foster decentration, reflectivity, integration, and so on.

An alternative strategy might be the one advocated by Farah and Kosslyn (1982) in the context of concept development (mental representations of knowledge). They write: "*Gedanken* experiments are a useful exercise before designing real experiments in this domain because . . . many interacting factors could determine which concept representations are used in a given situation" (p. 163). An example of the kind of experiment that might be done is exemplified in a study by Chletsos and DeLisi (1991). Using the balance beam task originally devised by Inhelder and Piaget (1955/1958) and modified by Siegler (1978), Chletsos and DeLisi (1991) used a pre–post design to determine the effectiveness of different teaching conditions to assess children's performance on proportional reasoning tasks. The children were assigned to three experimental teaching situations. One group received direct teaching in which an adult mentor used open-ended and direct tell-type questions; a second group was merely exposed to the problems over a period of time (this was the control group); a third condition created situations for students to make predictions and test their predictions concerning the mechanics of the balance beam scale. No instructions or feedback were used. Two grade levels were involved. Students were presumably self-regulating, receiving feedback from their own actions. In addition to age differences, the direct treatment group outperformed the other two groups. Direct telling did not help the younger students (sixth graders) as much as direct mentoring, however. Such a finding leads back to the basic question posed by the distancing model: What are the specifics of direct mentoring strategies and why do they work? More studies of this type should be conducted to test a basic premise of the distancing model—that discrepancies are necessary conditions for the emergence of representational thought, and experience in working with these discrepancies is the "how" of the cognitive change.

Experiments of the Chletsos and De Lisi type offer one approach to testing the distancing model experimentally. The evidence from correlational studies is strong enough to justify setting up experimental studies to answer a number of questions relevant to expanding the model. However, the issue is, which theory will assimilate the distancing model, or should the model and its theoretical base stand alone as a mini-theory, incorporating the necessary constructs from other developmental theories? Initially the impetus for this research came from a Piagetian orientation. Others may find the distancing model compatible with another perspective.

In time some consensus might be achieved and there will be a unified theory of the development of representational competence. For now the pieces are being developed and some of them are compatible with others, so that mini-steps in theory integration may be practical after all.

Developmental Concepts and the Distancing Model

The distancing model is based on a discrepancy construct of cognitive growth. The consequence of this assumption is that discrepant experiences as set up by distancing acts lead to cognitive restructuring. The type and intensity of the distancing act results in different kinds of discrepancies. Let me illustrate the issues with the following example: The teacher tells the child that one third can be represented in different ways: verbally, through descriptions, drawing of a pie and marking thirds, taking a group of items and putting them into thirds, by numerical notation. It is possible that a discrepancy is created indirectly, where the student learns to question, to evaluate, and to judge the teacher's comments. In effect, the student internalizes a distancing action mode and creates his or her own discrepancy.

If, however, the teacher asks the student to, for example, "Find as many ways as you can to indicate one third," the teacher is testing the child's comprehension of the concept and simultaneously stretching the child intellectually. To respond the child has to comprehend the task, decenter, and identify one representational form from another, and integrate these new discoveries into a more differentiated concept of one third.

This example illustrates the adversarial relation of the cognitive components as depicted in Fig. 9.2.

A related issue is whether the linear process once begun runs its course, or if individual differences affect its construction and follow through.

At this point in the development of distancing theory it is reasonable to conjecture that there is an inevitability of sequence if and when the child participates. It may be the case that some of the following contextual factors are involved: the developmental maturity of the participants, including their knowledge, their readiness and experience in employing each of these processes, their interpretation of the task, the distancing agent's choice of initial and follow-through distancing acts, the relationship between participants, and the nature of the task itself, including the goals of each of the participants. Each of these components in the distancing model, although conceptually interrelated, is also functionally related to the contextual conditions.

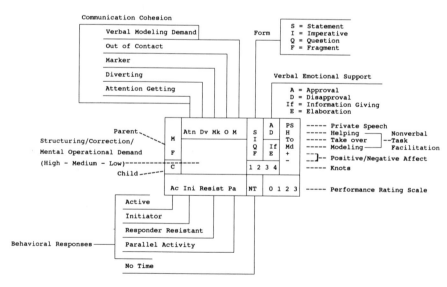

FIG. 9.2. Components of distancing acts.

Findings from the research reported here suggest that a distancing act may or may not set the process in motion. The distancing acts that evoke responses from the child cannot be identified a priori, although the nature of each cognitive demand can be described. It is only after the fact that one can be certain that the individual's cognitive processes have been stimulated. Hence Chapman is correct when he claims that how the child will respond becomes known after the fact. However, on the basis of distancing work it becomes increasingly clear that a child of a given age and social background will respond in predictable ways to different levels of the distancing act. For example, asking children to produce a response to an "if . . . then" question should yield a type of hypothetical answer. In fact, there may well be a correspondence between the distancing act and the response. However, it should be made clear that there are numerous constraints operating, such as the child's age, attention, and the like. However, predictions are possible. If a pattern of responses occurs to a particular distancing act, then this consistency becomes a basis for prediction of future behavior.

Because distancing acts make different cognitive demands, they can induce decentration, which in turn generates differentiation, which in turn generates reorganization of cognitive structures. In this way the individual integrates new experiences into already existing schemas or creates new ones. Further, the distancing acts function as instructions, as advocated by Vygotsky. The receptivity of the child to the distancing act may be in part a function of what the zone of proximal development is for that person. This exegesis describes the way the distancing model incorporates some of the key notions of cognitive development, equilibration, decentration, differentiation, integration, and the zone of proximal development. However, this presentation does not cover all of the factors of the distancing model.

Figure 9.2 reveals a more comprehensive depiction of distancing acts. The prototypic distancing act described here is verbal, although events and objects can instigate the discrepancy. Verbal utterances contain a number of features that make them salient, such as affective tone, clarity of expression, vocabulary level (relative to the addressee), length, and clarity of message.

CONCLUSIONS

The aim of this chapter was to present the distancing model as an analogical representation of processes and procedures depicting the development of representational competence.[3] The model has been built on an observational and

---

[3]In a sense I have done both, following the current psychological convention where the term model "has appeared in psychology as a synonym for 'theory.' In most scientific contexts a model is distinguished from a theory, in that a theory is taken to be a discourse about a model" (Harre & Lamb, 1983, pp. 397–398). In this chapter the more traditional approach was taken, in which the model is a representation of the processes involved in development.

empirical base limited to verbal distancing. There is need to frame the model developmentally. Amplification requires creating a three-dimensional model, taking time into account and denoting anticipated changes in cognitive competence. Thus a number of questions must be addressed to fill in the model. Addressing the particulars of representational competence, the how, what, when, and why requires further study. The "how" of representational competence has two referents: One is how to test all or some of the distancing model, and the other is the how referring to the mechanisms of distancing and the ways in which they function.

In addition, the "what" of the distancing theory that does influence the developing child has to be considered in the context of the "how." These are related questions since it is the "what" of the strategy that informs us about how it works. As indicated previously, the distancing interactional sequence is a complex multidimensional and multilevel process. Which components of the interaction sequence are of moment and which are of little consequence become the topic of study.[4] Two aspects of the event are relevant here. One is the content of the message, including the form of the message, and the other is the affect with which the distancing agent presents the demand of addressee action. In fact, in view of the multidimensionality of the entire social interaction, partitioning the event is the only way to determine the relative impact of any one or more components singly or in combination, for example, form and content (see Fig. 9.2).

When are distancing acts effective and, along with that, under what conditions? The findings reported in this chapter focus on the here and now, that is, the strategies parents use and the child's concurrent performance on a task involving some level of representational competence. Under that condition, analyses of the role of particular distancing acts within the sequence might be studied. Does it matter if a low-level strategy is followed by a high-level strategy as to how the child responds in the dialogue? Prior study has already identified the significance of the act used in the second turn in a dialogue compared to the first encounter (Zahaykevich, Sigel, & Rock, 1985). In that study, however, the type of strategy employed was not the focus. Studies of this type that address strategies are needed in order to identify the contextual effects of particular strategies—for example, is a distancing act's effect mitigated by what proceeds or follows it?

When particular strategies are used is also a critical consideration. Age level has also been shown to make a difference in terms of the strategies parents use (Sigel, Stinson, & Flaugher, in press) and the relative effectiveness of different

---

[4]To engage in this type of research requires some consideration of theory since without theory guiding the way such "what" questions can become too detailed and too idiosyncratic to provide guidance and myriads of trivial studies would be done. (Look at Fig. 9.2 for a process description as discussed here.)

strategies at different age levels, as reported in the Chletsos and De Lisi (1991) study. The child's history with particular classes of distancing acts is of particular importance, irrespective of age. Thus, when to use certain strategies in the course of the dialogue, as well as when in the developmental course of the child's life, become critical questions to further articulate the process of distancing and the theory on which it is based.

Another set of questions relates to the varied use of distancing acts by significant adults in the lives of children. Are they random nonreflective actions or are they reflective of particular values, beliefs, and performance routines? Knowing where these behaviors come from and their place in the psyche of the agent would presumably be informative for planning intervention or other change efforts on the part of teachers and/or other professionals.

Because identification of representational competence can occur only after the fact (i.e., on the basis of some performance), there is need to develop methods for assessment. These methods should be age related, that is, should involve increased difficulty so that assessment of competence can be determined. Although representational thought is generic to the human condition, competence to deal with signs, symbols, and their transformations into meaningful understandings and problem solving is not generic but learned. On this assumption then, it is reasonable to presume that assessment procedures can be devised that will define competency levels (Sigel, in press).

Finally, distancing, as a theoretical construct, is important to the degree that it furthers our understanding of the role of the sociocultural environment relative to the development of representational competence, for it is such a competence that is basic to effective cognitive functioning in our society. Representation is thought to be a universal competence, although its particular form may vary as a function of the media specific to cultures. The findings to date appear to support the importance of the distancing model for facilitating the development of representational competence. In turn, it is expected that maximal functioning will occur when and if the individuals are in a position to master the cultural symbols and, in turn, can appropriately engage in what representational thinking is for that culture.

ACKNOWLEDGMENTS

I acknowledge my gratitude to Rod Cocking and Ann Renninger for their efforts in organizing the "Conference on the Development of Psychological Distance." The ideas in this chapter (while at the moment my own) were derived from a wonderful set of colleagues including the organizers of the conference. I wish to call particular attention to Ann McGillicuddy-DeLisi, Jan Flaugher, James Johnson, Elizabeth Stinson, Brian Vandenberg, and Frederick Verdonik. Thanks go to Drew Gitomer for preparing the graphics. To Linda Kozelski I express gratitude in preparing the manuscript for publication.

REFERENCES

Brown, A. L., & Ferrara, R. A. (1985). Diagnosing zones of proximal development. In J. V. Wertsch (Ed.), *Culture, communication, and cognition: Vygotskian perspectives* (pp. 273–305). Cambridge, England: Cambridge University Press.

Chapman, M. (1988). Contextuality and directionality of cognitive development. *Human Development, 31*, 92–106.

Chletsos, P. N., & De Lisi, R. (1991). A microgenetic study of proportional reasoning using balance scale problems. *Journal of Applied Developmental Psychology, 12*, 307–330.

Cocking, R. R., & Copple, C. E. (1979). Change through exposure to others: A study of children's verbalizations as they draw. In M. K. Poulsen & G. I. Lubin (Eds.), *Proceedings of the Eighth Annual Conference on Piagetian Theory and the Helping Professions* (Vol. 2, pp. 124–132). Los Angeles: University of Southern California.

Copple, C., Sigel, I. E., & Saunders, R. (1984). *Educating the young thinker: Classroom strategies for cognitive growth*. Hillsdale, NJ: Lawrence Erlbaum Associates. (Original work published 1979)

Farah, M. J., & Kosslyn, S. M. (1982). Concept development. In H. W. Reese & L. P. Lipsitt (Eds.), *Advances in child development and behavior* (Vol. 16, pp. 126–167). New York: Academic Press.

Goodman, N. (1984). *Of mind and other matters*. Cambridge, MA: Harvard University Press.

Harre, R., & Lamb, R. (Eds.). (1983). *The encyclopedic dictionary of psychology*. Cambridge, MA: MIT Press.

Inhelder, B., & Piaget, J. (1958). *The growth of logical thinking from childhood to adolescence: An essay on the construction of formal operational structures* (A. Parson & S. Milgram, Trans.). New York: Basic Books. (Original work published 1955)

Johnson, J. E., & Hooper, F. H. (1982). Piagetian structuralism and learning: Reflections on two decades of educational application. *Contemporary Educational Psychology, 7*, 217–237.

Langer, J. (1986). *The origins of logic: One to two years*. Orlando, FL: Academic Press.

Lesh, R., Behr, M., & Post, T. (1987). Representations and translations among representations in mathematics learning and problem solving. In C. Janvier (Ed.), *Problems of representation in the teaching and learning of mathematics* (pp. 41–58). Hillsdale, NJ: Lawrence Erlbaum Associates.

McGillicuddy-DeLisi, A. V. (1982a). Parental beliefs about developmental processes. *Human Development, 25*, 192–200.

McGillicuddy-DeLisi, A. V. (1982b). The relationship between parents' beliefs about development and family constellation, socioeconomic status, and parents' teaching strategies. In L. M. Laosa & I. E. Sigel (Eds.), *Families as learning environments for children* (pp. 261–299). New York: Plenum.

McGillicuddy-DeLisi, A. V., & Sigel, I. E. (1982). Effects of the atypical child on the family. In L. A. Bond & J. M. Joffe (Eds.), *Facilitating infant and early childhood development* (pp. 197–233). Hanover, NH: University Press of New England.

Pellegrini, A. D., Brody, G. H., & Sigel, I. E. (1985). Parents' book-reading habits with their children. *Journal of Educational Psychology, 77*(3), 332–340.

Piaget, J. (1954). *The construction of reality in the child* (M. Cook, Trans.). New York: Basic Books.

Siegler, R. S. (Ed.). (1978). *Children's thinking: What develops?* Hillsdale, NJ: Lawrence Erlbaum Associates.

Sigel, I. E. (1970). The distancing hypothesis: A causal hypothesis for the acquisition of representational thought. In M. R. Jones (Ed.), *Miami symposium on the prediction of behavior, 1968: Effects of early experience* (pp. 99–118). Coral Gables, FL: University of Miami Press.

Sigel, I. E. (1971). Language of the disadvantaged: The distancing hypothesis. In C. S. Lavatelli (Ed.), *Language training in early childhood education* (pp. 60–76). Urbana, IL: University of Illinois Press.

Sigel, I. E. (1973). Intervention at age 2. In R. Piret (Ed.), *The Proceedings of the XVIIth International Congress of the International Association of Applied Psychology* (Vol. 2, pp. 1155–1164). Brussels, Belgium: EDITEST.

Sigel, I.E. (1982). The relationship between parents' distancing strategies and the child's cognitive behavior. In L. M. Laosa & I. E. Sigel (Eds.), *Families as learning environments for children* (pp. 47–86). New York: Plenum.

Sigel, I. E. (1984). A construcivist perspective for teaching thinking: A distancing strategy model. *Educational Leadership, 42*, 18–21.

Sigel, I. E. (1985). (Editor). *Parental belief systems: The psychological consequences for children.* Hillsdale, NJ: Lawrence Erlbaum Associates.

Sigel, I. E. (1986). Reflections on the belief-behavior connection: Lessons learned from a research program on parental belief systems and teaching strategies. In R. D. Ashmore & D. M. Brodzinsky (Eds.), *Thinking about the family: views of parents and children* (pp. 35–65). Hillsdale, NJ: Lawrence Erlbaum Associates.

Sigel, I. E. (1990). Journeys in serendipity: The development of the Distancing Model. In I. E. Sigel & G. H. Brody (Eds.), *Methods of family research: Biographies of research projects: Vol. 1. Normal families* (pp. 87–120). Hillsdale, NJ: Lawrence Erlbaum Associates.

Sigel, I. E. (in press). Representational competence: Another type? In M. Chandler & M. Chapman (Eds.), *Criteria for competence: Controversy in the assessment of children's abilities.* Hillsdale, NJ: Lawrence Erlbaum Associates.

Sigel, I. E., Anderson, L. M., & Shapiro, H. (1966). Categorization behavior of lower and middle class Negro preschool children: Differences in dealing with representation of familiar objects. *Journal of Negro Education, 35,* 218–229.

Sigel, I. E., & Cocking, R. R. (1977). Cognition and communication: A dialectic paradigm for development. In M. Lewis & L. A. Rosenblum (Eds.), *The origins of behavior: Vol. 5. Interaction, conversation, and the development of language* (pp. 207–226). New York: Wiley.

Sigel, I. E., & McBane, B. (1967). Cognitive competence and level of symbolization among five-year-old children. In J. Hellmuth (Ed.), *The disadvantaged child* (Vol. 1, pp. 433–453). Seattle, WA: Special Child Publications of the Seattle Sequin School.

Sigel, I. E., & McGillicuddy-DeLisi, A. V. (1984). Parents as teachers of their children: A distancing behavior model. In A. D. Pellegrini & T. D. Yawkey (Eds.), *The development of oral and written language in social contexts* (pp. 71–92). Norwood, NJ: Ablex.

Sigel, I. E., McGillicuddy-DeLisi, A. V., Flaugher, J., & Rock, D. A. (1983). *Parents as teachers of their own learning disabled children* (ETS RR 83-21). Princeton, NJ: Educational Testing Service.

Sigel, I. E., McGillicuddy-DeLisi, A. V., & Johnson, J. E. (1980). *Parental distancing, beliefs and children's representational competence within the family context* (ETS RR 80-21). Princeton, NJ: Educational Testing Service.

Sigel, I. E., & Olmsted, P. (1970a). The development of classification and representational competence. In A. J. Biemiller (Ed.), *Problems in the teaching of young children* (pp. 49–67). Toronto, Ontario, Canada: The Ontario Institute for Studies in Education.

Sigel, I. E., & Olmsted, P. (1970b). Modification of cognitive skills among lower-class black children. In J. Hellmuth (Ed.), *The disadvantaged child* (Vol. 3, pp. 300–338). New York: Brunner-Mazel.

Sigel, I. E., Roeper, A., & Hooper, F. H. (1966). A training procedure for acquisition of Piaget's conservation of quantity: A pilot study and its replication. *The British Journal of Educational Psychology, 36,* 301–311.

Sigel, I. E., Secrist, A., & Forman, G. (1973). Psycho-educational intervention beginning at age two: Reflections and outcomes. In J. C. Stanley (Ed.), *Compensatory education for children, ages two to eight: Recent studies of educational intervention.* Baltimore, MD: Johns Hopkins University Press.

Sigel, I. E., Stinson, E. T., & Flaugher, J. (1991). Socialization of representational competence in the family: The distancing paradigm. In L. Okagaki & R. J. Sternberg (Eds.), *Directors of development: Influences on the development of children's thinking* (pp. 121–144). Hillsdale, NJ: Lawrence Erlbaum Associates.

Sigel, I. E., Stinson, E. T., & Kim, M. (in press). Socialization of cognition: The distancing model. In K. W. Fischer & R. Wozniak (Eds.), *Specific environments: Thinking in contexts*. Hillsdale, NJ: Lawrence Erlbaum Associates.

Stinson, E. T. (1989). *Parental ideology: Implications for child academic achievement and self-concept.* Unpublished doctoral dissertation, The University of Pennsylvania, Philadelphia.

Vygotsky, L. S. (1962). *Thought and language* (E. Hanfmann & G. Vakar, Trans.). Cambridge, MA: MIT Press.

Werner, H., & Kaplan, B. (1963). *Symbol formation: An organismic-developmental approach to language and the expression of thought.* New York: Wiley.

Wertsch, J. V. (1985). *Vygotsky and the social formation of mind.* Cambridge, MA: Harvard University Press.

III PSYCHOLOGICAL DISTANCE AS AN ECOLOGICAL DEMAND

10 Representational Competence in Shared Symbol Systems: Electronic Media from Radio to Video Games

Patricia Marks Greenfield
University of California, Los Angeles

A central aspect of human cognitive processes is representational competence. Sigel and Cocking (1977) define representational competence as the capability of the individual to comprehend the *equivalence* of various modes of representation. At the same time, they see the development of an understanding of various media of representation, such as pictures, verbalizations, and gestures, as part of representational competence.

Cognitive processes—the basic processes by which we taken in, transform, remember, create, and communicate information—are universal. But a culture has the power to selectively encourage some cognitive processes, letting others stay in a relatively undeveloped state. As shared symbol systems, media are potent cultural tools for the selective sculpting of profiles of cognitive processes. A medium is not simply an information channel; as a particular mode of representation, it is also a potential influence on information processing. The notion of symbol systems as cultural tools for cognitive development can be traced back to, among others, Vygotsky (1962, 1978) and Bruner (1965, 1966). As applied to media, this notion was importantly expanded by Bruner and Olson (1974).

While individuals respond to and even create media, mass media are also cultural tools. They are both a shared cultural product and a shared cultural representation. To their audience, including children, media not only present culturally relevant content, they also present models and opportunities for particular representational processes.

Each medium has its particular design features such that it presents certain kinds of information easily and well and other kinds with difficulty and poorly. Each medium therefore presents certain opportunities to construct particular kinds of representations. As a consequence, each medium stimulates different kinds of representational processes. Therefore, a second aspect of representational competence must be the ability of an individual to comprehend differences between different modes of representation; such comprehension involves a metacognitive level of awareness. At the level of cognitive, rather than metacognitive, processes lies the ability to comprehend and use, to adapt to, different modes or media of representation.

The discrepancy between the perspectives of Sigel and those of Vygotsky and Bruner lies in Sigel's (1978, 1986) notion of conservation of meaning, the idea that "meaning is retained in spite of media transformations" (Sigel, 1986, p. 52). However, conservation of meaning across transformations of medium is only partial. In any transformation (including the classical Piagetian conservation tests), some things stay the same, while others change. This chapter addresses the meaning changes in the translation of a single content from one medium to another. Specifically, the term *cognitive socialization* is used to refer to the influence of cultural tools on the development and exercise of skills for processing and communicating information. Media are considered in terms of their role as tools of cognitive socialization.

Sigel (1970) identified psychological distancing strategies as a particular category of techniques for the cognitive socialization of representational competence. They are social behaviors that "create discrepancies and require representational thinking for their resolution" (Sigel, 1986, p. 52). In Sigel's research on distancing strategies, the emphasis is on the social experiences created by parents and teachers (e.g., Sigel, 1986). But children of today spend more time with video screens than with teachers and parents (National Institute of Mental Health, 1982). What are the implications of this fact for representational competence? The rest of my chapter attempts to answer this question.

A TRANSFORMATION OF MEDIUM YIELDS ONLY PARTIAL CONSERVATION OF MEANING

Two studies that compare the effects of an audio (radio) versus an audiovisual (television) medium on children's representational processes are summarized next (Greenfield, Farrar, & Beagles-Roos, 1986; Greenfield & Beagles-Roos, 1988). Using techniques based on Meringoff (1980), the studies explored the effects of adding moving visual imagery to an audio narrative. In essence, the questions being investigated involved the effects of external, cultural representations, produced in different media, on the internal representational processes of individual children.

For each study, the stimuli consisted of two narrated stories, based on children's picture books (Haley, 1970; dePaola, 1975). Each story had both a video version (produced at Weston Woods Studios) and an audio version with the exact same soundtrack. With appropriate counterbalancing of media and stories, each child in each study was exposed to one story in the audio version, the other story in the audiovisual version. One study focused on imaginal representation, the other on memory representation.

For the imagination study, the story was stopped a slight bit before its ending and first through fourth graders were individually asked to continue the story orally. The children's representational construction of elements that had not appeared in the stimulus story constituted our basic operational definition of imagination. The hypothesis was that television, the medium providing the richer information in an external representation, would be less stimulating to the children's internal, imaginal representations. It was expected that radio, leaving more to the imagination, would be more stimulating in this respect.

Table 10.1 shows those imaginal aspects of story continuations in which the medium of representation made a statistically significant difference. In accord with the hypothesis, the audio representations led to significantly greater representation of novel events, characters, and words (an overall measure of imagination), while the television representations led to significantly greater repetition of material from the preceding stimulus story.

In the study of memory representation, the children heard and saw the stories all the way through. Following each story, again presented as either an audiovisual or an audio representation, each child was asked to retell the story to another adult who, the child was told, had never heard or seen the story. After this free recall test, the child was asked a series of cued recall and inference questions. The inference questions did not have right or wrong answers; instead, the questions were posed in order to determine the representational sources for the children's answers.

Table 10.2 presents the statistically significant main effects of medium on memory and inference representations. Note that television leads to significantly better overall recall of information (central propositions, cued recall). It also leads to a greater focus on action representation (action recall and use of action information as a source of inferences). The advantages of the multimodal representation of television can also be seen in the greater use of audiovisual detail, both in direct recall and as a source of inferences, in comparison with the same

TABLE 10.1
Significant Medium Differences: Imagination

	Radio	TV
Imaginative events	11.30**	9.49
Imagined specific characters	0.87*	0.61
Imagined vague characters	0.49**	0.26
Imaginative words	107.87***	89.20
Repetitive words	8.17	20.16***

$*p \leq .05.$ $**p \leq .025.$ $***p \leq .01.$

TABLE 10.2
Significant Medium Differences: Memory and Inference

Memory	Radio	TV
Free recall		
Central propositions	7.40	8.95****
Actions	10.57	12.09**
Vague characters	2.12	2.80****
Direct dialogue	2.14*	1.61
Cued recall	8.56	11.73****
Picture sequencing	16.91	19.55****
Audiovisual detail	1.28	1.80****
Inference sources		
Audio	0.72**	0.56
Audiovisual	2.00	2.30***
Action	2.48	3.15****
Outside story	2.31****	1.73

$*p = .05.$ $**p \le .025.$ $***p \le .01.$ $****p \le .001.$

details presented in the audio medium alone. Radio, in contrast, led to greater focus on material presented only in the auditory channel (recall of dialogue and use of audio material as an inference source). Radio also led to less frequent vague reference (the vague characters variable) in which the subject used a pronoun or vague noun (e.g., "the man") without an antecedent. It appears that in some cases the visual image of the television representation serves as the unspoken antecedent, visually represented by the subject, but not communicated to the listener. The stimulation of visual representational processes by television is further indexed by the better performance in using pictures to retell the story (picture sequencing) after television than after radio (a not very surprising finding). Finally, radio once again proved more stimulating to the imagination (more frequent use of material from outside the stimulus story as an inference source).

Those features of a medium's representation that are communicated well also tend to be features that appear frequently in that medium. Thus, television programming emphasizes action information, and it communicates this well, whereas, over time, television programming has tended to deemphasize dialogue. (The television series "Miami Vice" was a good example of this trend.) An implication of such foci is that television will tend to provide its viewers with a great deal of practice in the comprehension of action information, but the corresponding representational processes involved in dialogue will get less practice.

In addition to the significant medium differences shown in Tables 10.1 and 10.2, there is also clearly a good deal of overlap in processes of imaginal and memory representation stimulated by the two media. There is not a single variable in which there is an all-or-none difference between the two media. Indeed, the margin of difference is, in every case, smaller than the overlap between average response to the two media. For this reason, it appears that there only is partial conservation of meaning across media. In the context of much overlap, each medium still leads to different emphases in representational processes and, consequently, different emphases in the communication of content.

IMPLICATIONS OF VIDEO IMAGERY FOR REPRESENTATIONAL COMPETENCE

The technology of television and, especially, that of video games augments skill in reading visual images as representations of three-dimensional space. The presence of print (and, later, photographic) technology is historically associated with the development of conventions of perspective. Such conventions both allow and require the three-dimensional interpretation of two-dimensional representations. Video technologies go beyond print and photography in their presentation of two-dimensional representations of three-dimensional space. The viewer must not only demonstrate an ability to interpret static two-dimensional images in the third dimension, but also skill in mentally transforming, manipulating, and relating dynamic and changing images. Thus, the video screen adds two new interrelated dimensions—time and motion—to the iconic imagery of pictorial representation. These two new dimensions have implications for the representation of three-dimensional space.

Television and the Mental Construction of Space

Television provides informal training in the representation of space. Figure 10.1 shows an item from the Space Construction Test developed by Gavriel Salomon (1979). In this test, the task is to put the four picture fragments together so that they form a single space, in this case a room. Salomon (1979) found that children who did well on this test were better able to understand edited films than children who did less well.

Why this correlation between performance on the Space Construction Test and skill in interpreting edited films? The answer lies in a visual technique that is intrinsic to the film and television media. When a three-dimensional space, such as a room, is filmed, the camera does not and cannot reveal the whole space in a single shot. Instead, the camera pans or cuts from one part of the room to another. It shows but one fragment at a time. To have a sense of the whole space, the viewer must mentally integrate the fragments, constructing the room for him- or herself. Apparently, learning to interpret and integrate the fragmentary shots in a film creates a cognitive skill, which then transfers to this paper-and-pencil test. This skill is also called into play by video games, the next medium to be discussed.

FIG. 10.1. Item from Space Construction Test. *Note.* From *Interaction of media, cognition, and learning* by G. Salomon, 1979, San Francisco: Jossey-Bass. Reprinted by permission of the author.

Video Games as a Representational Medium

The interactive television set called a computer has entered our society on a mass scale. Among all the forms of computer technology, the video game touches most directly a majority of people, and, even more important, touches them during the formative years of childhood, when socialization is taking place. A study in 1985–1986 by Rushbrook (1986) showed that 94% of 10-year-old children in Southern California (Orange County) had played video games. Eighty-five percent of these children considered themselves as good, very good, or expert players. Since that time the penetration of video games with young children has undoubtedly both increased in scope and decreased in age of first exposure: As of December 1991, there were more than 45 million Nintendos in homes in the United States.

Note that the reference is to video games, not to explicitly educational games, but primarily to the action games found in video arcades and played on home game sets. Indeed, the focus of this discussion is the cognitive implications of games that have commonly not been considered cognitive at all, but merely exercises in eye–hand coordination.

What are some of the implications of video games for representational processes and cognitive distance?

1. Unlike television, the player is not simply in the position of being a consumer of the representation: He or she is also a producer. The player not only interacts with the representation; through the joystick or game controller, the player is a partner with the computer in the construction of the representation. Through the joystick or controller, the player creates the movement patterns of the central character on the screen in an action game. In a simulation game, the player participates in the construction of a whole world. In a role-playing adventure game, the player participates in the creation of characters.

2. Therefore, the joystick (or controller) is itself a representational tool, for it creates its own mark, a moving signifier, on the screen. But it is a particular kind of representational tool, with a high degree of distance between tool and signifier. To get a notion of the representational distance, compare a joystick with a pencil. Unlike the joystick, the pencil creates a representation through spatial contiguity of tool and signifier. The joystick, in contrast, is at a distance from the screen representation it is controlling.

3. Action video games, like television, are a real-time medium. From the point of view of psychological distance, this characteristic probably has the most important implications. Because of the real-time movement of the video media, the player (or the viewer of television) cannot stop to reflect. If a pause to reflect occurs while watching television, the viewer misses the next event. If this is done while playing an action video game, the player's character will be lost or destroyed. This real-time quality finds its purest embodiment in arcade games,

where time is money (Harris, 1992). Consequently, arcade video games, like television, provide no opportunity to develop or practice the reflective or transcendent (Sigel, 1986) aspect of distancing strategies. There is time neither for the reflective abstraction emphasized by Piaget (1978), nor for the further symbolic transformation of ongoing experience emphasized by Sigel (1986).

4. Video games build upon and utilize the visual-spatial skills developed by television. For example, a number of video games require the very same cognitive process of spatial integration that is involved in the Space Construction Test (Fig. 10.1). It appears that the overlap in technology between the two media, television and video games, is also reflected in an overlap of requisite representational skills. For example, Fig. 10.2 shows the first three screens from a game called Castle Wolfenstein, which utilizes this skill. The goal of Castle Wolfenstein is to escape from the castle, which represents a Nazi prison. The castle consists of a series of mazes, only one of which is visible at a time. Yet the mazes are interconnected vertically by stairways (e.g., top right-hand corner of top maze) and horizontally by doorways (e.g., top middle of middle maze). In order to have an overview of the castle as a whole, the player must put together the individual mazes in his or her mind and mentally construct the space.

My own experience in playing the game indicates that this is not a skill to be taken for granted. After my first session with the game, I assumed each maze was independent of the others and that the order of mazes was essentially random. Essentially, I had not only failed to integrate the fragments, but failed to realize that the fragments *could* be integrated. My son Matthew was amazed at my ignorance. ("Most people realize *that,* even if they are not paying attention!") His amazement gave me a clue that spatial integration may be a well-understood convention, as well as a habit, for expert game players like him, more than for other people.

Figure 10.3a presents a map of Castle Wolfenstein that Matthew's friend, Paul Riskin, just sketched out for me when they discovered my interest in the spatial characteristics of the game. It shows quite clearly how developed these spatial integration skills can be in expert players. Although the original idea of a map had appeared in a magazine, Paul produced an initial sketch of the castle completely from memory. Matthew looked at it, thought there were a few errors, and then revised the sketch through a bit of game play. His revised sketch appears as Fig. 10.3b. Comparing the two maps, we see that Paul's map from memory, his internalized representation, although not perfect, was generally accurate. An informal survey in a communications studies class at UCLA confirmed that Castle Wolfenstein players do spontaneously develop mental maps of the castle as they play, even without ever seeing a map drawn out for them. The important point is that expert play requires spatial integration in the form of a mental map, and that expert players develop such representations. Note that the focus here is on iconic rather than symbolic (Bruner, 1965, 1966) modes of representation. That is, the map is iconic in that it bears a physical resemblance to its referent,

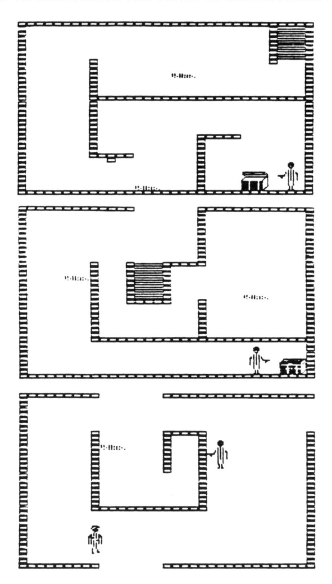

FIG. 10.2.   Three interlinked mazes from Castle Wolfenstein.

the castle. In this it differs from symbols such as words that bear, by definition, an arbitrary relationship to their referents.

One interesting point is that the need to integrate fragments of space into a single structure in the video game Castle Wolfenstein closely parallels the task of the Space Construction Test, performance on which was found to be related to an understanding of film. Thus, socialization by the visual media of television and

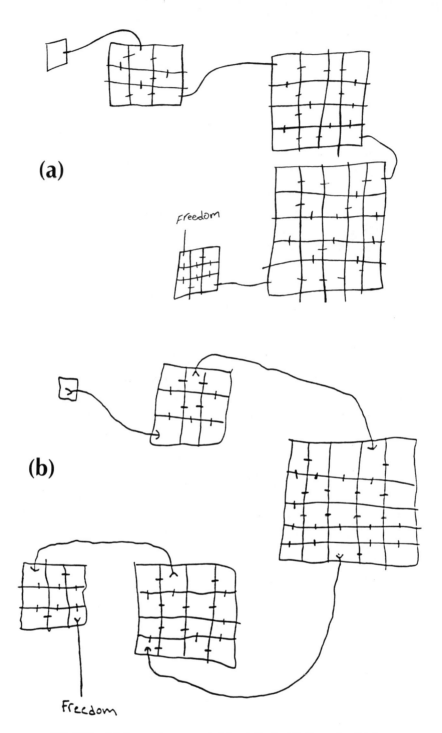

FIG. 10.3. (a) A spontaneous sketch of Castle Wolfenstein. (b) Revised sketch of Castle Wolfenstein.

film may provide informal training that is relevant to understanding (and operating in) the screen displays of video games.

With the advent of ever more complex video games, such as Nintendo's popular Legend of Zelda (1986), reference maps, an iconic metarepresentational guide to video representations of space, have become increasingly popular (Harris, 1992). *Nintendo Power,* for example, which regularly publishes such maps, currently boasts more than two million subscribers (Harris, 1992).

Spatial Integration and Computer Literacy

Spatial integration of computer screen displays, as required by the game Castle Wolfenstein or The Legend of Zelda, is a general requirement for using all sorts of computer programs. In a computer program, the user is not permitted to get to any part of the program, as indexed by a particular screen display, from any other part. There are certain, sometimes branching, paths between any two points in a program. A spatial model of these "paths" can help the user "move around" in the program. It is interesting to note how spatial metaphors such as "move around" have grown up to describe this process of understanding what is connected to what within a program. The situation is quite different in the older print medium. Consider the structure of a book, for example. The reader can move freely from any page to any other page. Unlike a computer program, the ordering is linear, and movement from one part to another is unconstrained.

The increasing utilization of the nonlinear organization of computer programs in software design is making the ability to construct iconic spatial representations ever more crucial for dealing with this medium. For example, the first computer databases were based on a print model: They are linear in their organization. However, in recent years, new types of databases, called hyperprint and hypermedia, have been developed; the information in these is arranged in complex, nonlinear spatial configurations. The ability to integrate fragments (individual screen displays) into a unified spatial representation is crucial to the efficient use of these futuristic systems, already in use. Most recently, there has been discussion of how to keep these systems from exceeding human capacities to represent nonlinear information (Loh, 1990).

There is Also Evidence that Games Further Develop the Spatial Skills That They Require.

The Empire Strikes Back, an arcade action game notable for requiring the player to navigate through three-dimensional space represented on a two-dimensional screen, was used in order to research visual-spatial skills (Brannon & Lohr, 1985; Greenfield, Brannon, & Lohr, in press). The researchers stood around the game in an arcade and tested players who had just finished playing. Their test of visual-spatial skills, mental paper folding (Shepard & Feng, 1972), was also one that demanded visualizing three-dimensional movement from a two-dimensional display. The test is shown in Fig. 10.4. Brannon and Lohr (1985; Greenfield, Brannon, & Lohr, in press) found that the better game players

Below are drawings each representing a cube that has been "unfolded." Your task is to mentally refold each cube and determine which one of the sides will be touching the side marked by an arrow.

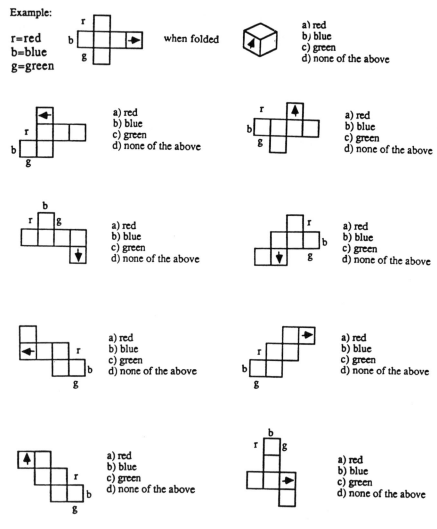

FIG. 10.4.   Mental paper folding test used by Brannon & Lohr (1985).

(scoring over 100,000 points) did significantly better on mental paper folding. This study confirms that a video game utilizes and/or develops related visual-spatial skills that are more general than the game itself.

   Perhaps most interesting in terms of the television–video game connection are results reported by Pezdek and colleagues (Pezdek, Simon, Stoecker, & Kieley, 1987). They found that skill in comprehending television (but not skill in comprehending radio or written material) is strongly correlated with performance on mental paper folding. In other words, in line with the hypothesis developed earlier, here is direct empirical evidence that players of three-dimensional video games are using and, perhaps, developing skills required by television information processing.

In an experimental follow-up to the correlational study (Greenfield, Brannon, & Lohr, in press), the relation between playing The Empire Strikes Back in the context of an experiment and improved mental paper folding was explored with a sample of university students. Although there was no effect from playing for an hour or two in our experiment, path analysis indicated that cumulative skill in The Empire Strikes Back, as indexed by initial performance, is a causal factor in the spatial representational skills of mental paper folding (see Fig. 10.5).

As Fig. 10.5 illustrates, gender is a causal factor in video game skill; video game skill, in turn, influences the spatial representational skills involved in mental paper folding. However, contrary to the notion that boys may be innately better at spatial skills, gender does not influence iconic spatial skills directly (see the nonsignificant dotted link in Fig. 10.5). Gender influences spatial representational skill through the medium of video game expertise. In a subsequent study, this knowledge was applied to reducing gender differences in visual-spatial skills.

In an experiment conducted with 10- and 11-year-old children, the age at which gender differences in visual-spatial skills first stabilize (Johnson & Meade, 1987), we investigated whether video game practice can reduce gender differences in iconic spatial skills (Subrahmanyam & Greenfield, in press). In the experiment, all children were first given a computerized battery of dynamic

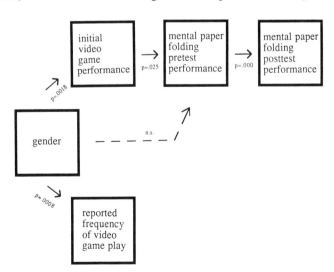

FIG. 10.5. Path model of causal relations between gender, video game behavior, and mental paper folding (Greenfield, Brannon, & Lohr, in press).

spatial skill tests developed by Pellegrino, Hunt, Abate, and Farr (1987). The tests involved judgments of distance and position, and memory for paths. Members of a randomly selected experimental group consisting of half the boys and half the girls then were given $2\frac{1}{4}$ hr of practice on a maze-based video game, Marble Madness (Harvey, 1986). Analysis of the game indicated that it required skills closely related to those tested. A control group played an unrelated word game, Conjecture, on the computer for the same amount of time. Finally in the posttest, all children were retested with two of the three tests given initially.

As expected, boys brought better iconic spatial skills into the experiment, as shown by their significantly lower error scores on the pretest. Also as expected, this gender gap in favor of boys seemed to get smaller on the posttest. The statistically significant pattern of experimental results graphed in Figure 10.6 provides one part of the explanation: Video game practice (but not the computerized word game used as a control condition) generally improved the dynamic spatial skills of anyone, male or female, who started out with relatively weak spatial skills (i.e., high spatial error in Figure 10.6). Those who started out with relatively strong skills (i.e., low spatial error in Figure 10.6) were, by contrast, unaffected by the experimental video game practice. The second part of the explanation lies in the fact that about two-thirds of the children who started out with relatively weak spatial skills were girls. As a consequence, the improvement in dynamic spatial skills that resulted from video game practice affected girls more than boys.

But the positive effect of video game practice on dynamic spatial skills was not a one-way relationship. Better spatial performance on the pretest also led to better video game performance at the end of the experimental practice period. These results indicate that skills in understanding a dynamic representation of

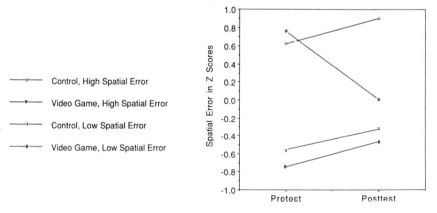

FIG. 10.6. The effect of video game practice on dynamic spatial test performance for children differing in pretest spatial skill (Greenfield & Subrahmanyam, in press).

spatial relations are a factor in the acquisition of video game expertise, as well as vice versa.

Discovering the Rules of a Dynamic Visual Representation

One of the most interesting points about video games as complex, dynamic representation systems is that no one tells you the rules in advance. The rules must be figured out by observation, trial-and-error, and a process of hypothesis testing. Several researchers have noted the problem-solving/discovery aspect of video games (Greenfield, 1983, 1984; Strover, 1984; Turkle, 1984).

In essence, the player creates a part of a dynamic representation using a joystick; he or she must figure out how his or her representation interacts with screen objects controlled by the computer. The rules go beyond the decoding of meaning for individual icons on the screen. More important than figuring out what the symbols mean is discovering how they act.

This process of making observations, formulating hypotheses, and figuring out the rules governing the behavior of a dynamic representation through a trial-and-error process is basically the cognitive process of inductive discovery. It is the process by which individuals learn much about the world, and, at a more formal level, it is the thought process behind scientific thinking and discovery. If video games function to train this process, they would have great educational and social importance.

To test this idea, the process of inductive discovery in the course of video game mastery was documented to determine whether video games could function as a method of informal training for scientific–technical thinking. The study had a cross-cultural aspect as well, involving a comparison between students in Los Angeles and Rome, where computer technology is less widespread (Camaioni, Ercolani, Perucchini, & Greenfield, 1990; Greenfield et al., in press; Sensales & Greenfield, 1991; Sensales & Greenfield, in press).

Learning and the Discovery Process

The experiment involved using the video game of Evolution, a "noneducational" action game for Apple computers (Sember & Mattrick, 1982), as an experimental treatment for university students studying psychology. Apart from being relatively nonviolent, this game had all of the design features of a normal action game found in video arcades, cafés, hand-held games, or home game sets. Most important for our purposes, it had a variety of levels, each one of which had a different set of rules and patterns to figure out.

In Evolution, the player "evolves" from ameba to human (this is *not* a realistic simulation!). At each stage, there are various inductive problems to solve: What is the goal? Who are the enemies? How does the joystick function to control movement? What are effective strategies?

In order to document results of the hypothesized discovery process, one of our experimental groups was given a series of questionnaires assessing their knowledge of answers to questions like those above. Twice in each game session (there were three sessions, totaling $2\frac{1}{2}$ hr in all), players were given such a questionnaire. Figure 10.7 shows the (statistically significant) development of knowledge of the game as game-playing experience increases. It appears that mastery of a video game does, indeed, involve the gradual discovery of rules, patterns, and strategies that allow mastery of a dynamic screen-based representation.

Furthermore, it appears that it was necessary for novices to learn the game inductively, rather than deductively. Before playing Evolution for the first time, a second group of subjects received detailed instructions on how to play the game. These explanations included verbal representations of rules, patterns, and strategies. It also included both static and dynamic iconic representations—slides of all of the Evolution screens (one from each level) and a video tape of the game screen as an expert player moved through all of the levels. However, in both Rome and Los Angeles, the group with these instructions failed to learn to play the game better than a third novice group who figured it out for themselves by trial and error. Nor did metacognitive awareness, presumably stimulated by the periodic questioning experienced by the first group, described above, make any

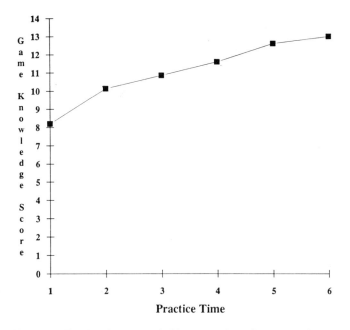

FIG. 10.7.   The development of video game knowledge as a function of practice (Greenfield et al., in press). The first point represents knowledge after about 15 minutes of play.

difference. It seems that video games necessitate not only inductive learning of the dynamic representational system, but interactive inductive learning. The instructional and questioning conditions showed that skill is not aided either by deductive application of verbal rules, by observation of a model, or by responding to verbal questions concerning rules and strategies. In terms of distancing theory, verbal and iconic strategies appeared to be of little use for conveying how to become skillful at the interactive dynamic representation called a video game. The interesting contrast, within this theoretical framework, is that strategies can be "too distant" for the performer or too far removed ("distant") from relevance to a particular medium.

On the other hand, Harris has observed that "In video game play, young children as novices are introduced to game play by more experienced players, and once the basics are mastered, the novice further develops his skills on his own through interaction with the game. . . . More experienced players share secrets with less experienced players, often modeling game strategies or providing verbal guidance through difficult moves" (Harris, 1992, p. 6). Given these observations concerning the role of expert instruction in the learning process, why did not visual demonstrations or periodic cuing through questions make a positive difference in mastering the video game Evolution? It may be the interactive and scaffolded nature of the novice-master relationship described by Harris (1992) that is crucial. In other words, the experienced player can observe the learner's level and specific needs for information as the learner plays the game, while the learner can communicate his/her specific informational needs to the master. The master-novice interaction described by Harris (1992) occurs while the learner is on-line with the game, receiving inductively relevant input. The learner creates a representational model of the game by interacting both with the game and with other players simultaneously. If this analysis is correct, our "training" conditions may have been unsuccessful for two reasons (1) training was not shaped by feedback from the learner, and (2) instruction did not occur while the learner was receiving induction-relevant experience by actually playing the game. Perhaps successful distancing strategies for interactive video games must include these two characteristics.

Transferring Discovery Skills from a Video Game to a Scientific/Technical Computer Simulation

Because video games have been widely considered to have little if any redeeming social value in themselves (e.g., "Rebellion Against Video Games," 1983), the next step was to determine if the processes of inductive discovery that they engage might transfer to problem solving in a scientific or technical context, an area of undisputed social importance (Camaioni, Ercolani, Perucchini, & Greenfield, 1990; Greenfield et al., in press). To investigate this, two parallel transfer tasks were developed, one given as a pretest, one given as a posttest; these involved animated simulations of the operation of electronic circuits presented schematically on a video screen (Robinett, 1982). Would the discovery of the rules governing one dynamic screen representation (the video game) help in discovering the meaning of another (animated electronic circuits) (Greenfield, 1990)?

Subjects were told nothing about the demonstrations, not even that what they were seeing were circuits; they were simply told to watch carefully so that they could answer questions later about what was going on. After every few demonstrations on the screen, subjects were given written questions to answer. The questions were such that the subjects not only had to understand what they had been shown on the screen, but also had to generalize their conclusions to new instances of circuits and to a new medium of representation, paper and pencil.

To test for transfer, our subjects were assigned to one of a number of experimental treatment groups. There were the three Evolution video game conditions already described, conceived as involving varying degrees of inductive discovery. A fourth condition involved playing a computer memory game. Like the video game Evolution, it used the computer medium; unlike Evolution, it was not thought to require inductive discovery for its mastery. Contrasting with the computer memory game, a fifth treatment condition was a mechanical memory game; it had the same rules and structure as the computer memory game, but utilized a different medium. Instead of the video screen used in the computer memory game, the mechanical memory game used a board. Finally, there was a "no treatment" control condition.

The experimental results (reported in more detail in Greenfield et al., in press) indicated that both computer games, the inductive action video game and the noninductive computer memory game, provided more transfer to comprehension of the scientific/technical stimulation on the posttest than did the noncomputer conditions. However, the pattern of experimental results suggested that, contrary to expectation, transfer was not mediated by general skill in inductive discovery, but rather by a medium-specific representational skill: ability to decode the iconic representation of computer graphics.

In order to further explore this possibility, a measure of the degree to which subjects used iconic diagrams versus symbolic (verbal) representations in answering questions about the simulated electronic circuits on pre- and posttest was developed. Statistical analysis showed that more use of iconic representation and less use of verbal representation in the pretest was significantly associated with greater initial skill in playing the action video game. More iconic and less verbal representation was also significantly associated with better comprehension of the simulated electronic circuits in the same pretest. Finally, subjects became significantly more iconic (and less verbal) in constructing their test answers after playing the computer memory game (Camaioni et al., 1990; Greenfield et al., in press). Therefore, it appears that one component in figuring out the rules of both an action video game and a technically oriented computer simulation is skill in iconic representation. Finally, the experimental results indicate that a computer game can develop just such representational skill.

Iconicity and Computer Literacy

Iconic computer interfaces were pioneered by Alan Kay, based on Bruner's (1965, 1966) concept of iconic representation. The increasing popularity of these interfaces, initially commercialized in Macintosh computers, has made iconic representational skills an ever more important component of computer literacy. Our study (Camaioni et al., 1991; Greenfield et al., in press) indicates that action video and other kinds of computer games utilize or enhance iconic representational processes.

Educational and Cultural Implications

In a 1977 article in *Science,* E. S. Ferguson pointed out that the language of technology is basically a nonverbal one and that people involved in technology need to be able to think in terms of visual images. He criticized engineering schools for their bias toward educating students to analyze systems using numbers rather than visual images, pointing out that this bias has produced a lack of people who have skills to deal with real machines and materials.

Ferguson's point has applicability way beyond engineering now that so many different kinds of learning and work involve computer screens. Our formal educational system ignores the visual requirements of the new technologies in both teaching and testing. It is concerned about verbal and other forms of symbolic representation, but not about the visual representation of space or other types of iconic representation. Until this situation changes, we shall be relying on television and video games to provide informal education in this important domain.

In many ways, however, the computer culture embodies and requires print as well as image literacy. With more than two million current subscriptions to *Nintendo Power* alone, "Young children not only learn to read complex maps and reference guides, but to understand the value of maintaining books for their reference value in answering questions to specific problems posed. In this respect, children's video game play and a reliance on technical support via print mirrors the behavior of adults within engineering and other technical fields" (Harris, 1992, p. 7).

Indeed, the anthropological study of games has demonstrated that a culture's games socialize children in accord with the needs and adaptational requirements of a particular society (Roberts & Sutton-Smith, 1962; Werner, 1979). Perhaps because video games are a product of the computer culture, as well as a socializing force for it, they have become a mass medium for cognitive socialization. In contrast, formal schooling, because of its historical base in the symbolic codes of print literacy, has been slower to adapt to the expanded requirements for universal technological literacy.

CONCLUSIONS

Video games are the first example of a computer technology that is having a socializing effect on the next generation on a mass scale, and even on a world-wide basis. Many of these effects seem to be preparing children (and adults) to deal with the world of computers in general. For example, in figuring out the rules and patterns of a game, a player is also figuring out the nature of the computer program behind the game, or what the programmer had in mind (Sudnow, 1983; Turkle, 1984). As the program is never visible, this is a mental representation. A willingness to figure out how the program works by interacting with the game rather than by reading instructions is a valuable skill in other computer tasks and environments. The skills in spatial or iconic representation developed by video and other computer games come into play in computer functions as diverse as word-processing (Gomez, Bowers, & Egan, 1982), programming (Roberts, 1984), and, as previously noted, understanding scientific simulations (Greenfield et al.) or decoding and finding your way around in a program.

What is the person like who has been socialized by the technologies of television and video games? So far, it appears that he or she may have more developed skills in iconic representation than the person socialized entirely by the older media of print and radio. The video game and computer, in adding an interactive dimension to television, may also be creating people with special skills in discovering rules and patterns by an active and interactive process of trial and error.

Video Game Violence

With respect to the thematic content of television and video games, there is at least one great problem with socialization by these media. The problem arises from the fact that so much content is violent. Indeed, the impact of playing a violent video game alone is exactly the same as watching a violent cartoon: It makes the young child's behavior more aggressive (Silvern & Williamson, 1987). Violent content is one reason why girls play action video games less frequently than boys (Malone, 1981); girls therefore receive less practice in the technologically relevant cognitive skills provided by the games. If the prevalence of violent themes in television and video games remains high, these media may reinforce or even forge an unfortunate link in society between violent social behavior and technologically oriented cognitive skills.

A New Person?

Are these technologies in the process of creating a new person? The cognitive skills are not new, although the particular combination may well be. In previous

180

generations a high level of development of these skills was probably restricted to people in certain relatively elite technical occupations—for example, pilots and engineers in the case of visual-spatial skills. Television and, especially, video games have made highly developed iconic-spatial representation potentially accessible to everyone. In this respect, they have much greater potential impact than the so-called "educational" software available mainly to those with access to personal computers.

The preceding chapter has emphasized real-time media and formats such as television and action video games. Although the action games studied by Greenfield and colleagues (Camaioni et al., 1990; Greenfield, 1990; Greenfield, Brannon, & Lohr, in press; Greenfield et al., in press; Greenfield, Dewinstanley, & Kaye, in press; Subrahmanyam & Greenfield, in press) clearly involve strategy and problem solving, they also emphasize quick and accurate manual responses to complex dynamic visual stimuli. This feature is typical of games originating in video arcades, where time is money (Harris, 1992). It is possible that the real-time nature of television and arcade-style video games interferes with the *reflective* function of distancing strategies.

In contrast to television and arcade games, however, video cassette players and home video games, do allow the consumer to stop, think, and replay the tape, or in some cases, the game action (Greenfield, 1984; Harris, 1992). Correlatively, a number of games originating for home game systems, such as the popular role-playing adventure games, require much more complex problem-solving and strategy, with less emphasis on speed. Although actual play still occurs in real time, players stop these games, discuss strategy, consult their *Nintendo Power* or other manuals, and redo unsuccessful moves (Harris, 1992, personal communication, 1992). We know little about which kinds of games are played more or will be in the future; nor do we know how frequently VCRs are actually stopped for replay or verbal discussion. Nevertheless, the modification of real-time media by stop-action and replay may, to some extent, keep these media from undermining the *reflective* function of distancing strategies, perhaps ultimately even supporting the development of this more traditional aspect of representational competence.

ACKNOWLEDGMENTS

I thank Peter Bentler, Laurel Smith, and Kaveri Subrahmanyam for help in data analysis and Deborah Land, Ralph Vogel, and Lisa Kendig for graphics. Various drafts of this chapter were prepared with the aid of a grant from the Office of Naval Research to Radcliffe College, a fellowship from the Bunting Institute, Radcliffe College, and a grant from the Spencer Foundation. Special thanks to Sharon Harris and Matthew Greenfield, who provided valuable criticism and suggestions for improving an earlier draft.

REFERENCES

Brannon, C., & Lohr, D. (1985). *Spatial abilities related to skill at a three-dimensional video game.* Los Angeles: University of California.

Bruner, J. S. (1965). The growth of mind. *American Psychologist, 20,* 1007–1017.

Bruner, J. S. (1966). On cognitive growth I. In J. S. Bruner, R. R. Olver, & P. M. Greenfield et al., *Studies in cognitive growth* (pp. 1–30). New York: Wiley.

Bruner, J. S., & Olson, D. R. (1974). Learning through experience and learning through media. In D. R. Olson (Ed.), *Media and symbols: The forms of expression, communication, and education* (pp. 125–150). Chicago: The University of Chicago Press.

Camaioni, L., Ercolani, A. P., Perucchini, P., & Greenfield, P. M. (1990). Video giochi e abilita cognitive: L'ipotesi del transfer. (Video games and cognitive ability: The hypothesis of transfer.) *Giornale Italiano Di Psicologia, 17*(2), 331–348.

dePaola, T. (1975). *Strega Nona.* Englewood Cliffs, NJ: Prentice-Hall.

Ferguson, E. S. (1977). The mind's eye: Nonverbal thought in technology. *Science, 197,* 827–836.

Gomez, L. M., Bowers, C., & Egan, D. E. (1982, March). Learner characteristics that predict success in using a text-editor tutorial. *Proceedings of Human Factors in Computer Systems,* Conference held in Gaithersburg, MD.

Greenfield, P. M. (1983). Video games and cognitive skills. In *Video games and human development: A research agenda for the '80's.* Cambridge, MA: Harvard Graduate School of Education.

Greenfield, P. M. (1984). *Mind and media: The effects of television, video games, and computers.* Cambridge, MA: Harvard University Press.

Greenfield, P. M. (1990). Video screens: Are they changing the way children learn? *The Harvard Education Letter, 6,* 1–4.

Greenfield, P. M., & Beagles-Roos, J. (1988). Radio vs. television: Their cognitive impact on children of different socioeconomic and ethnic groups. *Journal of Communication, 38,* 71–92.

Greenfield, P. M., Brannon, C., & Lohr, D. (in press). Two-dimensional representation of movement through three-dimensional space: The role of video game experience. *Journal of Applied Developmental Psychology.*

Greenfield, P. M., Camaioni, L., Ercolani, P., Weiss, L., Lauber, B. A., & Perrucchini, P. (in press). Cognitive socialization by computer games in two cultures: Inductive discovery or mastery of an iconic code? *Journal of Applied Developmental Psychology.*

Greenfield, P. M., Farrar, D., & Beagles-Roos, J. (1986). Is the medium the message?: An experimental comparison of the effects of radio and television on imagination. *Journal of Applied Developmental Psychology, 7,* 201–218.

Greenfield, P. M., deWinstanley, P., Kilpatrick, H., & Kaye, D. (in press). Action video games as informal education: Effects on strategies for dividing visual attention. *Journal of Applied Developmental Psychology.*

Haley, G. (1970). *A story, a story.* New York: Atheneum.

Harris, S. (1992, March). *Media influences on cognitive development.* Unpublished manuscript.

Harvey, W. (1986). *Marble madness* [computer program]. San Francisco: Electronic Arts.

Johnson, E. S., & Meade, A. C. (1987). Developmental patterns of spatial ability: An early sex difference. *Child Development, 58,* 725–740.

The Legend of Zelda [video game program] (1986). Redmond, WA: Nintendo.

Loh, B. (1990). Hypermedia: So many links, so little time. *Communication: The Communication Studies Journal, 1,* 18–26.

Malone, T. W. (1981). Toward a theory of intrinsically motivating instruction. *Cognitive Science, 5,* 333–370.

Meringoff, L. K. (1980). Influence of the medium on children's story apprehension. *Journal of Education Psychology, 72,* 210–249.

National Institute of Mental Health. (1982). *Television and behavior: Vol. 1, Ten years of scientific progress and implications for the eighties.* Washington, DC: Government Printing Office.

Pellegrino, J. W., Hunt, E. B., Abate, R., & Farr, S. (1987). A computer-based test battery for the assessment of static and dynamic spatial reasoning abilities. *Behavior Research Methods, 19,* 231–236.

Pezdek, K., Simon, S., Stoecert, J., & Kieley, J. (1987). Individual differences in television comprehension. *Memory and cognition, 15,* 428–435.

Piaget, J. (1978). *Success and understanding* (A. J. Pomerans, Trans.). Cambridge, MA: Harvard University Press.

Rebellion against video game spreads. (1983, April 24). *Los Angeles Times,* Part III, p. 3.

Roberts, J. M., & Sutton-Smith, B. (1962). Child training and game involvement. *Ethnology, 1,* 166–185.

Roberts, R. (1984, April). *The role of prior knowledge in learning computer programming.* Paper presented at the Western Psychological Association, Los Angeles.

Robinett, W. (1982). *Rocky's boots* [computer program]. Portola Valley, CA: The Learning Company.

Rushbrook, S. (1986). *Messages of videogames: Socialization implications.* Doctoral thesis, University of California, Los Angeles.

Salomon, G. (1979). *Interaction of media, cognition, and learning.* San Francisco: Jossey-Bass.

Sember, J., & Mattrick, D. (1982). *Evolution* [computer program]. Sydney Development Corporation.

Sensales, G., & Greenfield, P. M. (1991). Computer, scienza e tecnologia: Un confronto transculturale fra gli atteggiamenti di studenti italiani e statuitensi (Computers, science, and technology: A cross-cultural comparison of attitudes among students in Italy and the United States). *Giornale Italiano di Psicologia, 18,* 45–57.

Sensales, G., & Greenfield, P. M. (in press). Attitudes toward computers, science, and technology: A cross-cultural comparison between students of Rome and Los Angeles. *Journal of Cross-Cultural Psychology.*

Shepard, R., & Feng, C. (1972). A chronometric study of mental paper folding. *Cognitive Psychology, 3,* 228–243.

Sigel, I. E. (1970). The distancing hypothesis: A causal hypothesis for the acquisition of representational thought. In M. R. Jones (Ed.), *Miami symposium on the prediction of behavior, 1968: Effect of early experiences* (pp. 99–118). Coral Gables, FL: University of Miami Press.

Sigel, I. E. (1978). The development of pictorial comprehension. In B. S. Randhawa & W. E. Coffman (Eds.), *Visual learning, thinking, and communication* (pp. 93–111). New York: Academic Press.

Sigel, I. E. (1986). Early social experience and the development of representational competence. In W. Fowler (Ed.), *Early experience and the development of competence* (pp. 49–65). *New Directions for Child Development* (no. 32). San Francisco: Jossey-Bass.

Sigel, I. E., & Cocking, R. R. (1977). Cognition and communication: A dialectic paradigm for development. In M. Lewis & L. A. Rosenblum (Eds.), *Interaction, conversation, and the development of language: The origins of behavior* (Vol. 5, pp. 207–226). New York: Wiley.

Silvern, S. B., & Williamson, P. A. (1987). The effects of video game play on young children's aggression, fantasy, and prosocial behavior. *Journal of Applied Developmental Psychology, 8,* 453–462.

Strover, S. (1984, May). *Games in the information age.* Paper presented to the International Communication Association, San Francisco, CA.

Subrahmanyam, K., & Greenfield, P. M. (in press). Effect of video game practice on spatial skill in girls and boys. *Journal of Applied Developmental Psychology.*

Sudnow, D. (1983). *Pilgrim in the microworld.* New York: Warner.

Turkle, S. (1984). *The second self: Computers and the human spirit.* New York: Simon & Schuster.

Vygotsky, L. S. (1962). *Thought and language.* New York: Wiley.

Vygotsky, L. S. (1978). *Mind in society.* Cambridge, MA: Harvard University Press.

Werner, E. E. (1979). *Cross-cultural child development: A view from the Planet Earth.* Monterey, CA: Brooks/Cole.

11 Children's Conflicts: Representations and Lessons Learned

Carolyn U. Shantz
Wayne State University

The flow of everyday agreeable interaction of children with one another—at work and at play—is disrupted at times by episodes of quarreling and arguing. For observers and participants, such events may be viewed as a nuisance or as a serious confrontation, perhaps a threat to the relationship between the disputants or to the social order of a group. The likely impulse is to settle the matter as quickly as possible, and to get on with the goals or tasks at hand. Often, it seems, conflicts are seen as negative events, failures to "get along" and be sociable that are "best forgotten."

But are these events forgotten? One might well suppose they are not. Of the many social events that occur every day, interpersonal conflicts would seem to be particularly salient and memorable. Conflicts are, after all, social problems, and risky ones at that—in the sense that one never knows how they will turn out. And for the participants they often emerge unexpectedly. Conflicts are times when the self makes an issue of another person's behavior and protests, or, on the other hand, when the self's own behavior or wishes are thwarted by another person's opposition or refusal to comply. Such protests take effort by both parties, and carry both perils and promises for their relationship. In short, conflicts would seem to be memorable for some of the same reasons adults find certain events memorable to them (see Neisser & Winograd, 1988): because they are problematic social events, risky, demanding, often unexpected, and, at the moment they are occurring, are not matters of indifference to those involved.

They are not insignificant matters to developmental theorists, either. Virtually every major theorist has posited conflict as a significant force in development. Both Freud and Erikson viewed intrapsychic and interpersonal conflict or "crises" as propelling change, sometimes growth-enhancing change and sometimes regressive change in personality and identity. Further, the impact of conflict—as some theorists see it—is not limited to social and personality development. Piaget (1928) thought it a primary impetus to cognitive development in general, and reflective thought in particular. The child whose wants, intentions, or behaviors are challenged, for example, is prodded by the challenge to reflect on the merits of her own or his own position, and to communicate those merits of her own or his own position, and to communicate those merits in order to persuade others of their rightness or legitimacy. As further explicated by Sigel and Cocking (1977), such demands or prods—mild or strong, indirect or direct—encourage the child's psychological distancing from the here-and-now to represent the self, others, and the situation in order to meet the demand.

Given the significant social and cognitive effects social conflict is thought to have in development, the question arises as to how those effects might occur. The process may be one of simple extinguishing and strengthening of behaviors or relationships. However, a more constructive, social-cognitive process may be involved, one in which children create or abstract some kind of social message from their interactions. We chose to examine the latter possibility. Our focus, in contrast to theorists' emphasis on process, was to determine the substantive content of children's personal experiences of peer conflict: What do children recall of an encounter and what meaning or interpretation, if any, do children give such events? We asked children directly to describe two past conflicts with peers, and to tell what they had learned from the episodes. The answers we heard, to be reported later, reflect the meanings children give to these events, meanings that may influence, in turn, their future behavior and social cognitions.

It is surprising how little systematic study has been made of children's free-response descriptions of their social life, and particularly so in the case of their arguments and fights. Instead, there are substantial behavioral data on young children's actual, spontaneous conflicts—the common strategies used during such episodes and usual outcomes (for a review see Shantz, 1987). But what conflicts mean to those engaging in them can only be inferred by researchers from such behavioral data. There is also information about children's reasoning about conflicts, but, unfortunately, not their own conflicts. Rather, virtually all the social-cognitive research is based on hypothetical conflicts told in story or video form (e.g., Dodge, 1985; Selman, 1980; Shantz & Shantz, 1985). Not only are the events hypothetical, but the child is put in the position of being an "observer" of conflict rather than a participant in it.

How children represent social encounters in which they participated and what they learned from them can be more directly assessed by asking the children themselves. This method is premised on the tenets of attribution theory: The individual plays an active role in the creation of his or her experiences by selectively perceiving, interpreting, and remembering events, and by giving meaning to the behavior of the self and other largely through the perceiver's own causal schemes. Further, a wealth of empirical data indicates that attributions are influenced by whether an individual is an actor in or an observer of an episode (e.g., Schneider, Hastorf, & Ellsworth, 1979). How behavior is interpreted, then, might differ greatly between the researcher-observer and the child-actor, and, further, differ when the child is an observer of hypothetical events versus the child is an actor within actual events. Thus, children's reports of their perceptions and their reasoning about their own social experiences can provide new— and possibly significant—information on how children represent and give meaning to their social life.

To ask children about their own experiences touches on three primary empirical approaches: survey research, social event memory, and linguistic research on the narrative genre. First, the self-report method of survey research has focused on a variety of topics (e.g., perceptions of and feelings about various social relationships by Furman & Buhrmester [1985]) using a constrained, not a free-response, format. In order to respond to specific questions, children (usually age 8 and older) must summarize over time, situations, and/or individuals to report their general perceptions.

Because young children often have difficulty, however, summarizing over time and situations (e.g., Shaklee, 1976) and tend to conceptualize people and events in concrete, behavioral terms (e.g., Livesley & Bromley, 1973), such summarizing methods have limited validity for younger children. A preferable strategy is to ask children in a free-response format about specific events they have experienced. This has been the method of a good deal of social event (and autobiographical) memory research—both general (e.g., "scripts") and specific event representations (e.g., Todd & Perlmutter, 1980) as well as psycholinguistic research (e.g., Peterson & McCabe, 1983; Preece, 1987). These areas of study have revealed that children younger than 3 years spontaneously produce stories of their past experiences, and social memories are especially salient. By age 3–4 most children can produce them on request, and by age 6 most stories are well organized. These two areas of research, then, support the feasibility of eliciting memories of children's own experiences, especially social experiences, and in some organized form.

A study of children's recall about their conflicts with peers is reported in the following pages to provide initial data on how children represent such events. Beyond the descriptions, however, a major question was what children learn from their arguments, as a beginning effort to understand children's interpretations of social experiences of many kinds. The focus is on the specific social event of conflict because, as noted earlier, it has such theoretical importance in development. We selected children at age 7 because it is the age at which social conceptions are undergoing rapid development and it is a relatively neglected age in the three relevant research areas.

Given the theoretical importance Piaget placed on peer conflicts in development, we examined them rather than those with parents. Yet it seemed inadequate to merely examine "peers in general" because the social life of the child occurs in a matrix of different dimensions of social relationships, such as liking/disliking, power, and competency. The affectional dimension seemed especially important because of the potential impact conflict could have on it and how it might influence the ways conflict is conducted. Behavioral data confirm the importance of liking relations between adversaries. For example, Hartup, Laursen, Stewart, and Eastenson (1988) found that preschoolers' conflicts with their mutual friends compared to nonfriends were less emotionally intense, more often resolved by disengaging, and had more equal outcomes.

Thus, the second question of this study is, "With whom do children have their memorable conflicts?" We approached this question by examining "liking" relations at two levels: the dyadic relationship between the reporter and the reported adversary, and the sociometric status of the reporter and adversary in their classroom as a whole. Such data could begin to reveal the "social embeddedness" of conflict behavior as remembered by children.

A STUDY OF REMEMBERED CONFLICTS

This initial study of children's recall of peer conflicts and their social relations is based on one second-grade classroom of 27 children in a suburban public school. Children were asked to recall an "argument, fight, or disagreement" with any child in their classroom (general instructions), and, if necessary, were given additional encouragement to elicit recall. After the child's spontaneous recall, specific probes were asked to clarify the recall and elicit information not included spontaneously. Several weeks later, each child was asked to recall another, different conflict with a classmate. The narratives obtained in Interviews 1 and 2 were tape recorded, transcribed verbatim, and coded. (See the Appendix for the interview, codes, and reliabilities.)

Of the children who received parental permission to participate, 25 (16 girls, 9 boys) provided conflict descriptions in Interview 1, and 24 (15 girls, 9 boys) in Interview 2, yielding 49 total conflict descriptions. The data from the two interviews are analyzed separately at times to give an estimate of the replicability of the findings.

Content, Organization, and Lessons of Conflict

The majority of the second graders recalled and described a conflict after the initial request only (i.e., without further recall encouragement): 64% at Time 1, 83% at Time 2. This suggests that such memories are quite accessible to most children in this age group, more accessible than might be expected given the highly specific request to recall an argument with a classmate.

First we consider the question, "Of all the things children *could* report about their conflicts—outcomes, emotions, etc.—what *do* they focus on?" Here we examined only the initial, spontaneous descriptions prior to any questions asked by the interviewer. These data provide the clearest picture of how children represent conflicts and what they think is important to communicate about them, unsullied by the influence of the follow-up questions. Three aspects turned out to be central to conflict representations. First, the issue or "bone of contention" was stated in 96% of the descriptions. That is, these children had a clear idea of what the social problem was between them and their adversary and deemed it important to communicate. Second, children spontaneously cited their adversary by name (75%). This finding suggests that conflicts are socially embedded in memory, and part of their meaning is connected to who one's "partner in conflict" is. Third, in 65% of the cases the physical setting was mentioned spontaneously. In summary, children's memories are focused on what the problem was, who it was with, and where it all happened, features quite common to adults' event memories, too (Barsalou, 1988).

Now we turn to the full descriptions in which information given spontaneously is combined with answers to specific interview questions.

Onset. In 59% of the conflicts children had a clear notion of who started the conflict, and not surprisingly they most often said it was the other child (51%); conversely, in 8% they took responsibility. As every parent, teacher, and researcher knows, it is often difficult to determine who started a dispute, and children, too, seemed to have some difficulty making this judgment (or, perhaps, taking responsibility), 41% saying they were unsure.

Issues. The two primary, manifest issues of conflicts, as reported in each interview, were the control of a person's behavior (66%), and the possession and use of objects (33%). On the one hand, these proportions are highly similar to issues in preschoolers' actual conflicts as observed by Hartup et al. (1988), that is, 62% and 38%, respectively. However, a study of 6- to 7-year-olds' conflict behavior showed more object disputes than person control ones (Shantz & Shantz, 1985). Perhaps the different results are due to territorial/space issues being coded as behavioral in the Hartup et al. study but as object disputes in the Shantz and Shantz study. Thus, it is not clear whether the preponderance of recalled person control conflicts reflects the rate at which they actually occur in this age group, or whether person disputes are more memorable than are object disputes. Further, two types of person control issues were equally frequent: psychological harm such as teasing or name calling (20%), and physical harm such as hitting (20%). Violations of general social rules or rules of friendship were the bone of contention in 16%, and least often, facts or opinions (10%). Interview 1 percentages were very similar to Interview 2.

These are considered "manifest" issues in recognition that there are many latent (even symbolic) levels available for interpreting "what is at issue here?" For example, some object disputes may relate at a deeper level to the expectation/rule that "friends share their goodies with friends." In an ethnographic study of first graders' friendships, Rizzo (1988) found that disputes between friends often concerned violations of friendship expectations. Such violations could be the underlying issue in these second graders' conflicts, too, but we chose to code issues at the level children talked about them, and as such they accounted for a low proportion of the responses.

Strategies.   What children reported they and their adversary did and said during the episode (n = 87 strategies) were coded into three developmentally ordered categories based on a modification of the system reported in Shantz and Shantz (1985). Underlying the system is a proposed general dimension of the degree to which strategies appear to require the use of social knowledge of others' psychological functioning, that is, from minimal knowledge being needed to flee or use force to maximal knowledge to reason and compromise. Jose and Hennelly (1987) confirmed the developmental ordering of the categories for kindergartners through fourth graders.

The first level is the use of the most direct strategies: fleeing the interaction, using force through physical or verbal aggression or threats, or enlisting another person. Episodes involving such strategies accounted for more than half of all conflicts. The second category involves not flight or fight, but more conventional means such as apologizing, promising, saying "please," ignoring, and acting in a way to remedy the situation. These accounted for 28% of all strategies. Level 3 strategies (20%) appear to require less conventionality, more delay, and more intellectual means of solving conflicts: reasoning and compromising. These results indicate that second graders' memories of conflict with peers often involve, at some point, impulsive or forceful strategies being used by either themselves or their adversaries. Given the physical, psychological, and social implications of aggression, it is not surprising that its use in conflicts by either party makes conflicts memorable.

At the same time, nearly equal proportions of conflict involved "higher level" strategies, ones that presumably require more distancing from both the immediate situation and the thrust of one's wants in order to conform to more socially acceptable, conventional means, and even more so to justify, reason, and offer a compromise to settle the dispute. It is likely that children older than those interviewed here would show a greater number of the higher level strategies in comparison to forceful ones.

Emotions.   The emotions experienced during conflict by the self and other as reported by children themselves provide unique data in the conflict literature. All previous studies are observations of expressed emotion, and largely limited to preschoolers. Those studies provide a picture of neutral, low-intensity emotions. Specifically, during conflict, Hartup et al. (1988) found the majority (55%) to be low intensity. After 75% of conflicts, Dawe (1934) found little or no upset. In contrast, in this study children most often reported themselves to be mad or angry (43%), or bothered-upset (12%), or sad (12%). The rarer emotions (4%–8%) were "bad," blends of emotions, neutral, happy or good, and 8% did not attribute any emotion to themselves.

Mad and angry feelings were most often attributed also to the adversary (33%). Beyond that similarity of self and other, however, the results differ: 20% said they did not know how the other felt, 18% attributed happiness to the other, and at very low frequencies other emotions (sad, bothered, neutral, etc.). Some (10%) did not spontaneously report or answer the question.

In summary, children often experience anger and think their adversary does, too, at a rate higher than studies of expressed emotions suggest (at least among preschoolers). Feelings of frustration and anger would be expected in situations where one's goals are blocked, one's ongoing behavior is interrupted by opposition from another, or a peer does not comply with one's wishes. Social conflict, defined as mutual opposition, captures just such situations. It is interesting that the more internally oriented emotion of sadness is reported as frequently as being bothered or upset. Sadness and other emotions deserve further study to clarify individual differences in children's reported emotional reactions to conflict.

Endings.   Who or what ended the episode is seen quite often in this age group as "external" to the dyad (43%), usually intervening adults or peers (33%) or external events (such as the bell ringing to leave the playground). But equally often (44%), the conflict is settled within the dyad: the self ended it (22%), the other did (8%), or, interestingly, both were perceived as ending the episode (14%). The remaining endings were unspecified.

How the episode ended (the immediate "outcome") was frequently conceptualized as winning and losing (47%). Also, an unresolved ending (i.e., a stalemate) was often reported (35%). Compromises and collaborations occurred for only 14% of the conflicts, and in 4% children were not sure how it ended. We also asked, in effect, whether the argument had any long-term outcomes: no, 59%; yes, 16%; and unsure, 12% (with the remaining children not answering the question or the question not being asked). Thus, at this age, changes in the dyad's relationship are relatively rare, as they perceive it. In fact, for some children who answered "yes," these "long-term effects" lasted a day or so when they did not play with the adversary.

The larger picture emerging from these data is that children experience arguments and fights as part and parcel of social life, seldom seeing them as significantly altering their long-term relationships with others. And most children (80%) did not talk with their adversary about the argument. A few offered such rationales as it didn't occur to them to talk about it, they didn't think it was serious enough, the other probably forgot about it, or they wanted to avoid the topic for fear a new conflict would ensue.

Organization.   When children tell their conflict "story," how do they structure their representation of the event? To answer this question a three-category system was used based on the psycholinguistic work of Peterson and McCabe (1983), although their system was highly simplified for this study. The first type of structure, called *episodic,* is made up of stories organized as episodes along a time-line with some overall causal structure of how one event led to another to the final consequence (or goal-attainment). The second type, called *high point,* is a structure around a "centerpiece," a particularly salient event followed by elaborations, with minimal temporal ordering. The third, labeled *propositional,* is a narrative organized around a basic proposition followed by either evidence to support it or related propositions.

In the analysis, only the spontaneous part of the total narrative was examined because the interviewer's later specific probes could well influence the narrative organization. Of the 49 conflict stories, 55% were episodic; 24%, high-point; 18% had propositional organization; and 2% lacked any identifiable structure. Thus, most children seemed to adopt a reporter's stance toward an adult listener, starting at the beginning of the episode and describing it through its conclusion. The rarest were of propositional form (e.g., "She's so mean," followed by evidence of meanness). Unfortunately, these results cannot be compared directly to 7-year-olds' narratives gathered by Peterson and McCabe because their data were presented differently.

Lessons Learned.   In an earlier paper (Shantz, 1987), I raised a question concerning what lessons or messages participants in conflict draw from their peer arguments: "To what extent . . . do children construe messages about themselves as individuals, about specific peers, or about conflict behavior in general?" (p. 300). A major purpose of this present study was to begin to answer that question, specifically whether children draw any message at all, and, if so, what kind. The primary data come from the direct question toward the end of the interview: "What did you learn from (all of) this?"

Overall, children did draw a message in 76% of their conflicts. Their answers were uniformly immediate, as if (at least after relating the event) the question made sense and they had some clear idea of the meaning of their conflict. To code these messages, we devised a two-level system. The verbatim lessons were coded first into two broad categories: messages that focused on inhibition of behavior (the "don'ts") or on changing behavior (the "do's"). Within each broad category each message was further coded into three subtypes: lessons emphasizing specific behavior, friendship, or conflict. Lessons in this age group tended to be focused more on inhibiting (57%) than changing behavior (43%). Of these inhibition-focused lessons, most (55%) concerned specific behavior (e.g., "not to play with him again"); 30% drew inhibition messages about conflict itself ("I learned not to fight"); and 15% construed messages that emphasized friendship ("[I learned to] never fight with friends"). For those who focused on changing their behavior, 73% concerned different behaviors than those that had occurred during the conflict (e.g., "just ignore 'em"; "share stuff"); 20% friendship (e.g., "I learned that she has to make up her mind that she has to play with two people at a time or she's not getting any friends"), and the remainder, conflict messages (e.g., "I learned how to fight . . . if she hits me again, I'd probably flip her over my back").

Summing the subcategories across the two major categories indicates that this age group is likely to draw a behavioral message (63%): what they or the other should (do's) or should not do (don'ts). Less frequently children focused on conflict itself (20%) or friendship (17%).

The answers to my original questions appear to be that 7-year-olds most often draw messages about themselves—not in any abstract sense of the kind of person they are—but in the concrete sense of their behavior. These "guides to my behavior," which we see now that children are often constructing, may well influence their future interactions with peers, as suggested earlier. Such lessons, whether assessed at the time of conflict or recalled later, could be used both diagnostically and remedially in conflict intervention programs. Finally, few times did children draw "guides to my adversary's behavior": Only 2 of 46 conflict lessons were focused on what the adversary should have learned (e.g., "He should not be greedy").

In 24% of the conflicts, children said they had not learned anything from the encounter. A comparison between "no lesson" and "lesson" conflicts showed three distinctive features of the "no lesson" ones: strategies, outcomes, and gender of reporter. Physical and verbal aggressive strategies and threats occurred in 56% (vs. 17% in "lesson learned" conflicts); outcomes were wins/losses in 83% (vs. 35%); and 75% were reports by boys (vs. 24%). If, in these aggressive, win/loss conflicts, children often fail to draw a message (and not just fail to communicate one), the phenomenon would deserve further study. These are the very kinds of disputes from which adults would hope children learn the hazards of conflict, especially the hazards of aggressive behavior.

At the same time, it is important to note that the social context of these answers to "what did you learn?" was an adult asking a child. This may have pulled for socially approved maxims ("I should be nicer") or for inhibition lessons (the "don'ts") in the sense that the question is reminiscent of parents' and teachers' frequent statement, "Well, I hoped you learned your lesson from that!" to imply disapproval. Also, children may learn things of which they were completely unaware, or unable or unwilling to articulate.

Conflicts and Social Relationships

In order to explore the role conflict may play in the social life of children, we examined with whom children have their memorable conflicts. Specifically, we determined the social relationships between and among children: the dyadic relationship of reporter and adversary such as being friends, enemies, or only acquaintances; and, at a group level, their sociometric status as being popular, rejected, neglected, controversial, or average.

No theories of peer relations or conflict exist to guide hypotheses about conflicts between children having these different social relationships. But several reasonable possibilities come to mind. If one proposes that the conflicts remembered are a direct function of the frequencies of the types of social relationships that exist, then one might suppose that children have more conflicts with acquaintances than with friends or enemies because, in a classroom, there are more acquaintances with whom to dispute. Or, if the character of those relationships— rather than the number of them—is considered, then it might be that children who have an antagonistic relationship, for example, are especially prone to fights and those who are best friends seldom argue. Or, if the rate of interaction is weighted, it may be that ongoing antagonism between enemies encourages children to avoid one another so that conflicts with enemies are infrequent simply because there are few opportunities to dispute, and friends who interact with each other frequently are more prone to conflict, not less.

Another factor that greatly complicates the picture is to consider why children would remember some conflicts and not others, regardless of the number of relationships, their character, or rates of interaction. From nonsocial memory research we might posit that children are most likely to recall recent conflicts, for example, and thus the corpus of conflicts would be a random selection of existing relationships. Instead, however, it may be the social significance of the conflict—for the self and/or the relationship—that more often determines recall. One could posit, then, that children are least prone to recall fights with acquaintances and most prone to recall those with friends and enemies (i.e., those with whom they have a special relationship). By using such everyday rationales, many hypotheses can be entertained. Given the lack of theory and prior data on which to base hypotheses, this study is an exploratory examination of the issue.

Method.   About 2 weeks prior to the first interview to recall conflicts, children were individually interviewed about a theme called "things I like a lot and don't like a lot." They nominated their three "most liked" and three "most disliked" TV shows, foods, games, school subjects, and classmates, the latter providing the sociometric nomination data. During that phase, photographs of all class members were arrayed before the child to assist recall.

The nomination data yielded three dyadic relationships: mutual relations of liking (friends) and disliking (enemies); unilateral relations (e.g., X nominated Y as a best friend but Y did not nominate X as a best friend); and no special relations (i.e., "acquaintances," where neither child nominated the other as most or least liked). To calculate relations at the group level, the number of times each child was cited by class members as "liked most" (LM) and "liked least" (LL) were summed and used to yield each child's social impact (high to low visibility) and social preference (high to low liking). The scores were considered in combinations to yield five categories, as commonly defined in the field: Popular children are those highly liked (by 5 or more in this classroom), disliked by 1 or no classmates, and have a high social preference score ($n = 5$ children of 25); controversial children are highly liked by some classmates, highly disliked by others, and have a high social impact score ($n = 4$); neglected children receive 1 or no LM and LL scores, and low social impact scores ($n = 3$); rejected children have no LM citations, 3 or more LL citations, and negative social preference scores ($n = 3$); average children were all those who did not fit the criteria of the extreme groups ($n = 10$). The analyses reported here exclude seven adversaries in other classrooms whose status could not be assessed ($n = 42$ reports).

Results. First we consider the dyadic relation between the reporter and the adversary: 64% had mutual or unilateral relationships, and 36% had no special relationship. This suggests that recall is influenced (among many other factors) by the dyadic relationship between children.

Statistical tests were conducted to determine whether the predominance of special relationships for recalled conflicts is likely to be a direct function of the number of children who have these relationships. To avoid the dependencies in the data set summed across interviews and to determine the replicability of the findings, the interviews were examined separately. Each child had earlier nominated six classmates with whom there was a special relationship, leaving the majority with whom there was not. The distributions were used in a goodness-of-fit chi square as the basis for the theoretical probabilities of mention as an adversary (i.e., about two to three times more likely that there would be a "no special relationship" adversary). The results of Interview 1 showed, instead, a significant tendency to recall conflicts with those with whom children had a special relationship, the one-sample χ^2 (1, $n = 22$) = 18.56, $p < .001$.

Interview 2 replicated these findings. Based on the theoretical distribution of conflicts with possible classmates, it was shown again that "special relationship" conflicts were much more frequent, χ^2 (1, $n = 20$) = 8.57, $p < .01$, than acquaintance conflicts.

In sum, then, the dyadic analysis shows that children have a clear tendency to recall conflicts with classmates whom they especially like or dislike, and not to recall adversaries as a direct function of the number of children liked, disliked, or acquaintances. Further, the 64% of "special relationship" adversaries was composed of 38% unilateral relationships and 26% mutual ones. The unilateral ones were highly skewed toward one-way liking (88%) compared to disliking (12%). Of the mutual ones, 55% were friends, 18% were enemies, and 27% were opposite mutual relations (i.e., X especially liked Y whereas Y disliked X). These findings, in contrast to some common expectations, indicate that conflicts between friends are more likely to be recalled than those between enemies.

The sociometric status of children in the classroom as a whole was the second means to assess the social relationships. First we examined the reporter's and adversary's classroom status in the 42 conflicts. The number of reporters versus adversaries in each category were as follows: 8 popular reporters versus 11 popular adversaries; controversial, 7 versus 11; average, 18 versus 14; neglected, 5 versus 3; rejected, 4 versus 3. Given the number of reporters of different statuses, the most marked deviations were overrepresentation of popular adversaries and controversial adversaries, and underrepresentation of average status adversaries.

Further, the greatest number of reporters were of average status and their adversaries were not randomly distributed among the status classes; rather, they recalled the most conflicts with popular and controversial children in each interview (1, 66%; 2, 56%). Binomial tests of each interview of average status reporters confirmed a significant deviation from chance ($p_s < .002$). (Other distributions of reporters could not be tested for significance due to insufficient numbers in each interview.) The predominance of popular and controversial children as adversaries in reporters' conflicts may reflect, in part, the high interaction rates these children tend to have within the group (Dodge, 1983), and, in part, their social significance.

In summary, children tend to recall conflicts with peers with whom they have a special dyadic relationship, and particularly a "most liked" one (either unilateral or mutual). The effect of liking relationships on recall was also evident in the sociometric status analysis in which the two categories of children with the highest liking scores—popular and controversial—were overrepresented as adversaries for their absolute numbers in recalled conflicts. Thus, the possibilities that children's recalled conflicts, as a whole, are distributed randomly or only reflect the numbers of different relationships (e.g., the number of friends, acquaintances, average status, etc.) are not supported by these data. The findings require more extensive research with larger samples and at other ages. At the same time, these indications of the inherently social nature of conflict representation and recall are buttressed by the unanticipated finding that children also spontaneously cite their adversary, and do so by name.

REFLECTIONS

Children have provided in their accounts a unique window on their social world. We can see the emotions they experience and the meanings they attribute to their conflicts with peers. The modal messages they constructed are guides to the "do's" and "don'ts" of the self in conflict. But there was great diversity, too, in the "lessons" these encounters afforded. No single coding system does justice to that diversity. Consider some of the following quotations:

- I'm not sure (what I learned) but if I ever get a friend like that again, I'm not going to be a friend at all.

- Treat people how they want to be treated.
- Don't get in line by him.
- Not to make fun of people.
- I learned not to be left out or worried.
- Probably just walk away instead of playing with the person that we're fighting over.
- If somebody is playing with another person, don't think they don't like you no more . . . don't be sad or anything.
- To help each other.
- I learned how it felt to have everyone call me names.
- We shouldn't crowd an ocean (concerning a dispute where children had drawn too many jellyfish in a classroom ocean mural).

As the last lesson illustrates, some lessons are very concrete whereas others are as abstract as the "golden rule." Some focus on the avoidance of conflict or a particular peer. Some are lessons of emotions and empathy, and many are lessons of self-regulation.

The lessons reveal the dynamics of social life that have important developmental implications. Consider the issue of whether or not to comply with a peer's request or demand: One child did and wished he had not, and another did not and wished she had. In the first case, the lesson was "I learned not to just give something, give somebody whatever they want." In the second case a girl said, "I'll do (next time) what the person wants who gets mad," a clear statement of her intimidation by others' anger, and her willingness to comply with others in the future. These lessons, I suggest, reflect two developmental themes: being "connected" with others (a sense of belonging, being accepted and valued) while at the same time being "separated" (a sense of being a unique person, one with legitimate needs and rights). Conflictual interaction, we have suggested (Shantz & Hobart, 1989), is a particularly important process in children's ongoing development of their self-concept and their sense of being in close relationships with others. These children, and others, appear to be working on these fundamental themes, reflecting on the hazards and benefits of resisting or complying in their everyday encounters.

Not only did children's lessons vary widely, but so did their perceptions and representations of their adversarial encounters. The reported strategies, for example, ranged from offering remedial actions to subtle sarcasm or direct threats to the friendship. Some strategies could be inferred from children's virtual re-enactment of their conflicts, with the majority quoting themselves and other as their conflict story unfolded. The strategies reported and inferred are much more in keeping with the tactical complexity and diversity sociolinguists have observed of children's conflict talk (see Shantz, 1987, for a review) than they are with the simple strategies offered for hypothetical conflicts (e.g., Dodge, 1985; Selman, 1980).

Although it would be of interest to compare the recalled conflicts with the actual conflict behavior, it is impossible to do so because the conflicts were not observed. Interest in such comparisons is often based on researchers' underlying concern about self-report data: How accurate are children's descriptions of what actually occurred? This simple question is moot because of the problem—a perennial one in psychology—of the criteria of accuracy. It can not be assumed, for example, that adult observers are always more accurate than children, especially when it comes to child–child interactions. For example, children are privy to their history of interactions with their peers, their peers' reputations, and have certain expectations, all of which can influence the meaning of their conflict behavior. (In fact, adversaries' past behavior or reputation was explicitly and spontaneously described in 21% of the reports.) In contrast, observers bring their own perspectives on social events—as adults and as outsiders to the interactions and, perhaps, to the specific classroom culture.

Rather than posing the question as one of accuracy, a more productive approach might be to determine the similarities and differences among perspectives: the observing adult's, the child's immediate recall of a conflict (perhaps by on-the-spot interviewing as soon as the conflict ends), and the child's delayed recall. The triangulated comparisons could reveal how adults and children interpret each component of conflict, and which the child forgets, changes, and perhaps adds only later in time. Although such an endeavor is fraught with difficulty, it is especially important when one is dealing with social events. The interpretive and memorial processes are omnipresent—as events occur sequentially, as they are recalled immediately, and as they are remembered later in time. Freeman, Csikszentmihalyi, and Larson (1986) have suggested: "recollection . . . should not be looked upon as a detached summation of the past, nor as a distortion of reality, nor as 'merely subjective' reality. Instead, it should be seen as . . . concerned more with the interpretation of experience. . . Recollection, far from displacing objectivity, may actually facilitate it: It can bring the distance and perspective needed for a more comprehensive appraisal of what . . . happened" (p. 183).

This framework emphasizes the roles interpretive and memorial processes themselves have in fostering psychological distance and perspective taking. In addition, the "content" of the event—social conflict—may well facilitate distancing because conflicts are times of being challenged and challenging others that induce reflection on one's own wishes and behaviors. By doing so some psychological distance is gained from the immediate interaction. Indeed, such distancing may account, in part, for children's ease in describing their conflicts and responding to the question about the lessons learned. If theorists are correct, these are significant processes and events for fostering social and cognitive development.

Challenges to the self and by the self are seldom matters of indifference to those involved. Whether they are over trivial or substantial issues, they are moments of true social engagement and involvement. Thus, it was not surprising to find—although to my knowledge, the first time demonstrated—that recalled conflicts are embedded within important social relationships between children. Liking relations predominated at both the dyadic level (unilateral and mutual ones) and the group level (popular and controversial children as adversaries). These findings underscore and expand observational studies that document how conflicts influence the formation of friendship (e.g., Gottman, 1983) and how friendship influences the way conflicts are conducted (Hartup et al., 1988).

The "remembrance of conflicts past" offers a promising research area for understanding children's representations of their social interactions because they provide the insiders' views. Particularly revealing is the more enduring meaning children give to such events, that is, the lessons learned. Such lessons touch on many areas of long-standing concern to developmentalists—for example, self-understanding and regulation, peer and friendship relations, aggression, empathy, social competence, compliance, assertiveness, and experienced emotions. Sometimes the lessons children draw may be perplexing or may not be ones that adults would hope for, but that is all the more reason to give children their own voice. Their perspective, along with the perspectives of parents, teachers, and researchers, can begin to reveal more fully children's social and social-cognitive life and development.

ACKNOWLEDGMENTS

The research reported here was supported by a grant from the Spencer Foundation. Appreciation is extended to Christine Butler, Barbara J. Maier, and Cynthia A. Shantz for their sensitivity and care in interviewing, transcribing, and assisting in coding the data. My thanks are given to Dr. James Cambridge, Ms. Lynne Hendricks, and the children at Lobbestael Elementary School, Mt. Clemens, Michigan, for their enthusiastic participation in this project. I would like to express, too, special gratitude to Irv Sigel for his encouragement of this research, and his support throughout my academic career.

REFERENCES

Barsalou, L. W. (1988). The content and organization of autobiographical memories. In U. Neisser & E. Winograd (Eds.), *Remembering reconsidered: Ecological and traditional approaches to the study of memory* (pp. 193–243). Cambridge, England: Cambridge University Press.

Dawe, H. C. (1934). An analysis of two hundred quarrels of preschool children. *Child Development, 5,* 139–157.

Dodge, K. A. (1983). Behavioral antecedents of peers social status. *Child Development, 53,* 1386–1399.

Dodge, K. A. (1985). A social information processing model of social competence in children. In M. Perlmutter (Ed.). *Minnesota symposium on child psychology* (Vol. 18, pp. 77–125). Hillsdale, NJ: Lawrence Erlbaum Associates.

Freeman, M., Csikszentmihalyi, M., & Larson, R. (1986). Adolescence and its recollection: Toward an interpretive model of development. *Merrill–Palmer Quarterly, 32*, 187–203.

Furman, W., & Buhrmester, D. (1985). Children's perceptions of the personal relationships in their social networks. *Developmental Psychology, 21*, 1016–1022.

Gottman, J. M. (1983). How children become friends. *Monographs of the Society of Child Development, 48*(3, Serial No. 201).

Hartup, W. W., Laursen, B., Stewart, M. I., & Eastenson, A. (1988). Conflict and the friendship relations of young children. *Child Development, 59*, 1590–1600.

Jose, P. E., & Hennelly, S. (1987, April). *Measures of social cognitive development: Interpersonal conflict resolution and social rule understanding.* Paper presented at the meeting of the Society for Research in Child Development, Baltimore, MD.

Livesley, W. J., & Bromley, D. B. (1973). *Person perception in childhood and adolescence.* London: Wiley.

Neisser, U., & Winograd, E. (Eds.). (1988). *Remembering reconsidered: Ecological and traditional approaches to the study of memory.* Cambridge, England: Cambridge University Press.

Peterson, C., & McCabe, A. (1983). *Developmental psycholinguistics: Three ways of looking at a child's narrative.* New York: Plenum.

Piaget, J. (1928). *Judgment and reasoning in the child.* London: Routledge & Kegan Paul.

Preece, A. (1987). The range of narrative forms conversationally produced by young children. *Journal of Child Language, 14*, 353–373.

Rizzo, T. A. (1988). *Friendship development among children in school.* Norwood, NJ: Ablex.

Schneider, D. J., Hastorf, A. H., & Ellsworth, P. C. (1979). *Person perception* (2nd ed.). Reading, MA: Addison-Wesley.

Selman, R. (1980). *The growth of interpersonal understanding: Developmental and clinical analyses.* New York: Academic Press.

Shaklee, H. (1976). Development in inferences of ability and task difficulty. *Child Development, 47*, 1051–1057.

Shantz, C. U. (1987). Conflicts between children. *Child Development, 58*, 283–305.

Shantz, C. U., & Hobart, C. (1989). Social conflict and development: Peers and siblings. In T. J. Berndt & G. W. Ladd (Eds.), *Peer relationships in child development* (pp. 71–94). New York: Wiley.

Shantz, C. U., & Shantz, D. W. (1985). Conflict between children: Social-cognitive and sociometric correlates. In M. W. Berkowitz (Ed.), *Peer conflict and psychological growth: New directions for child development* (pp. 3–21). San Francisco: Jossey-Bass.

Sigel, I. E., & Cocking, R. R. (1977). Cognition and communication: A dialectic paradigm for development. In M. Lewis & L. A. Rosenblum (Eds.), *The origins of behavior* (Vol. 5, pp. 207–226). New York: Wiley.

Todd, C. M., & Perlmutter, M. (1980). Reality recalled by preschool children. In M. Perlmutter (Ed.), *Children's memory: New directions for child development* (pp. 69–85). San Francisco: Jossey-Bass.

APPENDIX: INTERVIEW, CODING DEFINITIONS, AND RELIABILITIES

Note: The interviewer's questions and comments are in capitals; the codes and explanatory comments are in lower case; topics and reliabilities are in brackets.

After a general introduction, I WANT YOU TO THINK BACK, TO REMEMBER A TIME WHEN YOU HAD AN ARGUMENT WITH SOMEONE IN YOUR CLASS. TELL ME ALL ABOUT IT. If necessary, WE'LL JUST TAKE OUR TIME . . . THINK BACK TO SOME FIGHT OR DISAGREEMENT YOU HAD WITH SOMEONE IN YOUR CLASS. TELL ME IN YOUR OWN WORDS ABOUT IT . . . WHAT HAPPENED. If needed, TELL ME MORE ABOUT IT. WHAT ELSE HAPPENED? More specific prompts given, as needed. THAT WAS VERY GOOD. I HAVE A FEW QUESTIONS TO BE SURE I UNDERSTAND IT ALL. The following questions were asked next if the information was not provided in the spontaneous description.

[Start; 82%] WHO STARTED THIS ARGUMENT/FIGHT, DO YOU THINK?
  Self, other, both, third party, unsure/don't know
[Issue; 80%] WHAT WAS THIS DISAGREEMENT/FIGHT ABOUT, EXACTLY?
  Object/space: possession or use of object or space person lays claim to
  Physical harm: intended or unintended harm such as hitting or kicking (if the initial focus in dispute; if it occurred later, coded as strategy)
  Psychological harm: ego insults, derogation, hurtful teasing
  Rule violation-general social rules: violation of classroom, school, or general cultural rules other than friendship rules (e.g., breaking into line, violating game rules)
  Rule violation-friendship: violations of friendship rules (e.g., not to tell secrets, to play with X when X wants to play, etc.)
  Beliefs, opinions, facts: arguments about such matters as whether Nintendo is easy or hard, what the teacher did or didn't say, etc.
[Strategies; 78%] WHAT DID YOU DO OR SAY DURING THIS ARGUMENT? WHAT DID X DO OR SAY DURING IT?
  Level 1: Flee or abruptly leave interaction
    Physical aggression: intended harmful act to person (hit, slap, etc.) (coded as a strategy if it was not the original issue of dispute)
    Verbal aggression: insulting, derogating, mocking
    Third-party intervention: adult or other peer is brought or enter into the dispute spontaneously
  Level 2: Insistence: original wish/demand is repeated with no elaboration
    Apologize/promise: saying "sorry," promise not to do X again

Ignore: purposeful lack of response to perceived behavior of other
Act to remedy: offer to do something to undo or compensate
Level 3: Reasons: explanations or justifications for position/wish
  Compromise: statement by either child suggesting a way to settle dispute
  in which each would partially get what each wanted (e.g., sharing
  toy).

[Emotions; self, 92%; other, 83%] WHEN YOU WERE FIGHTING/
ARGUING WITH X, HOW DID YOU FEEL? After answer, AND HOW DID X
FEEL WHEN YOU TWO WERE ARGUING? For self and other: angry/mad;
sad; bad (only); bothered or upset; happy, feeling good, having fun; no particular
feelings/neutral; blends; unsure.

[Who ended; 83%] WHO ENDED THIS DISAGREEMENT/ARGUMENT,
DO YOU THINK?
Dyad: Self, other, both; External-to-dyad: third party, physical event (bus leaves,
bell rings to leave playground, etc.)

[How ended; 82%] HOW DID THIS ARGUMENT/FIGHT END? (And, if
needed, DID YOU GET WHAT YOU WANTED; DID X GET WHAT HE/SHE
WANTED?)

Win/loss: one person yielded or complied with other's original position

Stalemate: no clear resolution, no clear win/loss, argument abandoned

Compromise: each person got, partially, what they wanted

Collaboration: settlement that maximizes each person's gain; often a "we"
  focus rather than "you versus me"

Unsure/don't know

AFTER IT ALL ENDED, WHAT DID YOU DO? WHAT DID X DO? Not
coded.

[Long-term effects; 91%] HAVE YOU TALKED WITH OR PLAYED WITH
X SINCE THE ARGUMENT? Yes, no, unsure/not asked; if yes, asked to
elaborate.

[Talk about conflict; 80%] DID YOU EVER TALK TO X ABOUT THIS
DISAGREEMENT? Yes, no, can't remember/unsure/don't know/not asked.

IF (this situation as described) HAPPENS AGAIN (or IF X DOES Y
AGAIN), WHAT WOULD YOU DO? Not coded for this report.

[Lessons learned; 90%] WHAT DID YOU LEARN FROM (ALL OF) THIS?
If no answer, WHAT DID YOU LEARN FROM HAVING THIS ARGUMENT?

A. Inhibition focused: coded (1) on behavior, usually "not to do X again"; (2)
   on friendship relation; (3) on conflict

B. Change focused: coded (1) on behavior, usually "to do Y next time," that
   is, alternate strategy; (2) on friendship relation; (3) on conflict

C. No lesson learned: nothing learned or don't know

[Organization of spontaneous description; 100%] See text for definitions.

12

The Social Origins of Individual Mental Functioning: Alternatives and Perspectives

James V. Wertsch
Frances L. Hiatt School of Psychology, Clark University

Jennifer A. Bivens
University of Northern Iowa

Over the past decade there has been a major resurgence of interest in developmental psychology and related disciplines in the issue of how social activity gives rise to individual mental functioning. This interest grew out of a dissatisfaction with theoretical approaches grounded in individualistic assumptions—assumptions that resulted in a tendency to either ignore or trivialize the contribution of social factors to the development of mind. The growing recognition that essential aspects of mental functioning in the individual derive from social activity has led to a reevaluation of the ideas of theorists such as Piaget (1928, 1950, 1960, 1985) and Vygotsky (1978, 1987), and it has led to the emergence of constructs such as distancing (Sigel, 1970, 1982), which posit that participation in certain forms of social interaction with adults allows children to develop crucial representational abilities.

Various efforts to address this issue have been united in their claim that social processes play an essential role in the formation of individual mental functioning. However, they differ over what they count as social processes, how they analyze social processes, and how they view these processes as giving rise to cognition or other forms of psychological functioning in the individual. Because these sources of difference typically remain unexplicated, it is often difficult to detect how approaches differ with regard to the role of social factors in the formation of individual mental functioning.

In an attempt to address this problem we outline three perspectives on the relationship between social interaction and individual mental functioning. These perspectives are distinguished from one another on the basis of: (a) assumptions about the nature of social interaction, and (b) assumptions about how social interaction influences individual mental functioning. Some of the differences

203

among these perspectives amount to complementarities rather than contradictions (e.g., a focus on adult–child vs. child–child interaction). In such cases the perspectives do not involve conflicting accounts of the same basic phenomena, but instead focus on different kinds of social interaction and anticipated psychological correlates. In other cases the perspectives are complementary in that they focus on different aspects of the same set of social or individual processes. In these cases the lesson might be that the perspectives should be combined into a more comprehensive account. And in yet other cases there may be genuine contradictions in interpretations of the same basic phenomena.

PIAGETIAN ANALYSES OF THE ROLE OF SOCIAL PROCESSES IN THE FORMATION OF INDIVIDUAL MENTAL FUNCTIONING

Over a half century ago, Piaget outlined an account of intellectual development that incorporated social interaction as an essential component. A fundamental assumption underlying his approach is that social interaction fosters intellectual growth by causing some sort of conflict or "discrepancy" (Sigel & Cocking, 1977; Sigel & Kelley, 1988) in an individual's cognitive system.

According to Piagetian theory (1950), individual cognitive development arises out of experiences that induce cognitive conflict or disequilibrium. In fact, Piaget (1985) argued that one of the sources of progress in development of knowledge is found in states of disequilibria because this "forces the subject to go beyond his current state and strike out in new directions" (p. 10). One way in which this cognitive conflict can occur is when an individual's established schemes come into contact with information from the outside world that does not fit into these schemas. However, it is not simply individuals' experience with objects that results in such conflict. Indeed, individuals are quite capable of distorting information from experience with objects such that it fits with preexisting schemes. It is when the conflict stems from social exchanges that it appears most beneficial to cognitive development, at least during middle childhood.

Piaget (1928) attributed the difficulty that children have in observing their own thought processes to egocentrism. He observed that it is often only when children engage in the process of proving and justifying to others the thoughts they have asserted that they become conscious of these thoughts and are able to free themselves from egocentrism. Thus, he claimed that it is through social interaction, especially with other children, that children find themselves forced to reexamine their own concepts in contrast with those of others. Gradually, this process of social interaction allows the child to overcome the egocentric tendencies that characterize early thought.

For this reason Piaget posited that open-ended social exchange among peers, rather than social interaction with adults, is an important factor in the growth of thought and the use of language. He focused on exchanges among peers because such exchanges are based on mutual, rather than unilateral, relations. That is not to say that Piaget viewed social exchanges between child and adult as serving no useful function. Indeed, he argued that both adults and peers play an important role in the child's development. However, they do so in different ways.

> Through imitation and language, as also through the whole content of adult thought which exercises pressure on the child's mind as soon as verbal intercourse has become possible, the child begins, in a sense, to be socialized by the end of its first year. But the very nature of the relations which the child sustains with the adults around him prevents this socialization for the moment from reaching that state of equilibrium which is propitious to the development of reason. We mean, of course, the state of cooperation, in which the individuals, regarding each other as equals, can exercise a mutual control and thus attain objectivity. In other words, the very nature of the relation between child and adult places the child apart, so that his thought is isolated, and while he believes himself to be sharing the point of view of the world at large he is really still shut up in his own point of view. (Piaget, 1960, p. 26)

Thus, Piaget argued that because of the distance between child and adult, genuine cognitive growth occurs when children are able to engage in social interaction with other children of equal status. He contended that unilateral relations with adults foster heteronomous moral concepts, while the mutual relations provided by peers foster autonomous ones (Damon & Phelps, 1987). Indeed, recent research by Damon and Phelps suggests that adult–child interaction supports particular types of mental sets from which we can expect such cognitive products as planning, goal-directedness, means–ends reasoning, and a centering on the existing order of things, whereas peer relations foster "autonomous thinking."

For our purposes, there are several major points to be made about Piagetian accounts of the role of social interaction in the formation of individual mental functioning. First, a fundamental strength of this approach is that it highlights the active role that children take in social processes. The individuals involved are not viewed as passive observers or passive recipients of information from others. Instead, the process is understood in terms of how one perspective comes into active contact with another. It is precisely through such contact that inherent conflicts or discrepancies become apparent.

We would like to argue, however, that even though social interaction is viewed as being essential to this process, the analysis of this interaction is ultimately grounded in analytic units tied to the individual. Specifically, social interaction is considered from the perspective of how effective it is in creating conflict in individuals' cognitive systems. This tendency reflects an underlying assumption that the individual is to be given analytic priority. The basic move in constructing an analytic framework is to begin with the individual and then to consider the social; in order to understand the latter, the former must be invoked, but not vice versa.

Third, the kind of social interaction envisioned in this approach is presumed to exist in roughly the same form across cultural, historical, and institutional contexts. This assumption is grounded in the individualistic assumption just mentioned.

VYGOTSKIAN ANALYSES OF THE ROLE OF SOCIAL PROCESSES IN THE FORMATION OF INDIVIDUAL MENTAL FUNCTIONING

Vygotsky's approach to the relationship between social and individual processes contrasts with Piaget's in several essential ways. Primary among these is the analytic priority Vygotsky gave to social phenomena. In Vygotsky's view, "the social dimension of consciousness is primary in time and in fact. The individual dimension of consciousness is derivative and secondary" (1979, p. 30). This assumption on his part grew out of his attempts to formulate a psychological theory that would be consistent with Marxist theory, but it also was grounded in the ideas of other social scientists of his day such as Janet (1926–1927, 1928) and Baldwin (1906).

Vygotsky's assumption that the understanding of individual mental functioning begins with an account of social life underlay all of his work, and it continues to be a thread in the theoretical perspectives that are present in contemporary studies in Soviet psychology. For example, several decades after Vygotsky's death, Luria (1981) wrote:

> In order to explain the highly complex forms of human consciousness one must go beyond the human organism. One must seek the origins of conscious activity and "categorical" behavior not in the recesses of the human brain or in the depths of the spirit, but in the external conditions of life. Above all, this means that one must seek these origins in the external processes of social life, in the social and historical forms of human existence. (p. 25)

The kind of sociality to which Luria was alluding here concerns the historically evolved institutional structure characteristic of a society. Such phenomena are often viewed as falling under the heading of "macrosociological" processes in modern parlance, processes to which we return later. The primary focus of Vygotsky and his colleagues, however, was on dyadic and small group forms of sociality, that is, forms that fall under the heading of what we term social interactional processes. This focus is reflected at many points in his writings, for example, in his account of the transition from social to egocentric to inner speech. Perhaps his most succinct, concrete formulation of this point as it applies to ontogenesis can be found in his "general genetic law of cultural development":

> Any function in the child's cultural development appears twice, or on two planes. First it appears on the social plane, and then on the psychological plane. First it appears between people as an interpsychological [intermental[1]] category, and then within the child as an intrapsychological [intramental] category. This is equally true with regard to voluntary attention, logical memory, the formation of concepts, and the development of volition. . . [I]t goes without saying that internalization transforms the process itself and changes its structure and functions. Social relations or relations among people genetically underlie all higher functions and their relationships. (Vygotsky, 1981, p. 163)

In the West many of the most important applications of the general genetic law of cultural development have emerged in connection with the "zone of proximal development." This zone is defined as the distance between a child's "actual developmental level as determined by independent problem solving" and the higher level of "potential development as determined through problem solving under adult guidance or in collaboration with more capable peers" (Vygotsky, 1978, p. 86).

Vygotsky outlined the zone of proximal development in order to deal with two related issues. First, he saw it as a palliative to a view of psychological testing that focuses exclusively on the intramental plane (Brown & Ferrara, 1985; Wertsch, 1985), and second, he saw it as a key to understanding the effects of instruction. Our concern is primarily with the latter issue. In attempts to apply his ideas in this sphere, subtle yet major differences have emerged in interpreting the nature and function of intermental processes and how they give rise to intramental processes. In what follows we outline two of these interpretations: a modeling view and a text mediational view.

As we outline these views it is essential to keep in mind that they represent interpretations of Vygotsky's ideas by others. Just as Piaget has been interpreted by various scholars in various ways, the same fate awaits Vygotsky. This need not be a bad thing. Indeed, it indicates the generative power of a major thinker. In this connection it is essential to remember that Vygotsky himself (Wertsch, 1991) expressed the desire to have his writings serve as a starting point for further theoretical development rather than as a finished product. However, the nature and implications of differing interpretations must be clarified if we are to explicate a theoretical framework such as Vygotsky's in a coherent manner.

---

[1]Following the practice of Minick in the translation of Vygotsky (1987), we use the terms "intermental" and "intramental" rather than "interpsychological" and "intrapsychological," respectively. The latter terms have been used in earlier translations, but are less consistent with other aspects of the English translations of Vygotsky's terminology.

A MODELING INTERPRETATION OF VYGOTSKY

In a modeling interpretation of Vygotsky's comments on the social origins of individual mental processes, intermental functioning is view primarily in terms of how it can provide a model for tutees' individual mental processes. According to this view the regulative role played by tutors is gradually taken over and "internalized" (Wertsch & Stone, 1985) by tutees on the intramental plane.

This transition has sometimes been described as the transition from "other-regulation" to "self-regulation" (Wertsch, 1979; Wertsch, McNamee, McLane, & Budwig, 1980). These terms have been found to be useful in analyzing the social origins of individual mental functioning (e.g., Wertsch & Sammarco, 1985; Wertsch, Minick, & Arns, 1984). However, a few points of caution should be raised in connection with their use. First, although Vygotsky used terms quite similar in meaning to "self-regulation," he never employed the term "other-regulation." Second, the use of this pair of terms is often grounded in certain assumptions, some of which may not be consistent with Vygotsky's intent. Specifically, their use implies a kind of direct parallelism between intermental and intramental functioning, something that Vygotsky (1981; Wertsch, 1985) actually cautioned against in his comments on internalization. Finally, this parallelism implies a kind of modeling: The tutor models the appropriate forms of regulation to the tutee and the latter takes them over.

Although it is far from clear that Vygotsky had some notion of modeling in mind when he spoke of the social origins of individual mental functioning, modeling interpretations of his ideas have been quite productive in generating contemporary research. In this research the process whereby the transfer of the locus of control or regulation takes place for the most part is still quite under-specified. In most cases, the claim is that by participating in intermental functioning, tutees come to organize their mental processes around the questions and directives used by the tutor. In some cases claims have been made about the role of egocentric speech in this process. For example, Wertsch (1979) argued that in the transition from other-regulation to self-regulation, children's egocentric speech took on the form of answers to internalized questions—questions that had previously been posed in overt social speech directives of adults. In other cases the precise forms of semiotic mediation have not been elaborated, but empirical evidence has supported the claim that psychological processes emerge on the individual plane through mastering patterns involved in the intermental process of guided participation (e.g., Rogoff, 1990).

In most of these studies the implicit claim is that the transition from intermental to intramental functioning takes place spontaneously, that is, without the need for outside motivation or explicit instruction. Although there are certainly exceptions (e.g., Wertsch and Sammarco, 1985), the children who have been studied have generally been found to enter into intermental functioning and to master those aspects required for appropriate functioning on the intramental plane.

208

Investigators such as Rogoff (1990), Sigel (1982), and Wertsch (1985) have tried to identify some of the complex processes involved in this transition. For example, Rogoff has examined some of the concrete social interaction patterns of "guided participation" involving adults and children in planning and other problem solving settings; Sigel has outlined a range of adult–child interaction patterns from the perspective of how "distancing" is created and maintained; and Wertsch has attempted to describe the various forms of adult–child interaction and their potential for fostering self-regulation on the part of children. In the end, however, we still know very little about exactly how or why the transition occurs.

Some of our implicit assumptions about the dynamics involved in a modeling interpretation of the transition from intermental to intramental functioning come to light when one considers special groups of tutees who apparently need additional assistance in making the transition from the intermental to the intramental plane. Precisely these kinds of cases have recently been studied by Palincsar and Brown (1984, 1988) in their account of reciprocal teaching. In the practice of reciprocal teaching, students are explicitly instructed in how to lead a dialogue (i.e., pose questions usually posed by teachers) in a reading task.

Palincsar and Brown have focused specifically on devising a set of training and assessment procedures for students at various grade levels who had been identified as having major problems in developing reading skills. The core of these procedures revolves around the practice in which students and teachers take turns leading dialogues about texts, generating summaries and predictions, and clarifying misleading or complex sections of the text.

Reciprocal teaching has produced some quite striking results. Palincsar and Brown report that at the end of a relatively small number of sessions, poor readers show remarkable improvement, noting that "by the end of ten sessions [they] were providing paraphrases and questions of some sophistication . . . by the end of the sessions, unclear questions had dropped out and were replaced with questions focusing on the main idea of each text segment. A similar improvement was found for summary statements" (1984, p. 125). From the perspective of the general genetic law of cultural development the most important result was that student improvement was not limited to performance in the reciprocal teaching sessions. Improvement extended to intramental functioning as well.

Each day, before (baseline), during, and after (maintenance) training, the students took an unassisted assessment, where they read a novel passage and answered ten comprehension questions on it from memory. From their baseline performance of 15% correct, they improved during training to accuracy levels of 85%, levels they maintained when the intervention was terminated. Even after a 6-month delay, the students averaged 60% correct without help, and it took only 1 day of renewed reciprocal teaching to return them to the 85% level achieved during training. . . . Remember that these scores [on unassisted assessment measures] were obtained on privately read assessment passages, that is, different texts that the students read independently after their interaction with the instructor. What was learned during the instructional sequence was used independently [i.e., on the intramental plane] by the learners. (Palincsar & Brown, 1984, p. 125)

As in the case of authors who interpret the general genetic law of cultural development in terms of a transition from other-regulation to self-regulation, the formulation of reciprocal teaching rests on, or at least is quite consistent with, a modeling interpretation of Vygotsky's claims. In both cases the assumption is that functioning evolves on the intramental plane through a process of taking over a set of strategically organized directives originally used by a tutor.

At first glance this may appear to amount to a reduction of social to individual processes, something that clearly goes against Vygotsky's claims about the analytic and genetic priority of social practices. However, it is important to keep in mind that the modeling involved is of a very specific sort; it specifically involves *participation in dialogic interaction*. Most studies on this topic have assumed that this active participation in dialogue is a prerequisite for the transition to the intramental plane to occur. They do *not* assume that a viable alternative would be to model or train tutees in isolation from such dialogue. Thus, in reciprocal teaching it appears that a crucial ingredient is the actual experience of engaging in dialogue with others.

Such an approach contrasts with others such as Meichenbaum's (1977), which focus on training and modeling directives for tutees. Such training efforts assume that the directives can be learned in relative isolation from the kind of dialogic social interaction envisioned by Palincsar and Brown. The basic formulation is one in which the training is viewed as focusing directly on intramental functioning without the need to ground it in an intermental plane of action. Thus the focus of Meichenbaum's self-instruction training has been to provide subjects with a model who demonstrates the self-instruction verbalizations while performing a task. The subjects are then asked to imitate the behavior of the model while performing the same task.

The modeling interpretation of Vygotsky represents a second interpretation of how social interaction is related to individual mental functioning. As in the case of the Piagetian account, we would argue that the point is not to assess it simply in terms of whether it is correct or incorrect. Instead, it should be understood as a perspective that can provide important insights into how at least certain forms of intermental functioning can give rise to individual psychological processes. Of particular importance in this respect is the fact that it seems to provide insights into interaction where there is a clearly defined expert and a clearly defined novice. Its pragmatic value in generating research findings and practical implications is beyond dispute in our view, as studies by investigators such as Palincsar and Brown (1984) and Rogoff (1990) have demonstrated. One of its weaknesses is that it tends to view the tutee as inherently passive. Rogoff's apt term "guided *participation*" is motivated by a desire to emphasize the tutee's active engagement in intermental functioning, but the tendency to view the processes involved in terms of modeling means that the tutee often continues to be viewed as a passive recipient.

A TEXT MEDIATIONAL VIEW OF VYGOTSKY

A second interpretation of Vygotsky's ideas is what we shall term the text mediational view. It rests heavily on the assumptions that: (a) intermental and intramental functioning is fundamentally shaped by mediational means such as forms of language (Wertsch, 1985, 1991), and (b) all participants in intermental functioning are actively engaged in shaping this functioning.

The claims we outline in connection with the text mediational view of Vygotsky are grounded heavily in the writings of the Soviet semiotician Lotman (1988a, 1988b). Lotman argues that two functions are characteristic of all "texts."[2] The functional dualism he envisions involves what we shall term a univocal function on the one hand and a dialogic function on the other. The univocal function focuses on how it is possible "to convey meanings adequately" (1988b, p. 34), and the dialogic function is concerned with how it is possible "to generate new meanings" (1988b, p. 34).

> The first function is fulfilled best when the codes of the speaker and the listener most completely coincide and, consequently, when the text has the maximum degree of univocality. The ideal boundary mechanism for such an operation would be an artificial language. . . . Since it is this aspect of a text that is most easily modeled with the means at our disposal, this aspect of text has been the most noticed. It has become an object of study, and at times has been identified with a text as such, obfuscating the other aspects. (Lotman, 1988b, pp. 34–35)

The kind of single-minded focus on this function noted by Lotman is similar to what Reddy (1979) was criticizing in his account of the conduit metaphor of communication. In Reddy's view this powerful but misleading metaphor underlies many contemporary theories of communication with their emphasis on encoding, transmission, decoding, and so forth.

In contrast to this first, transmission-like function of a text—a function that "requires maximal semiotic ordering and structural uniformity of the media used in the process of reception and transmission" (Lotman, 1988b, p. 41)—the

---

[2]As used by Soviet scholars such as Lotman, a text is any semiotic corpus that has significance. It may be verbal (e.g., a single utterance, a book-length treatise) or nonverbal (e.g., a painting, a costume). Our focus will be on verbal texts, especially ones that are spoken in the flow of intermental functioning.

second function of text is grounded in the kind of multivoicedness, or dialogic-
ality that concerned one of Lotman's intellectual mentors, M. M. Bakhtin (1981,
1984; Wertsch, 1991). According to Lotman:

> The second function of text is to generate new meanings. In this respect a text
> ceases to be a passive link in conveying some constant information between input
> (sender) and output (receiver). Whereas in the first case a difference between the
> message at the input and that at the output of an information circuit can occur only
> as a result of a defect in the communications channel, and is to be attributed to the
> technical imperfections of this system, in the second case such a difference is the
> very essence of a text's function as a "thinking device." What from the first
> standpoint is a defect, from the second is a norm, and vice versa. (Lotman, 1988b,
> pp. 36–37)

In Lotman's view virtually any text is characterized by both the univocal and
the dialogic function. However, the degree to which one or the other dominates
may vary widely. Among other things, then, his account of functional dualism
implies that when a text is serving a dialogic function, it cannot be adequately
understood in terms of the transmission model of communication. This is so
because a transmission model presupposes that a single, univocal message is
transmitted from sender to receiver, whereas Lotman and Bakhtin view the
process as involving multiple voices from the outset. As Wertsch (1991) has
noted, Bakhtin argued that the very process of understanding, or comprehension
is one in which the active listener "strives to match the speaker's word with a
counter word" (Volosinov, 1973, p. 102).

The insights of Lotman and Bakhtin suggest that the dominant tendency to
focus on the univocal function of text makes it very difficult to see some of the
essential mechanisms whereby semiotically mediated social interaction transpires. In their view it is essential to appreciate the dynamics associated with the
dialogic function as well. For our purposes, a further implication of the exclusive
focus on the univocal function will be that the failure to take into account the
dialogic function of text makes it difficult to understand the processes whereby
the transition from intermental to intramental functioning occurs.

Taking the dialogic function of text into account means that spoken utterances, written utterances, and other forms of text are viewed in terms of their
capacity to be thinking devices or objects to which one can respond. This function is distinct from, and complements, the function of texts to serve as con-
tainers of information transmitted from sender to receiver. In Lotman's words:

> . . . in its second function a text is not a passive receptacle, or bearer of some
> content placed in it from without, but a generator. The essence of the process of
> generation, however, is not only an evolution but also, to a considerable extent, an
> interaction between structures. Their interaction in the closed world of text be-
> comes an active cultural factor as a working semiotic system. A text of this type is
> always richer than any particular language and cannot be put together automatically

from it. A text is a semiotic space in which languages interact, interfere, and organize themselves hierarchically. (Lotman, 1988b, p. 37)

The general point of Lotman's account of functional dualism is *not* that communication is best understood in terms of either a univocal or dialogic model in isolation. Instead, virtually every text is viewed as involving an irreducible tension between these two poles. At the same time, he views certain kinds of texts as being more heavily weighted on one or the other side of this tension. Certain texts are primarily univocal and transmissionlike in their function, with a reduced emphasis on the dialogical function, and others have the opposite set of characteristics.

Lotman's account of the functional dualism of text has major implications for a Vygotskian account of the transition from intermental to intramental functioning. Specifically, it can help distinguish between interpretations that presuppose a predominantly univocal or a predominantly dialogic function of text. It addresses whether the communication in intermental functioning is viewed in terms of the transmission of information, or whether it is viewed in terms of texts that can serve as thinking devices (i.e., as texts with which one is to come into dialogic contact by questioning, rejecting, appropriating, and so forth). Thus, the two orientations toward communication have profound implications for what one is likely to see going on in social interaction and having an impact on intramental functioning.

The kind of contrast we envision here can be seen in different modes of classroom discourse. Investigators such as Mehan (1979) have reported that a great deal of classroom discourse occurs in the form of interaction consisting of: (a) teacher Initiation, (b) pupil Reply, and (c) teacher Evaluation. For example, this I–R–E sequence often revolves around "instructional questions" (i.e., questions to which the teacher knows the answer) as in:

Teacher: What is the capital of the U.S., Jack?
Pupil: Washington, D.C.
Teacher: Good.

In such exchanges, the text comprised by each utterance functions primarily as a means to transmit information or a directive; it is not intended to serve as a thinking device capable of generating new meanings. Thus each utterance is treated as a kind of unalterable whole that is to be "received," "decoded," and responded to by transmitting some message in return.

In contrast to this heavy emphasis on producing univocal texts, some recent attempts at reshaping classroom discourse have been motivated by a desire to produce what Lotman would term dialogic texts. A fundamental indication of this tendency is that the utterances produced by the discourse participants are treated as starting points for conversation, as being capable of generating new meanings, as thinking devices. For example, the emphasis Tharp and Gallimore (1988) place on beginning reading discussions by building on pupils' statements about experience outside the classroom reflects this tendency. Instead of viewing such statements as the transmission of correct or incorrect information (or ruling them out as irrelevant), the goal is to view them as capable of generating new meanings that can serve as a bridge between everyday experience and formal instruction.

Another example of a program with an emphasis on taking utterances as thinking devices can be found in the Hypothesis–Experiment–Instruction method of science instruction developed by Itakura (1986). In this case, debate among pupils and teams of pupils is fostered around a particular scientific problem. Specifically, it is fostered by asking pupils to make predictions about the anticipated outcome of an experiment and then to question those who make other predictions and defend their own predictions before the experiment is carried out. Investigators such as Hatano and Inagaki (1991) and Wertsch and Toma (1990) have noted the extremely active debate that transpires in this setting. Furthermore, Hatano and Inagaki have analyzed the interaction in terms of the "partisanship" that may emerge, and Wertsch and Toma (1990) have noted pupils' tendency to invoke others' stated ideas (i.e., to use others' utterances as thinking devices) in formulating their own utterances.

In many respects the text mediation interpretation of Vygotsky's ideas about the transition from intermental to intramental functioning might be viewed as quite similar to what Piaget had in mind when talking about the conflict or discrepancy among perspectives generated by social interaction. And indeed there are important affinities. The kind of conflict or discrepancy envisaged by Piaget has much in common with Lotman's discussions of the "interaction between structures" or the "semiotic space in which languages interact, interfere, and organize themselves hierarchically" (Lotman, 1988b, p. 37). For Piaget, this interaction between structures is viewed as occurring primarily on what we are calling the intramental plane, whereas for authors such as Tharp and Gallimore, Hatano and Inagaki, and Wertsch and Toma, the focus is on intermental functioning. However, these latter authors would all agree that such intermental functioning is tied to intramental functioning. Differences still may remain with regard to the precise nature of the relation between these two planes of functioning, but this does not contradict the affinity between Lotman and Piaget at a more general level.

Where major differences do appear, however, is in the nature of the texts that mediate social and individual performance. In the Vygotskian perspective we have been discussing, the notion of mediation is central. Indeed, Vygotsky's notion of mediation provides the key to understanding how his approach differs from many others (Wertsch, 1985, 1991). The centrality of this notion is reflected in the fact that for Vygotsky human agency is not a property of individuals or of groups of individuals alone. Instead, it always involves mediational means as well, a point expressed in the equation of agency with "individual(s)-operating-with-mediational-means," or "mediated agency" for short.

Furthermore, the forms of mediation (e.g., discourse forms, pictures and graphs) used by humans to carry out conversation, group and individual problem solving, and so forth are fundamentally shaped by the sociocultural setting in which activities are carried out. Building on Bakhtin's (1984) notion of "ventriloquism," Wertsch (1991) has argued that this does not mean that individuals are reduced to being conduits for mediational means. However, it does mean that they are not completely free to appropriate any mediational means imaginable. Thus the mediational means that shape intermental and intramental functioning are usually not invented de novo by the individuals using them. Instead, they are provided largely by the cultural, historical, and institutional settings in which these individuals exist. As a result we are empowered as well as constrained in specific ways by the mediational means of a sociocultural setting.

This point is reflected in the research of investigators such as Hatano and Inagaki (1991). The nature of social interaction and thinking in the Hypothesis–Experiment–Instruction method is fundamentally shaped by the mediational means employed in the science classroom, and what is employed is determined in large measure by what is allowed and encouraged in that setting. Investigators such as Gee (1988), Michaels (1981), and Wertsch and Minick (1990) have argued in general that the forms of discourse employed in classrooms are subject to all kinds of constraints that have little to do with the cognitive tasks at hand or may even inhibit functioning on these tasks. For example, Gee and Michaels have argued that middle-class American ideology about proper forms of language and argumentation is often a criterial factor in determining whether an utterance is acceptable or not, and Wertsch and Minick have argued that one of the major criteria that defines appropriate classroom discourse is a unique set of boundaries that define topics. Such studies point to ways in which classroom discourse is constrained in fundamental ways and hence is quite distinct from that found in other sociocultural settings.

Thus, the point here is that the text mediational view of Vygotsky's approach differs from the Piagetian approach we outlined earlier in what it sees as the nature of the texts employed. The tradition of Vygotsky, Bakhtin, and Lotman emphasizes the sociocultural origins and situatedness of the texts used as mediational means, and this tradition views these mediational means as fundamental components of the agency involved in human activity. In contrast, the general notion of mediation is at least not emphasized in Piagetian approaches, and it certainly is not grounded in the notion of sociocultural situatedness.

CONCLUSION

Where does this leave us? We believe that the most important conclusion is that the three views we have outlined of the social origins of individual mental functioning differ in fundamental ways in what they view as social interaction, what they view as individual functioning, and how they view the relationship between these two forms of functioning.

In some cases, these differences derive from subtle yet essential discrepancies in assumptions about the analytic priority given to individual or social processes. The notion of priority is crucial here because the issue is not simply one of whether or not social processes are included in the account; it is an issue of the role they play in an analytic strategy. Thus the question is whether an account of individual processes is viewed as providing the starting point from which social processes can be understood or vice versa. As outlined earlier, we view most Piagetian strategies as following the first path, and we view Vygotsky as following the second.

As we have noted, however, this does not mean that there is a single interpretation of Vygotsky's claims about the social origins of individual mental processes. Just as Piaget's writings have spawned a variety of interpretations, there are at least two interpretations that can be given to Vygotsky's ideas about the social origins of individual mental functioning. We have labeled these the modeling interpretation and the text mediational interpretation. In our view, both of these interpretations accord priority to intermental processes, but they differ in the attention they give to mediational means and to sociocultural situatedness.

As we noted at the beginning of our chapter, many of the differences we have outlined arise because various authors have focused on different types of social or individual functioning. For example, one perspective may be quite useful when dealing with adult–child interaction but less relevant when trying to explicate child–child interaction. In the end, this means that in many instances the perspectives do not reflect different interpretations of the same basic phenomenon, but pieces of a more comprehensive approach that has yet to be developed.

ACKNOWLEDGMENT

The writing of this chapter was assisted by a grant from the Spencer Foundation to James V. Wertsch. The statements made and the views expressed are solely the responsibility of the authors.

REFERENCES

Bakhtin, M. M. (1981). *The dialogic imagination: Four essays by M. M. Bakhtin* (Ed. Michael Holquist, Trans. Caryl Emerson and Michael Holquist). Austin: University of Texas Press.
Bakhtin, M. M. (1984). *Problems of Dostoevsky's poetics* (C. Emerson, Ed. and Trans.). Minneapolis: University of Minnesota Press. (Originally published in Russian, 1929)
Baldwin, J. M. (1906). *Mental development in the child and the race.* New York: Macmillan.
Brown, A. L., & Ferrara, R. A. (1985). Diagnosing zones of proximal development. In J. V. Wertsch (Ed.), *Culture, communication, and cognition: Vygotskian perspectives* (pp. 273–305). New York: Cambridge University Press.
Damon, W., & Phelps, E. (1987, June). *Peer collaboration as a context for cognitive growth.* Paper presented at Tel Aviv University School of Education annual symposium.

Gee, J. P. (1988). Legacies of literacy: From Plato to Freire through Harvey Graff. *Harvard Educational Review, 58,* 195–212.

Hatano, G., & Inagaki, K. (1991). Sharing cognition through collective comprehension activity. In L. B. Resnick, R. Levine, & A. Behrend (Eds.), *Perspectives on socially shared cognition* (pp. 331–348). Washington, DC: American Psychological Association.

Itakura, K. (1986, August). *The hypothesis-experiment-instruction method of learning.* Paper presented at the International Conference on Trends in Physics Education, Tokyo, Japan.

Janet, P. (1926–1927). "La pensee interieure et ses troubles." Course given at the College de France.

Janet, P. (1928). *De l'angoisse a l'extase: Etudes sur les croyances et les sentiments. Vol. 2: Les sentiments fondamentaux.* Paris: Librairie Felix Alcan.

Lotman, Y. M. (1988a). The semiotics of culture and the concept of a text. *Soviet Psychology, 26,* 52–58.

Lotman, Y. M. (1988b). Text within a text. *Soviet Psychology, 26,* 32–51.

Luria, A. R. (1981). *Language and cognition* (J. V. Wertsch, Trans.). New York: Wiley.

Mehan, H. (1979). *Learning lessons.* Cambridge, MA: Harvard University Press.

Meichenbaum, D. (1977). *Cognitive-behavior modification: An integrative approach.* New York: Plenum.

Michaels, S. (1981). "Sharing time": Children's narrative styles and differential access to literacy. *Language Socialization, 10,* 423–442.

Palincsar, A. S., & Brown, A. L. (1984). Reciprocal teaching of comprehension-fostering and comprehension-monitoring activities. *Cognition and Instruction, 1,* 117–175.

Palincsar, A. S., & Brown, A. L. (1988). Teaching and practicing thinking skills to promote comprehension in the context of group problem solving. *RASE, 9*(1), 53–59.

Piaget, J. (1928). *Judgment and reasoning in the child.* New York: Harcourt, Brace.

Piaget, J. (1950). *The psychology of intelligence.* London: Routledge & Kegan Paul.

Piaget, J. (1960). *The moral judgment of the child.* Glencoe, IL: The Free Press. (Original work published 1932)

Piaget, J. (1985). *The equilibration of cognitive structures: The central problem of intellectual development* (T. Brown & K. J. Thampy, Trans.). Chicago, IL: University of Chicago Press.

Reddy, M. J. (1979). The conduit metaphor: A case of frame conflict in our language about language. In A. Ortony (Ed.), *Metaphor and thought.* Cambridge, England: Cambridge University Press.

Rogoff, B. (1990). *Apprenticeship in thinking: Cognitive development in social context.* New York: Oxford University Press.

Sigel, I. E. (1970). The distancing hypothesis: A causal hypothesis for the acquisition of representational thought. In M. R. Jones (Ed.), *Miami Symposium on the Prediction of Behavior. 1968: Effect of early experiences* (pp. 99–118). Coral Gables, FL: University of Miami Press.

Sigel, I. E. (1982). The relationship between parental distancing strategies and the child's cognitive behavior. In L. M. Laosa & I. E. Sigel (Eds.), *Families as learning environments for children* (pp. 47–68). New York: Plenum.

Sigel, I. E., & Cocking, R. R. (1977). Cognition and communication: A dialectic paradigm for development. In M. Lewis & L. A. Rosenbaum (Eds.), *The origins of behavior. Vol. 5. Interaction, conversation, and the development of language* (pp. 207–226). New York: Wiley.

Sigel, I. E., & Kelley, T. D. (1988). A cognitive developmental approach to questioning. In J. Dillon (Ed.), *Classroom questioning and discussion: A multidisciplinary study* (pp. 105–134). Norwood, NJ: Ablex.

Tharp, R. G., & Gallimore, R. (1988). *Rousing minds to life.* New York: Cambridge University Press.

Volosinov, V. N. (1973). *Marxism and the philosophy of language* (L. Matejka & I. R. Titunik, Trans.). New York: Seminar Press.

Vygotsky, L. S. (1978). *Mind in society: The development of higher psychological processes* (M.

Cole, V. John-Steiner, S. Scribner, and E. Souberman (Eds.). Cambridge, MA: Harvard University Press. (Original works published 1930, 1933, 1935)

Vygotsky, L. S. (1979). Consciousness as a problem in the psychology of behavior. *Soviet Psychology, 17*(4), 3–35.

Vygotsky, L. S. (1981). The genesis of higher mental functions. In J. V. Wertsch (Ed.), *The concept of activity in Soviet psychology* (pp. 144–188). Armonk, NY: M. E. Sharpe.

Vygotsky, L. S. (1987). Thinking and speech. In R. W. Rieber & A. S. Carton (Eds.), & N. Minick (Trans.), *The collected works of L. S. Vygotsky: Vol. 1 Problems of general psychology.* (pp. 37–285). New York: Plenum. (Original work published 1934)

Wertsch, J. V. (1979). From social interaction to higher psychological processes: A clarification and application of Vygotsky's's theory. *Human Development, 22,* 1–22.

Wertsch, J. V. (1985). *Vygotsky and the social formation of mind.* Cambridge, MA: Harvard University Press.

Wertsch, J. V. (1991). *Voices of the mind: A sociocultural approach to mediated action.* Cambridge, MA: Harvard University Press.

Wertsch, J. V., McNamee, G. D., McLane, J. B., & Budwig, N. A. (1980). The adult–child dyad as a problem-solving system. *Child Development, 51,* 1215–1221.

Wertsch, J. V., & Minick, N. (1990). Negotiating sense in the zone of proximal development. In M. Schwebel, C. A. Maher, & N. S. Fagley (Eds.), *Promoting cognitive growth over the life span* (pp. 71–88). Hillsdale, NJ: Lawrence Erlbaum Associates.

Wertsch, J. V., Minick, N., & Arns, F. J. (1984). The creation of context in joint problem-solving. In B. Rogoff & J. Lave (Eds.), *Everyday cognition: Its development in social context* (pp. 151–171). Cambridge, MA: Harvard University Press.

Wertsch, J. V., & Sammarco, J. G. (1985). Social precursors to individual cognitive functioning: The problem of units of analysis. In R. A. Hinde, A. Perret-Clermont, & J. Stevenson-Hinde (Eds.), *Social relationships and cognitive development* (pp. 276–293). Oxford: Clarendon Press.

Wertsch, J. V., & Stone, C. A. (1985). The concept of internalization in Vygotsky's account of the genesis of higher mental functions. In J. V. Wertsch (Ed.), *Culture, communication, and cognition: Vygotskian perspectives* (pp. 162–179). New York: Cambridge University Press.

Wertsch, J. V., & Toma, C. (1990, April). *Discourse and learning in the classroom: A sociocultural approach.* Paper presented at the University of Georgia Visiting Lecture Series on Constructivism in Education.

13 Psychological Distance and Underachievement

Robert B. McCall
Lynn Kratzer
University of Pittsburgh

Three decades ago, a book (1961) and a paper (1963) by Joseph McVicker Hunt symbolized a major transition in thinking about early experience in the development of mental ability and performance. Contrary to the prevailing thought that general mental ability (i.e., IQ) was an innate, constant, pervasive characteristic of individuals, Hunt suggested that it underwent qualitative as well as quantitative development and was potentially influenced by the early environments in which children grew up.

A good deal of research at that time was done with animals, and attempts were made to rear animals, especially rats, in "massively enriched" environments, which consisted, for example, of the presence of various objects and other animals with which to "play." The early results suggested that massively enriched rats displayed better learning ability and some neurological and biochemical benefits.

Only a few investigators, however, then wondered what specific components of such enriched environments improved development in general and improved which specific skills in particular. Certainly, not all stimuli and early experiences are equal in their potential to improve development; some must be "more equal than others." For example, McCall and Lester (1969) studied the potential differential benefits of visual experience with angles versus curves, and McCall (1967) explored whether experience with movable (i.e., responsive) objects was more beneficial than experience with identical but immovable (i.e., nonresponsive) objects. These studies were promising, but, as Kagan (personal communication, 1967) observed at the time, "they were manipulations in search of a dependent variable." The rat, alas, was a poor model for human intelligence, and psychologists were at a relative loss to measure general "intelligence" or even many

219

specific mental skills in the rat. So the issue of specificity in animal enrichment studies was abandoned.

At the same time, substantial amounts of money became available for study-ing children, including "massive enrichment" programs for poor infants, tod-dlers, and preschool children. Again, the early results suggested that such gener-al experiences could indeed improve the IQs of "disadvantaged" children (at least temporarily). Also again, few people studied the specific components of the "massive enrichment" that might have produced the IQ gains or that might improve more specific mental skills.

An exception was Sigel who was more interested in particular thought pro-cesses of children than in IQ, and in what the crucial early experiences were that promoted effective thought processes (Sigel, 1970). Much of this work has revolved around Sigel's concept of *distancing*.

Sigel recalls (Sigel, 1990) that as his airplane took off from Detroit one day he experienced many of the known perceptual constancies as the distance increased between him and the objects on the ground. The unique insight was that viewing an object from a great distance is an experience that presents a contradiction between what we sense and perceive (e.g., the reduced retinal size of an object) on the one hand and what we have experienced and know (e.g., the actual size and function of an object) on the other. Such experiences, Sigel reasoned, force us to recognize that our sensory and perceptual data are only representations or symbols of objects. Experiencing objects at a distance and from different percep-tual perspectives, then, might be a crucial experience in the development of symbolic and representational thought. Further, perhaps children from poor en-vironments have less opportunities for such experiences, not simply less oppor-tunities to fly in airplanes but to have adults provide and mediate more common distancing experiences in ways that help them recognize and rely on symbols of reality rather than only on direct perceptual contact with and physical manipula-tion of concrete objects. Sigel has demonstrated that such experiences potentially do play this role.

But scientists with a good idea tend to apply that idea to as many different circumstances as possible. Not only did Sigel design programs to provide experi-mentally children with what he felt were distancing experiences, but the ap-proach was unique in that it included the naturalistic attempts of parents and teachers to provide (or to fail to provide) distancing experiences for children. These observations gave insight into what particular distancing experiences could be presented to children, and they suggested that the concept of distancing also could be applied to interpersonal relations. For example, not every "advantaged" child flowers mentally, and it was reasoned that the crucial component was the propensity of parents and teachers to structure and mediate experiences in ways that force the child to deal with the distancing component of those experiences (Sigel, 1990).

Specifically, children who grow up in homes where parents use distancing strategies develop a more positive sense of self as problem solvers and as independent thinkers, and such children should have the self-confidence to risk failure and to persist in the presence of challenge, two crucial requirements for achievement in mental as well as interpersonal realms (Sigel, 1984, 1990).

In this chapter, we explore this proposition as it applies to a specific group of children and youth, namely, underachievers. Underachievers, as the term is typically used in educational circles, are individuals who perform more poorly in school than one would expect on the basis of their mental abilities. They are not simply poor performers (indeed, some can be quite good), but they achieve less than one would predict on the basis of their abilities. Further, they are often thought to lack persistence in the face of challenge, to have little self confidence, and to fear failure—precisely the characteristics Sigel feels might be the result of inadequate social distancing experiences. Moreover, underachievers are a group of individuals who represent a crucial test of the idea that distancing can influence the motivational, not simply the mental, side of achievement, because, by definition, these individuals are performing disproportionally poorly relative to their mental ability.

Of course, no retrospective or prospective studies exist that demonstrate that underachievers come from those families that fail to provide appropriate distancing experiences. Therefore, in this chapter we first summarize the literature on underachievers as that literature has been compiled, and then we look back on that literature from the conceptual perspective of distancing. It is important to note that the focus in this review is on underachievement per se, and therefore, the literature covered is based predominantly on studies and reports from the fields of counseling, school psychology, clinical psychology, and special education. It does not embrace the mainstream psychological study of achievement in general or the sociological field of educational and occupational status achievement.

A PRIMER ON UNDERACHIEVEMENT

The literature on underachievement is old, and much of it antedates Sigel's theorizing. Underachievement became an educational issue, at least by that name, in the middle 1950s (Shoff, 1984). By that time, the measurements of ability and achievement were refined and accepted (Fine, 1967), which was necessary to define underachievement. Further, in 1957 the United States failed to duplicate the Russian feat of launching a satellite, which threatened the collective American scientific prowess and caused the nation to notice that many of its most gifted students did not perform in school as well as one would expect. As a result, research and applied programs focused on improving the performance of lagging but otherwise intellectually superior students—that is, on gifted underachievers.

Interest in underachievement within the educational community then atrophied during the 1970s, overshadowed in part by concern over learning disabilities and other specific disorders. More recently, however, assessments of the performance of the nation's high school students have redirected public attention to the fact that one fourth of the nation's young people do not graduate from high school on time (Ekstrom, Goertz, Pollack, & Rock, 1986), and many of those who do graduate perform at minimum levels of competency. Presumably, many of these students are "underachieving" their mental potential.

Clinical interest in underachieving students also has increased recently. We suspect this is partly a consequence of greater public acceptance of psychological services for less serious problems plus (1) the value upper- and middle-class parents place on education as a route to success, (b) the intolerance they have for their children's lack of achievement, and (c) their frustration with the schools to do much about their children's underachievement. As a result, well-to-do parents have sought private clinical services, franchised tutoring services have sprung up nationwide, and at least one chain of psychological services especially designed to treat underachievement (i.e., Institute for Motivational Development) has been established in numerous cities across the country.

But this resurgence of public interest actually has two thrusts that should be distinguished. One is a push to improve the schools in general, especially to minimize the dropout rate and upgrade the basic educational achievement level of students nationwide. Technically, this is a concern over "low achievement" with the assumption that these students are underachieving their potential. Only some of these students, however, will be "underachievers" by the technical definition presented later in this chapter.

The other thrust is a push for the school system to provide special services for true underachievers. This concern is driven by individual parents of underachieving children, typically those who are well educated and affluent who are frustrated at the inability and sometimes unwillingness of the school system to provide special services or otherwise cope with their youngsters' problems. Indeed, although underachievement is typically a necessary criterion to receive certain special services (e.g., for learning disabilities), it is usually not sufficient. As one irate mother said, "If my kid ran around the room and hit other children he would be 'emotionally disturbed,' or if he got his letters mixed up he might be 'learning disabled.' Then they would provide a special program for him. But since he is only 'not getting an education,' nothing is done."

Methodological Issues

The educational and psychological literature on underachievement is voluminous, diverse, and chaotic, and studies generally are poorly executed from a scientific standpoint. It has been reviewed several times, even though it defies serious integration (e.g., Dowdell & Colangelo, 1982; Krouse & Krouse, 1981;

Mandel & Marcus, 1988; McCall, Evahn, & Kratzer, 1992; Whitmore, 1980). What follows, then, is a brief analysis of that literature, which does not do justice to its complexity.

Measurements and Definitions

The conceptual definition of an underachiever is a student who performs more poorly in school than would be predicted on the basis of assessments of his or her mental ability. It is usually also assumed that this disparity is associated with motivational and behavioral factors, not organic disorders.

Underachievement should be distinguished from low achievement. Low achievement may refer to any student, regardless of mental ability, who performs poorly by some definition. In contrast, underachievement refers to students who exhibit a discrepancy between their school performance and indices of mental ability. Presumably, many poor achievers—and perhaps some students with learning disabilities—are also underachievers, but this must be verified by finding an ability–performance disparity.

Although there is relative agreement about the conceptual definition of under-achievement, little uniformity exists in the way it is operationally defined. Grade point average is the most accepted measure of school performance, but a great variety of variables have been used to assess mental ability, from teacher judgments to IQ tests. While a Wechsler or Binet is preferred, standardized group ability or educational achievement tests are most common. They are justified as IQ substitutes on the conceptual ground that there is no meaningful distinction between "aptitude" and "achievement" tests (e.g., Humphreys, 1973; Kaplan & Saccuzzo, 1982; Sternberg, 1982) and on the practical and ecological ground that schools use group ability and achievement tests, not IQ tests (McCall et al., 1992).

The discrepancy between measures of ability and performance also has been operationally defined in numerous ways, and even the more commonly used methods vary so greatly that substantial percentages of students classified as underachievers by one approach would not be so classified by another (Annesley, Odhner, Modoff, & Chansky, 1970; Asbury, 1974; Dowdall & Colangelo, 1982; Farquhar & Payne, 1964; Pirozzo, 1982).

Although not the most common, the most accepted and statistically sophisticated definition is to designate as underachievers those students who fall more than one standard deviation below the regression of grades on an ability measure (Farquhar & Payne, 1964; Gowen, 1957; Willson & Reynolds, 1985). This definition has several advantages, including relative ease and consistency in applying it from sample to sample and across different measures of ability and performance, plus the statistical fact that it produces a common percentage of underachievers spread evenly across nearly the entire range of abilities and grades.

Despite these advantages, this definition has several limitations (see later), and it has been criticized (e.g., Thorndike, 1963; Wood, 1984) as capitalizing, both statistically and clinically, on what otherwise would be considered chance or error. Specifically, according to this argument, underachievers defined by this regression procedure are simply "errors of prediction," and it is possible that no meaningful concept of underachievement exists. But underachievers and non-underachievers matched for mental ability or matched for grades can be discriminated on the basis of psychological characteristics (e.g., for a review, see Mandel & Marcus, 1988; McCall et al., 1992), so the concept is more than simply prediction error.

Sampling

Most studies, especially older ones, have focused on only one segment of the ability dimension, namely, gifted underachievers, defined in various ways. Correlates of underachievement might be quite different if the sample were restricted to the gifted than if it included underachievers across the entire range of ability.

Comparison Groups

The use of comparison groups is not common. Comparison groups should consist of students who fall close to the regression line. Typically, when a comparison group has been employed, it is composed of students who have approximately the same mental ability as the underachievers but whose grades are commensurate with that ability. Few studies also add a group of students who have the same grades as the underachievers but lower, appropriately matched mental ability (e.g., McCall et al., 1992). Without a same-grades comparison, it is not possible to discern whether correlates are associated with underachievement per se or with poorer grades, and, therefore, whether a true specific syndrome of underachievement exists.

These methodological issues have been belabored here because they make studies incomparable and nearly render the entire literature uninterpretable. With due respect to these complexities, however, here is what we think we know about the psychology of underachievement.

Extent, Timing, and Demographics

Frequency. Even when underachievement is defined by the preferred regression procedure, the percentage of students classified as underachievers will be arbitrary, because the extent to which performance must deviate from that predicted by ability in the definition is arbitrary. If one standard deviation below the regression line is selected as this arbitrary criterion, approximately 16% of the population of all students will be underachievers, and this will be true at each age. Therefore, no meaningful answer exists to the otherwise reasonable question, "How many underachievers are there?"

Age of Onset.   Similarly, since the regression procedure defines a constant proportion of children as underachievers at every age, there will be no particular age at which underachievement first appears.

Nevertheless, it is commonly reported in the clinical and counseling literature that underachievement begins during the late elementary grades and certainly by junior high school. This conclusion derives from two sources. First, academic demands, especially homework, increase during these grades, and unmotivated students are more noticeable to teachers and parents when they fail to complete these assignments. Second, a few studies show that the year-to-year stability of underachievement becomes apparent at this time, somewhat earlier for boys than for girls (Mandel & Marcus, 1988; Shaw & McCuen, 1960). Other studies, however, show relatively little age-to-age consistency, for example, between the third, sixth, and ninth grades (Kowitz & Armstrong, 1961).

Sex Ratio.   A rather uniform finding in the literature is that two or three males are found to be underachievers for every female. The question is, why? A substantial portion of this sex differential could be produced by the fact that girls tend to have better grades than boys, while ability tests are generally constructed to minimize sex differences (McCall et al., 1992; Thorndike, 1963). In a mixed-sex sample, then, fewer girls would have low grades at a given ability level.

Although this statistical circumstance may "explain" the sex ratio, it does not necessarily wash away the psychological implications. Marathons may be scored separately for the sexes but rank in class is not, and no male student and his parents judge a poor report card to be "OK for a boy."

Parental Socioeconomic Class.   Even though some review articles report underachievers to have parents of lower socioeconomic status (SES), the empirical evidence is mixed. Inconsistencies between studies derive partly from differences in how underachievement is defined and the nature of socioeconomic circumstances in the sample studied. For example, gifted children who are identified as underachievers are more likely to have parents who have high SES. One might also expect that parents who bring their children to private clinicians will have high SES. Conversely, samples of "low achieving students" have low-SES parents, whereas studies based on large samples in which underachievement is defined by the regression method across the entire range of ability tend to show that underachievement is not associated with SES (McCall et al., 1992).

Birth Order.   Although it has been suggested that underachievers tend to have high-achieving older siblings, little consistency exists in the literature regarding parity, and large-scale studies with broad samples find no relation to birth order (McCall et al., 1992).

Divorce.   Also, it is typically asserted that underachievers are more likely to come from disrupted and single-parent households (Dowdall & Colangelo,

1982), but some large-sample studies show no differences in this regard (e.g., McCall et al., 1992).

Behavioral Characteristics of Underachievers

The reviews already mentioned also indicate certain characteristics of underachievers and their parents. However, comparison groups are typically absent, so it is not clear whether these characteristics pertain to underachievers per se or, for example, to students with poor grades. The largest study with the broadest sample and the best comparison groups suggests that at least some of the contemporary characteristics described next may be associated with the grades underachievers receive, not their status as underachievers (McCall et al., 1992).

Self-Perception. Underachievers are commonly said to have poor self-perceptions of their abilities, poor self-concepts in general, and low self-esteem. Often they are self-critical, have a fear of failure and a fear of success, and are anxious or nervous, especially when asked to perform.

Goal Orientation. Underachievers often have faulty and unrealistic orientations toward goals. The standards they set for themselves may be unrealistic, or they may completely lack goals and aspirations.

Lack of Persistence. Behaviorally, underachievers lack persistence, especially in the face of challenge. They may dash off any response to school assignments and call them done, or they will give up in the middle of a task when things are not going well. One study (McCall et al., 1992) demonstrated that lack of persistence—at higher education, holding a job, and marriage—was an enduring characteristic of underachievers for at least 13 years after high school compared both to students who had the same ability and to students who had the same grades but who were not underachievers.

Peer Relations. Although a few are highly skilled socially, most authors report underachievers to have very poor peer relationships. They lack friends, and they are lonely and socially withdrawn. When they do have friends, their friends do not value education and have a negative attitude toward school. As adolescents, some studies show they date less and have problems with heterosexual adjustment, while other studies indicate they date more and have more intense heterosexual relations (Kurtz & Swenson, 1951; Rocks, Baker, & Guerney, 1985).

Authority Relations. Some underachievers have problems relating to authority—parents, teachers, and other adults. They may be overtly aggressive and hostile, have discipline problems and high rates of delinquency, lack self-control, and be irresponsible and unreliable. They may also have serious problems establishing independence from their parents. While some underachievers are overt in these tendencies, others are more passively aggressive.

Loss of Control. Underachievers generally have an external locus of control, especially in terms of blaming other people rather than themselves for their problems or failures and being hypercritical and negativistic toward others.

Emotional Expression. Underachievers are sometimes said to be apathetic and affectively flat, unhappy or depressed, or emotionally explosive and poorly controlled. Extremely serious emotional problems, however, are rarely mentioned.

Types of Underachievers. Not all underachievers display all of these symptoms, and some authors have attempted theoretically to categorize underachievers into different types. Unfortunately, few empirical studies have tried to factor characteristics or cluster underachievers into syndromes that would validate these types.

Whitmore (1980), in a large study of gifted elementary-school-age underachievers, distinguished between *aggressive underachievers* (e.g., disruptive, talkative, clowning in class, rebellious, and hostile), *withdrawn underachievers* (e.g., disinterested, bored, do not try or participate), and a *combination of aggressive and withdrawn underachievers* (e.g., erratic, unpredictable, vacillate between aggression and withdrawal).

Pecaut (1979), on the basis of clinical experience, outlined four types of underachievers. One, the *trust seekers,* are lonely, isolated, withdrawn, impulsive, and emotionally explosive. *Approval seekers* are indecisive, try to fulfill the expectations of others but may stop attempting to do so, have serious test anxiety, need praise, and are afraid of authority. *Dependency seekers* are selectively disinterested in certain basic subjects in elementary school, ambivalent to authority, passive–aggressive, socially gregarious, and project responsibility for their failures onto others. Finally, *independence seekers* are in conflict about independence and dependence from parents, value whatever is opposite to that emphasized by parents and other adults, and are hostile and rebellious against adult authority.

The most comprehensive and long-lived diagnostic scheme is the Developmental Theory Model, originally proposed by Roth, Berenbaum, and Hershenson (1967) and recently summarized by Mandel and Marcus (1988). The Developmental Theory Model relies on standard psychiatric diagnoses (DSM–III) and proposes that different types of underachievers are produced when fixation in psychological development occurs at different stages of the normal developmental sequence. The five categories of underachievers (with DSM–III references) are the Overanxious Disorder (313.00), the Conduct Disorder (312.00, 312.2.

and 312.90), the Academic Problem or the Non-Achievement Syndrome (V62.30), the Identity Disorder (313.82), and the Oppositional Defiant Disorder (313.81).

Mandel and Marcus (1988) review the literature regarding the differential diagnosis of these types and argue that it can be done reliably, that patterns of nonachievement and symptomatology differ as a function of these categories, and that the symptomatology of each type corresponds to that specified by DSM-III (Mandel & Mandel, 1992).

Parental Characteristics

Parents of underachievers often have been described as being either too indifferent to or too preoccupied with their children's achievement. Most descriptions of parents are based on clinical experience, not systematic empirical research, and comparison groups are nearly totally absent.

Indifference.   Parents may be disinterested, have distant relationships with their children with minimum affection, and possess neutral-to-negative attitudes toward education. These characteristics may exist alone or in combination with two other themes. One theme is an authoritarian, restrictive, and rejecting style, especially by fathers. The other involves extreme permissiveness and freedom, perhaps bordering on neglect or, in the case of a gifted child, treating the child as an independent, miniature adult.

Overemphasis on Achievement.   There may be too much parental pressure and a preoccupation with achievement to the exclusion of all other characteristics of the child. Alternatively, one may have an overindulgent, oversolicitous, over-protective parent who is simply too helpful and who thereby prevents the child from developing independence, responsibility, self-sufficiency, and feelings of self-fulfillment and self-worth.

Parental Inconsistency.   These different styles of parents may exist in the same family. For example, Rimm (1984) describes several types of such families. In one, the father is restrictive, authoritarian, and controlling, but the mother supports the child in compensation for her husband. In a second type, the sex roles are reversed. A third type involves a mother who is educated and feels she knows how to rear the children and who has a husband who is not educated or who relinquishes parental influence to her dominance.

School Characteristics

Although underachievement is defined to be a problem of performance in school, almost no empirical attention has been paid to describing the characteristics of schools, classrooms, or teachers that might contribute to underachievement, perhaps because underachievers exist in all schools. The exceptions are gifted underachievers, who are said to be bored or unstimulated in school (Pirozzo, 1982; Sahler, 1983), perhaps because of a disparity between the gifted child's creativity, imagination, and exploratory nature and the schools' traditional lock-step, autocratic style and emphasis on convergent rather than divergent thinking (Myers, 1980; Torrance, 1962; Pirozzo, 1982; Whitmore, 1980).

Prognosis and Treatment

Long-Term Consequences. If left untreated, what is the prognosis for under-achievers? Only one study has addressed this issue systematically and over a long period of time (McCall et al., 1992).

Chronic high school underachievers defined by the regression method across the entire ability spectrum were compared to two groups of non-underachieving students, one group matched for grades and the other matched for mental ability. During high school, underachievers as a group were poorer than those controls matched for mental ability but essentially identical to non-underachieving students who had the same grades but lower mental ability with respect to over 90 demographic and personal-social factors. Similarly, after high school, the educational attainment and job status of underachievers were consistent with their grades, and not with their abilities. However, 13 years after high school, under-achievers showed signs of continuing their inability to persist at a task in the face of challenge. Compared to both control groups, underachievers demonstrated less persistence in completing their college degrees, holding onto the same job, and maintaining their marriages (McCall et al., 1992). This result shows that a syndrome of underachievement does exist that differentiates underachievers from those with poorer grades. The defining element of the syndrome seems to be lack of persistence in the face of challenge.

Some underachievers, of course, did "catch up" to their abilities with respect to educational and occupational achievement. Approximately 10%–15% of un-derachievers, those with parents who had relatively high educational levels and those who themselves during high school expected to achieve educationally and occupationally, did so, at least in one subsample but not as impressively in another. But serious underachievers—those receiving grades approximately two grade points below expectancy—were among the poorest achievers as adults regardless of their mental ability or other characteristics (McCall et al., 1992). Thus, while some underachievers may "recover" or "catch up," most do not; an underachieving diamond in the rough tends to stay in the rough.

Treatment. Most reviews of research agree that the effects of intervention and treatment are modest and that no single approach can claim consistent results (Dowdall & Colangelo, 1982; Krouse & Krouse, 1981; Mandel & Marcus, 1988; Pirozzo, 1982; Whitmore, 1980).

More specifically, Krouse and Krouse (1981) classified treatments into four categories: (a) remediation with an emphasis on study skills; (b) psychotherapy; (c) promoting self-control through self-monitoring, self-reinforcement, and stimulus control; and (d) reducing interfering anxiety (e.g., test anxiety). Results have been mixed for each approach, and when benefits are reported they have not been substantial. Generally, private clinical therapy and franchised tutoring services have not been evaluated or publicly reported.

More recent attempts, however, have produced more consistent results, but there is a tendency for intervention programs to emphasize one characteristic, produce positive consequences for that characteristic, but not improve grade point average and thereby fail to eliminate the defining element of underachievement (McCall et al., 1992). Programs that combine different approaches, begin early, and are comprehensive tend to have better outcomes (McCall et al., 1992).

The most direct approach is the periodic progress report system, a daily or weekly report card listing each behavior to be encouraged (e.g., homework, test performance, class participation, self-control). It is completed by each teacher, brought to a counselor, and then sent home for the parent to dispense rewards for appropriate behavior and progress. The approach has been documented to improve academic and deportment behavior in students across the age span (Atkeson & Forehand, 1978, 1979). Reportedly, it is the most frequently used approach in the schools. Some clinicians (e.g., Pecaut, 1979), however, have doubts about the effectiveness of this approach (or of tutoring) with youth who are in advanced stages of underachievement (i.e., whose parents have sought private clinical services).

UNDERACHIEVEMENT AND DISTANCING

Is underachievement the result of lack of appropriate distancing experiences in the families and schools of these youngsters?

As indicated, the underachievement literature largely antedates and has been conducted quite independently from the distancing literature. Therefore, no studies, prospective or retrospective, have directly addressed the possible relation between distancing strategies and underachievement. However, it is certainly the case that some of the purported characteristics of underachievers could be the consequence of inappropriate distancing experiences.

Parents

Parents of underachievers, for example, were described as being either indifferent or overly involved with their children, perhaps in an authoritarian, restrictive manner. In either case, it might be supposed that such parents are less likely to provide appropriate distancing experiences for their children.

More specifically, a particular kind of parent, one who appears to be exceptionally devoted, may be the protypical upper-class parent who fails to foster appropriate distance between him- or herself and the child, producing a lack of self-fulfillment, self-sufficiency, self-worth, and independent achievement. This is a parent who values achievement, encourages his or her child, and provides all the appropriate experiences—but is too helpful, too concerned lest the child fail, always showing the child how to do it better, and never allowing the child to go off on his or her own without guidance and a safety net. The parent is well-meaning but provides too much parenting and not enough independence.

Let me illustrate with an informal example told by one mother of an underachiever:

> He never learned to be self-reliant and responsible. Even as an adolescent, I'd wake him up in the morning, instead of letting him do it himself with an alarm clock. Then I'd nag to get him out the door on time and remind him to take the key.
>
> Then, I suppose, he had enough and rebelled. He was not going to study or do anything we wanted the way we wanted it. And we perceived this as obnoxious, adolescent independence and storm and stress. It was, but it was also a cry for help, a signal that we had gone too far. We didn't hear it that way. (McCall, 1988)

Schools

Certainly the schools also have "distanced" themselves from this problem. Most school systems and states have no special programs to help underachievers, unless an underachieving student has other identifiable problems, such as mental retardation, physical disabilities, learning disabilities, or social-emotional problems. Serious lack of motivation in an otherwise competent student is usually not sufficient reason for special programming. Schools, however, often implement the periodic progress report system for students having a variety of problems including underachievement, although "underachievers" may not be identified in any very systematic or precise way.

Anecdotally, underachievers report that their schools are "distant" from them in another respect. They dislike school, find it "dumb," believe their teachers are "stupid," and find the whole enterprise irrelevant. While some of this perception may be attributed to defensiveness and projection, the match between these student's interests and abilities and the material and tasks presented by the school is quite disparate.

This distance between what underachievers believe they can and want to do and the demands and characteristics of the school context needs to be shortened. Clinically, underachievers believe that they cannot perform the required tasks at an acceptable standard of performance. Rather than marshalling their courage and energy to meet the challenge, they do not try, thereby avoiding failure and preserving self-esteem by permitting them to believe that they could have done it if they had wanted to. By reducing the distance between what underachievers want and feel they can do and the demands of the task, underachievers are more likely to experience real success at a valued task, which is probably the main effective cure for lack of self-esteem and motivation.

This might be accomplished by breaking down the curriculum into small, manageable units or "modules" and permitting students to proceed at their own pace. Progress as well as proficiency would be measured by performance, and students would stay within a unit until they became proficient.

The military takes this approach in much of its training, and it can be argued that many contemporary recruits are at least poor students if not underachievers. Recruits, for example, study weaponry, practice riflery, and train physically until reaching an acceptable level of performance. Except in extreme cases, they do not "fail"; they simply receive more training until they pass. Some recruits graduate from basic training in the minimum time permitted, while others take longer, but most eventually learn and accomplish up to a minimum standard. This strategy could be applied to traditional academic material, especially mathematics and science, which can be easily divided into modules and progress readily assessed. Also, the approach could be implemented on computers. Recall, for example, that one of the purported advantages of computerized instruction is that it permits students to move at their own pace and to be assessed constantly for proficiency, with review and extra training added as needed. However it is implemented, it is an approach public schools, or at least alternative schools specializing in underachievers, might consider.

CONCLUSIONS

Underachievement is a complex problem typically involving family dynamics, personal characteristics of the child, and the educational environment to which the child is exposed. Appropriate distancing experiences might be an integrating dynamic theme across these domains.

Research Agenda

Much research is yet to be done:

1. More longitudinal studies of underachievement are needed, because so little is known empirically about its developmental course.

2. Instruments need to be designed to directly assess the characteristics of underachievers, their parents, and their schools. It is only in this way that what little theory exists, including the distancing hypothesis, can be evaluated, and different types or syndromes of underachievers can be described empirically.

3. New treatment programs need to be created and evaluated. The periodic progress report system is promising but it should be evaluated directly and

specifically with underachievers. Other treatments need to be combined to form a comprehensive approach to the problem dealing with personal, family, and school issues. Private therapists and alternative schools specializing in treating underachievers should have their approaches documented and outcomes evaluated.

Advocacy Agenda

Much also remains to be done in the schools.

1. Schools need to be aware that most underachieving students do not "get their acts together on their own when they leave home," as parents are often reassuringly told. Schools need to make underachievement a priority and to establish procedures that systematically and objectively detect underachievers, because research shows that counselors are poor judges of underachievement in the absence of objective information (McCall et al., 1992).

2. Some creative solutions need to be explored. A modularized curriculum as described above should be studied, for example, perhaps in alternative schools that claim to specialize in helping underachievers.

Of course, most underachievers do graduate from school, do find a niche, and do live normal and self-sufficient lives. But, at a time when the academic and intellectual demands of society are rapidly increasingly, "a mind is a terrible thing to waste."

REFERENCES

Annesley, F., Odhner, F., Modoff, E., & Chansky, N. (1970). Identifying the first grade underachiever. *Journal of Educational Research, 63*, 459–462.

Asbury, C. A. (1974). Selected factors influencing over- and underachievement in young school-aged children. *Review of Educational Research, 44*, 409–428.

Atkeson, B. M., & Forehand, R. (1978). Parents as behavior change agents with school-related problems. *Education and Urban Society, 10*, 521–540.

Atkeson, B. M., & Forehand, R. (1979). Home-based reinforcement programs designed to modify classroom behavior: A review and methodological evaluation. *Psychological Bulletin, 86*, 1298–1308.

Dowdall, C. B., & Colangelo, N. (1982). Underachieving gifted students: Review and implications. *Gifted Child Quarterly, 26*, 179–184.

Ekstrom, R. B., Goertz, M. E., Pollack, J. M., & Rock, D. A. (1986). Who drops out of high school and why? Findings from a national study. *Teachers College Record, 87*, 410–429.

Farquhar, W. W., & Payne, D. A. (1964). A classification and comparison of techniques used in selecting under- and overachievers. *Personnel and Guidance Journal, 42*, 874–884.

Fine, B. (1967). *Underachievers: How they can be helped.* New York: Dutton.

Gowan, J. C. (1957). Dynamics of the underachievement of gifted students. *Exceptional Children, 24*, 98–122.

Hunt, J. McV. (1961). *Intelligence and experience.* New York: Ronald Press.

Hunt, J. McV. (1963). Motivation inherent in information processing and action. In O. J. Harvey (Ed.), *Motivation and social interaction* (pp. 35–94). New York: Ronald Press.

Humphreys, L. G. (1973). The misleading distinction between aptitude and achievement tests. In D. R. Green (Ed.), *The aptitude-achievement distinction* (pp. 262–274). Monterey, CA: CTB/McGraw-Hill.

Kaplan, R. M., & Saccuzzo, D. P. (1982). *Psychological test: Principles, applications, and issues.* Monterey, CA: Brooks/Cole.

Kowitz, G. T., & Armstrong, C. M. (1961). Underachievement: Concept or artifact. *School and Society, 87,* 347–349.

Krouse, J. H., & Krouse, H. J. (1981). Toward a multimodal theory of academic underachievement. *Educational Psychologist, 16,* 151–164.

Kurtz, J. J., & Swenson, S. J. (1951). Factors related to overachievement and underachievement in school. *School Review, 59,* 472–480.

Mandel, H. P., & Mandel, D. E. (1992). *Along the path: Case histories of differentially diagnosed underachievers.* Toronto, Canada: Institution Achievement and Motivation, York University.

Mandel, H. P., & Marcus, S. I. (1988). *The psychology of underachievement: Differential diagnosis & differential treatment.* New York: Wiley.

McCall, R. B. (1967). Movable and immovable object experience and exploratory behavior. *Psychonomic Science, 8,* 473–474.

McCall, R. B. (1988, February). Kids who won't try. *Parents,* pp. 116–121, 199–200.

McCall, R. B., Evahn, C., & Kratzer, L. (1990). *High school underachievers. What do they achieve as adults?* Newbury Park, CA: Sage Publications.

McCall, R. B., & Lester, M. L. (1969). Differential enrichment potential of visual experience with angles versus curves. *Journal of Comparative and Physiological Psychology, 4,* 644–648.

Myers, R. K. (1980). *Underachievement in gifted pupils.* Proceedings of a workshop at Slippery Rock State College, Slippery Rock, PA, July 23–27, 1979. (ERIC Document Reproduction Service No. ED 185 773)

Pecaut, L. S. (1979). *Understanding and influencing student motivation,* Vols. 1–2. Glen Ellyn, IL: Institute for Motivational Development.

Pirozzo, R. (1982). Gifted underachievers. *Roeper Review, 4,* 18–21.

Rimm, S. (1984). Underachievement. *G/C/T, 31,* 26–29.

Rocks, T. G., Baker, S. B., & Guerney, B. G. (1985). Effects of counselor-directed relationship enhancement training on underachieving, poorly communicating students and their teachers. *School Counselor, 32,* 231–238.

Roth, R. M., Berenbaum, H. L., & Hershenson, D. (1967). *A developmental theory of psychotherapy: A systematic eclecticism.* Unpublished paper, Department of Psychology, Illinois Institute of Technology, Chicago.

Sahler, O. J. Z. (1983). The teenager with failing grades. *Pediatrics in Review, 4,* 293–300.

Shaw, M. C., & McCuen, J. T. (1960). The onset of academic underachievement in bright children. *Journal of Educational Psychology, 51*(3), 103–108.

Shoff, H. G. (1984). *The gifted underachiever: Definitions and identification strategies.* (ERIC Document Reproduction Service No. ED 252 029.) Champaign, IL: ERIC.

Sigel, I. E. (1970). The distancing hypothesis: A causal hypothesis for the acquisition of representational thought. In M. R. Jones (Ed.), *Miami symposium on the prediction of behavior, 1968: Effects of early experiences.* (pp. 99–118). Coral Gables, FL: University of Miami Press.

Sigel, I. E. (1984). Reflections on action theory and distancing theory. *Human Development, 27,* 188–193.

Sigel, I. E. (1990). Journeys in serendipity: The development of the distancing model. In I. E. Sigel & G. H. Brody (Eds.), *Methods of family research: Biographics of research projects (Vol. 1): Normal families* (pp. 87–120). Hillsdale, NJ: Lawrence Erlbaum Associates.

Sternberg, R. J. (1982). Lies we live by: Misapplication of tests in identifying the gifted. *Gifted Child Quarterly, 26,* 157–161.

Thorndike, R. L. (1963). *The concepts of over- and underachievement.* New York: Teachers College, Columbia University.

Torrance, E. P. (1962). Who is the underachiever? *NEA Journal, 58*(8), 15–17.

Whitmore, J. R. (1980). *Giftedness, conflict, and underachievement.* Boston: Allyn and Bacon.

Willson, V. L., & Reynolds, C. R. (1985). Another look at evaluating aptitude–achievement discrepancies in the diagnosis of learning disabilities. *Journal of Special Education, 18,* 477–487.

Wood, R. (1984). Doubts about 'underachievement,' particularly as operationalized by Yule, Lansdown & Urbanowicz. *British Journal of Clinical Psychology, 23,* 231–232.

14 Putting the Distance into Students' Hands: Practical Intelligence for School

Lynn Okagaki and Robert J. Sternberg
Yale University

What do students need to succeed in school? Traditionally, educators and psychologists have addressed this question by focusing on skills that are required to do academic tasks—skills such as comparing similarities and differences, making inferences, clarifying problems. In this chapter, however, we propose that besides having the abilities to do academic tasks, there are practical skills and practical knowledge that students need in order to do well in school. This body of practical knowledge and skills is similar to the practical knowledge that investigators of nonschool settings have called tacit knowledge, the generally unexplained knowledge that one needs to function appropriately within any social setting (Polanyi, 1946, 1976; Wagner & Sternberg, 1986). Gardner's (1983) multiple intelligences theory and Sternberg's (1985) triarchic theory of human intelligence are used to provide the basis of a theory of tacit or practical knowledge for school. Gardner's theory identifies the intellectual domains in which tacit knowledge for school is needed. Sternberg's theory specifies the mental processes that are required for handling practical school problems. The two theories combined provide a strong theoretical description of the knowledge and abilities required to handle tacit problems for school.

In keeping with the theme of this book, this chapter addresses the ways in which a theory of practical knowledge for school is relevant to the issue of psychological distance. In particular, two aspects of distance are discussed: (a) the distance or difference between what the learner can already do and what the learner could do with help (i.e., the learner's zone of proximal development [Vygotsky, 1978]), and (b) distancing strategies or processes that require the individual to separate him- or herself from the immediate context. Distancing strategies include actions, such as imagining how something that is broken would work if it were fixed, reflecting on how a message might be interpreted by other people, and relating a past event to a present event. Generally, in teaching/ learning situations, the teacher is the person who monitors the instruction so that it falls within the zone of proximal development (see Rogoff & Wertsch, 1984). Similarly, the teacher or adult is typically the person who uses distancing strategies to encourage the development and enrichment of the learner's conception of a given phenomenon. Sigel's comprehensive and rich research on parents' use of distancing strategies to promote the intellectual development of their children (e.g., Sigel, 1982, 1985; Sigel, Stinson, & Flaugher, 1991) has aptly demonstrated the importance of distancing strategies in the family learning environment. However, from the perspective of a theory of practical intelligence, the goal is to get students to take the distance into their own hands. The premise of this chapter is that young adolescents can take responsibility for giving teachers cues that will draw the level of instruction into their own zones of proximal development and for using distancing strategies to help them examine, think about, and resolve problems.

Why is this approach to learning interesting? To teach within students' zones of proximal development in the classroom requires that the teacher closely monitor the learning and performance of the students individually. Unfortunately, in public schools in the United States, such monitoring is virtually impossible, particularly at the junior and senior high levels. In junior and senior high schools, instead of a self-contained classroom in which a teacher is solely responsible for a group of 20–30 children, each teacher may have five or six different classes and be responsible for well over 100 students. Both class size and responsibility for multiple classes limit the monitoring that the teacher can do.

When class structure makes it impossible for the teacher to monitor students individually, can students learn to take more responsibility for monitoring their learning? Can students learn to evaluate their own performance, so that they can ask questions to bring the teacher's instruction into their zone of proximal development? These problems are tacit problems underlying a group learning situation, and we believe that the answer to these questions is "yes." However, if students are going to carry more responsibility for their education, then it is necessary to provide them with the knowledge and skills to do so effectively. Our curriculum, entitled Practical Intelligence for School, is one attempt to equip students with the tools they need to plan and monitor their education.

A TACIT KNOWLEDGE FOR SCHOOL

Within any social setting, there are rules that guide behaviors, social roles, and interpersonal interactions, and rules that dictate how tasks within that setting ought to be done (e.g., Moore, 1981). Some of these rules are explicitly taught to individuals within that setting. For example, in many elementary school classrooms, there is chart on the wall that lists the classroom rules (e.g., "Raise your hand before speaking," or "No pushing, hitting, or name calling"). These rules are part of the explicit classroom rules. But also, in every classroom, there are implicit rules that guide behavior—that is, there are rules that are not explicitly taught to the children. For example, in a sociolinguistic analysis of classroom interaction, Green and Weade (1985) determined that not only was it important for the child to raise his or her hand before speaking, but that the teacher only acknowledged raised hands at certain times during a demonstration. Appropriate times for raising one's hand were cued by the teacher pausing in his or her speech and looking from one side of the classroom to the other. Waiting for the teacher to pause and to look around the class before raising one's hand with a question was one of the unspoken classroom rules. Some children quickly pick up on these implicit rules—perhaps, for example, because they have already learned to wait for a pause in their parents' speech before interrupting with a question. Other children do not easily identify and follow these unspoken rules.

Polanyi (1946, 1976) used the term "tacit knowledge" to identify the unspoken, unexplained knowledge that one needs to function properly within a setting. Wagner and Sternberg (1986) have further elaborated the concept of tacit knowledge to include three specific types of knowledge: (a) knowledge about oneself, (b) knowledge about tasks, and (c) knowledge about interpersonal relationships. Their research indicates that level of tacit knowledge is a good predictor of job performance (Wagner & Sternberg, 1985, 1986) and of academic performance among college students (Sternberg & Wagner, 1989).

Our belief is that utilization of tacit knowledge in the school setting can enable junior high students to improve their academic performance, in part by enabling them to communicate with teachers when the level of instruction is outside their zone of proximal development. Two important questions need to be considered: (a) how do we identify the tacit knowledge that is important for school performance, and (b) what skills and abilities do students need to develop to monitor their understanding of a concept and their teachers' instruction? In the following section, we discuss the theories that enable us to address these questions.

UNDERLYING THEORIES FOR DEVELOPING A TACIT KNOWLEDGE FOR SCHOOL

During the past 3 years, investigators from both Yale University and Harvard University have been engaged in a joint effort to develop a practical, theory-based curriculum for teaching children at the intermediate level the skills they need to succeed in school (Sternberg, Okagaki, & Jackson, 1990). This curriculum is based on Gardner's theory of multiple intelligences (1983) and Sternberg's triarchic theory of intelligence (1985). Briefly, the theory of multiple intelligences identifies the intellectual domains in which tacit knowledge for school is needed and helps students to recognize a variety of abilities, both in themselves and in others. The triarchic theory specifies the mental processes that operate in the intellectual domains and identifies contextual factors that affect the application of those processes to immediate problems and the transfer of skills to new problems. Rather than providing a detailed discussion of these theories, this chapter focuses only on how the theories address the present interest in: (a) tacit knowledge about school tasks, (b) tacit knowledge about oneself, and (c) tacit knowledge about school relationships.

Tacit Knowledge About School Tasks and Theory of Multiple Intelligences

First, consider how multiple intelligences informs our understanding of a tacit knowledge about school tasks. Gardner's theory identifies the domains in which intelligence manifests itself: (a) linguistic, (b) logical-mathematical, (c) spatial, (d) musical, (e) bodily-kinesthetic, (f) intrapersonal, and (g) interpersonal. The first five domains comprise areas of school curriculum and help us identify the types of tasks which students must be able to do. For example, the linguistic domain maps onto English, reading, and literature classes. The logical-mathematical domain is expressed in mathematical classes. The spatial domain typically cuts across academic domains, and spatial ability is called on, for example, in math, geography, and physical education classes. Musical knowledge is required in both music theory and music performance classes. Finally, the bodily-kinesthetic domain is related to physical education classes and other movement-oriented classes, such as drama, dance, and music performance. Discussion of all of these different domains enables students to recognize different abilities that they themselves have and to recognize that others can be gifted in many different ways, too. It also introduces distance between what they know and could know and provides a way for talking about representing information to self.

Students need to understand how the structure of knowledge within each of the intellectual domains affects learning and use of that knowledge. For example, just as there are multiple ways of describing a concept on an English essay, there may be multiple ways of solving an algebra problem. In contrast, there may be more than one correct answer to a question on an English exam, and only one correct answer to a question on a math test. By getting students to look at the nature of the information that they are learning, it is hoped that they will recognize when, for example, precision is important. Similarly, it is expected that if students perceive similarities in processes—for example, how identification of the theme of a novel is similar to identification of the political themes or causes that provoked the American Revolution—then students will begin to see that "thinking tools" (i.e., problem-solving processes) can be useful in multiple contexts. Discussion of the different intellectual domains posited in the theory of multiple intelligences enables teachers to direct students' attention to comparisons of different subject-matter content and increases their awareness of the varying effectiveness of learning strategies in each domain.

Within each domain, the student is faced with the fundamental problems of learning the information that the teacher presents and then demonstrating that learning (knowledge) on a test, or perhaps by writing a report. Tacit knowledge comes into play when we consider the "hidden" problems within the general task of learning the information. For example, the student must figure out: (a) how to learn the information, (b) which information is most important to learn, (c) how to determine if he or she understands the concepts in the same way that the teacher intends for him or her to understand them, (d) how to check whether or not he or she has actually learned the information, and (e) how to allocate his or her time so that he or she has enough time to learn the information for one class and still do the other things that are required. If the student is required to take a test to demonstrate what he or she has learned, then there are other aspects of tacit knowledge that may be addressed. But the goal is to get students to identify test-taking as a problem for which they themselves can generate solution strategies, implement these strategies, evaluate the results, and further refine their strategies. It is not to give students a list of strategies for test-taking or strategies for studying. Discussion of domains and the abilities that are utilized within each domain helps students recognize that having one generic approach to learning may not be the best way to handle the differential demands of their classes, and, as discussed later, Sternberg's theory will provide the mental components that can be used to build the problem-solving strategies for meeting these demands.

Tacit Knowledge About Oneself and the Multiple Intelligences

Gardner's intrapersonal domain directly relates to tacit knowledge about oneself. Intrapersonal knowledge that is important to the student's role in school includes knowledge about the strengths and weaknesses of one's intellectual abilities, and knowledge about the conditions under which one works best. For example, in order to be most effective at school, a student might need to know: (a) what motivates him or her, (b) what social context is most productive (e.g., does he or she study best alone or in a small group), (c) what type or combination of sensory input facilitates learning the best for the individual (e.g., does he or she learn best by seeing and reading information or by listening to lectures), (d) what memorization strategies work best and for which purposes, and (e) how can he or she manage time so that everything gets done. Knowledge about oneself also needs to be considered vis-à-vis the individual intellectual domains. Although it might seem obvious to a teacher that the strategies one uses to learn material in a literature class might be different from strategies that are effective in a science class, students do not necessarily realize it.

Tacit Knowledge About School Relationships and the Multiple Intelligences

The final intellectual domain in Gardner's theory is the interpersonal domain— knowledge about other people and one's relation to others. Many students have to get past their primary image of teachers as adversaries to see teachers as providers of information, as resources when academic or other problems occur, or simply as individuals who have a particular role within a social system. Students need to learn that within any social setting (e.g., school, work, home) there are both explicit and implicit rules that govern behavior and that to violate even arbitrary social conventions produces a certain amount of friction within the system. For example, there are more and less annoying ways for students to ask questions in a class. If the student only wants to be annoying, then it may not matter how irritated the teacher becomes when a question is asked. However, if the student genuinely wants clarification or further information, then knowing how to ask questions becomes important. Learning how to identify the social conventions used in a particular system and how to apply those conventions can have important consequences when the system is a work setting and part of one's job evaluation rests on knowing how to work well with others.

Tacit Knowledge and the Triarchic Theory of Intelligence

Whereas the theory of multiple intelligences corresponds to the three areas of tacit knowledge and articulates the types of tacit-knowledge problems students face in school, Sternberg's triarchic theory speaks to the development, use, and transfer of the tacit-knowledge skills needed to handle these problems. The triarchic theory is comprised of three subtheories: (a) the componential subtheory, which identifies the mental processes that are exercised in acquiring and applying tacit knowledge, (b) the contextual subtheory, which defines the practical, "relevant-to-life" ways in which the componential processes are applied, and (c) the experiential subtheory, which deals with the transfer of knowledge and skills to new situations. We briefly discuss the implications of each of these subtheories.

Componential Subtheory. Sternberg describes three types of cognitive processes: metacomponents, performance components, and knowledge-acquisition components. *Metacomponents* are higher-order executive processes used to plan, monitor, and evaluate one's task performance (e.g., defining the nature of the problem; selecting lower-order processes to accomplish the task). *Performance components* are lower order processes that execute the plans created by the metacomponents (e.g., inferring relations between stimuli; applying previously inferred relations to new situations). *Knowledge-acquisition components* are lower order processes that are used in gaining new knowledge (e.g., selective encoding, by which information that is relevant for one's purposes is distinguished from information that is not relevant for one's purposes; selective combination, by which selectively encoded information is put together in a usable way).

The present discussion on the development of a tacit knowledge for school focuses on metacomponents. Sternberg posits seven metacomponents that oversee information processing: (a) identifying the problem, (b) selecting the components or steps needed to solve the problem, (c) selecting a strategy for ordering the problem-solving steps, (d) selecting a mental representation for information, (e) allocating resources, (f) monitoring the solution process, and (g) evaluating the results and external feedback. The central focus of our curriculum is teaching students to capitalize on their metacognitive abilities and by doing so to monitor their learning, their interactions with other people, and, in general, their behavior in a wide range of situations. In this section, as an example, the metacomponent of problem identification is used. In the section on the curriculum, the general problem-solving strategy is applied to various tacit-knowledge problems.

Throughout the curriculum, students are asked first to identify the problem or question that they are facing. For example, suppose a teacher has called on a student to answer a question and the student gives an incorrect answer, what problem is the student facing? What went wrong? This first step of recognizing and defining the problem is critical if students are going to take responsibility for monitoring their learning. In this particular situation, it means the student cannot sit back, shrug his or her shoulders, and forget about the incident. Students need to take responsibility for their learning by asking themselves what went wrong. There are at least three possible explanations of "what went wrong" that reveal a range of tacit knowledge. One explanation is that the student had not learned the information and had just guessed at the answer. Given this hypothesis, junior high students are quick to generate ideas about the "problem behind the problem." For example, the student did not have time to study the night before because he or she had so much homework from other classes. In this case, the tacit-knowledge problem may be one of managing time or being organized. Alternatively, perhaps the student read the book, but did not remember what he or she had read. The tacit-knowledge question is: How might students take in new information so that they will remember it and be able to use it in the future?

A second explanation is that the student knew the correct answer, but misunderstood the question. In this instance, the tacit-knowledge problem may be one of communication skills: How might students ask teachers to clarify their questions?

Finally, a third explanation is that the student misunderstood the teacher's lecture or material in a book and did not recognize that there was a difference between his or her perception of the concept and the teacher's perception. This situation is more difficult for students, and it does hit at the heart of problems related to teaching within the zone of proximal development. When a teacher presents a concept to a class, the teacher begins with an understanding, a picture or mental representation of that concept in his or her mind, and then describes the various aspects of the concept or picture to the students. Even if the students understand each separate aspect of the concept, they can still be putting the whole picture together incorrectly and not realize it. A theory of tacit knowledge for school suggests, for example, that when new information is presented, the first step is to connect it to old information—that is, to something the students already know. By building on previous knowledge, the students can ask themselves when something does not fit with what they already know. Students are asked to take responsibility for asking questions such as: "When you said X, did you mean that this is what is happening?" A basic premise of this program is that the students do not wait until the teacher gives a test to find out if they have learned something. Rather, the students are constantly monitoring their understanding of what is being presented, and check their understanding by asking the teacher and other students questions.

When the level of instruction is far beyond the student's zone of proximal development, it is often easier for students to recognize that they do not understand what the teacher is talking about than when they are following threads of the instruction. When the students are totally lost, the tacit knowledge problem is usually one of how does one ask a question without antagonizing the teacher and without feeling like a fool. When students are developing a misperception of a concept, it is more difficult for them to identify that they are having a problem with the learning. By getting the students to check their understanding by articulating what they think the teacher has said and then asking for verification or further explanation during the lecture, the teacher can clarify or modify the level of instruction. What students often fail to realize is that without feedback from the students—through questions, comments, and even puzzled looks—the teachers may not know that the discussion is beyond the students.

In essence, getting students to monitor their learning and to compare their developing conception of a problem to the teacher's conception is an attempt to have students initiate the use of distancing strategies. Typically, the adult or experienced person uses distancing strategies to prod the learner to step back and reflect on his or her understanding of problem (Sigel, 1982). The aim here is to get students to prod themselves through self-monitoring to look for inconsistencies in their conceptions and conflicts between their understanding and the teacher's understanding of the problem. The students cannot passively assume that they are correctly taking in the information and correctly building the mental representation of the problem. Instead, they are asked to assume that there will be misunderstandings and that they must constantly monitor their learning.

Contextual Subtheory.   The contextual subtheory places intelligence within a cultural context. In this subtheory two concepts are emphasized. The first concept is that "intelligent" behavior depends on the relation between the individual and the surrounding environment. The implication is that what works for one person may not work for someone else. Moreover, within the same situation, people's goals may differ—and what is intelligent for one person may not be an intelligent choice for someone else. According to the contextual subtheory, in any given situation, the individual may choose: (a) to adapt or change him- or herself to better meet the demands of the situation, (b) to shape or change the environment to better suit his or her needs, or (c) to select an alternative environment that better meets his or her needs. The intelligent choice will depend on the individual's abilities, needs, and relation to the situation.

Second, the contextual subtheory proposes that context affects cognition. That is, we believe that the same componential processes are applied to different types of content domains with differing results. Performance in any particular domain is a function of experience, motivation, and an interaction between the cognitive processes and the content domain. We believe that the same cognitive processes are used across domains but in different combinations and to different degrees. In addition, we suggest that the interaction among the demands of the domain (e.g., literature may rely more heavily on analytical skills, but art may require more use of spatial skills), the cognitive processes, and the individual's prior knowledge in the domain and in the social context in which performance is being required, along with other factors (e.g., practice and motivation), will produce differing degrees of expertise across domains within the individual. Recognition of the interaction between cognitive processes and knowledge domains is important to our development of tacit knowledge for school because it implies that students need to approach different courses in different manners—what they do to study for math may not work in history. Some subjects may be easier for them than others are, and how much time they allot to studying each subject should differ.

Experiential Subtheory. Finally, the third subtheory is the experiential subtheory. It proposes that a task measures "intelligence" to the extent that it requires either or both of two skills: (a) the ability to deal with novel kinds of task and situational demands, and (b) the ability to automatize information processing. According to the experiential subtheory, one's intelligence is most taxed when one is learning how to handle a new type of problem or when one is automatizing a learned skill.

With respect to tacit knowledge for school, it should be emphasized that the ability to deal with novel situations is critical. A primary difficulty that students have is that when they are faced with a new situation they do not immediately and naturally transfer learned skills or problem-solving strategies to the new situation. Part of the problem may stem from skills that become imbedded or contextualized into the contexts in which they were first developed (Okagaki & Sternberg, in press). For example, a student can learn how to compare new information to previously learned information in a math class in order to see the relations between different algebraic formulas. Later, this same student does not think to apply the same strategy to an English class in order to see similarities in different writing genres. In order to facilitate transfer of skills to new situations, skills must be developed and used in multiple contexts so that students can recognize the utility of a particular strategy in different situations. Second, students have to be asked to apply the strategy to a new problem that they themselves have identified. Students need to see the strategy as a skill they can apply on their own initiative and not simply when a teacher is directing them to use it. If dealing with novelty is when our intellectual capabilities are most taxed, then we cannot expect students to function optimally when faced with new problems. To help them, we need to get them to recognize new problems on their own and to become accustomed to trying out a variety of problem-solving strategies in those situations.

Summary of Theoretical Framework. To summarize, Fig. 14.1 shows a diagram of the relation between the components of the two theories of intelligence. The processes specified in Sternberg's componential subtheory are the basic cognitive processes that can be applied to tacit problems arising in school. The experiential subtheory posits that mental resources will be taxed to varying degrees as a function of one's experience with a given situation and serves as the basis for designing strategies to facilitate transfer of skills to new problems. Gardner's multiple intelligences theory identifies the intellectual domains in which tacit knowledge for school should be developed. Finally, the contextual subtheory provides a framework for understanding how individuals can use skills in multiple contexts for different purposes with varying results.

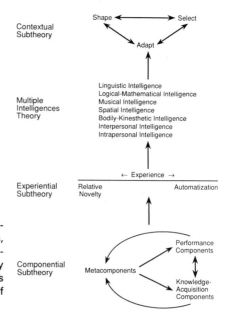

FIG. 14.1. Integration of theory of multiple intelligences, which specifies domains of intelligences, with triarchic theory of intelligence, which specifies processes that occur in each of these domains.

These two broad theories of intelligence naturally complement and strengthen each other to form a theory of tacit knowledge for school. Gardner's theory represents a domain-specific view of cognition and focuses our attention on specific problems arising in each of the intellectual domains. It does not, however, specify cognitive processes that would be applied to each of the domains. In contrast, Sternberg's theory primarily emphasizes domain-general mental processes, although the contextual subtheory posits that there will be contextual or domain-specific factors influencing the operation of these mental processes. The importance of both domain-specific and domain-general influences on thinking has been established by research on cognitive processing in real world contexts (see Rogoff, 1982; Rogoff & Lave, 1984; Sternberg & Wagner, 1986) and with research on teaching thinking skills (see Bransford, Sherwood, Vye, & Rieser, 1986; Brown et al., 1989; Perkins & Salomon, 1989). It is on the basis of this work that the practical intelligence for school curriculum was developed.

THE PRACTICAL INTELLIGENCE
FOR SCHOOL CURRICULUM

Many types of curriculum have been proposed to improve students' thinking skills (see Adams, 1989; Baron & Sternberg, 1987; Bransford et al., 1986; Greeno, 1989; Nickerson, Perkins, & Smith, 1985). Other programs are specifically designed to improve students study skills and test-taking skills (e.g., Carrier & Titus, 1981; Kiewra, 1988; Stevens, 1988). The present curriculum is designed to both improve thinking skills and improve skills related to specific school tasks such as studying and test-taking. However, a curriculum based on a theory of tacit knowledge for school must also include, for example, the development of interpersonal skills (e.g., communication skills and group problem-solving skills) and the development of intrapersonal knowledge (e.g., learning what one's strengths and weaknesses are).

The Practical Intelligence for School (PIFS) curriculum is the result of a collaboration between research teams at Harvard and Yale Universities. The Harvard group, led by Howard Gardner, has focused on the development of units that emphasize individual subject-matter infusion of skills within content courses (e.g., The lesson entitled "finding the right math tools" directly applies some of the basic problem-solving strategies to doing math problems). The Yale team, under the direction of Robert J. Sternberg and Lynn Okagaki, has designed a curriculum that develops skills to be used across content areas. The eventual goal is to combine the two curriculum into a total program that will allow students to develop and practice skills in multiple contexts. The remainder of this chapter, however, focuses solely on the Yale portion of the curriculum, which was field-tested in the spring of 1989.

The Yale PIFS curriculum is organized according to the three types of tacit knowledge described earlier: managing oneself, managing tasks, and working with others. Table 14.1 presents an outline of the curriculum.

TABLE 14.1
Outline of Practical Intelligence for School,
Yale University

Introduction to Teachers
Introduction to Practical Intelligence for School
Overview of Topics
Introduction to Students
   1. Introductory Lesson

I. Managing Yourself
  A. Overview of Managing Yourself
    2. Kinds of intelligence: Definitions and principles
    3. Kinds of intelligence: Multiple intelligences
    4. Kinds of intelligence: Academic or practical intelligence
    5. Understanding test scores
    6. Exploring what you may do
    7. Accepting responsibility
    8. Collecting your thoughts and setting goals
  B. Learning Styles
    9. What's your learning style?
   10. Taking in new information
   11. Showing what you learned
   12. Knowing how you work best
   13. Recognizing the whole and the parts
  C. Improving Your Own Learning
   14. Memory
   15. Using what you already know
   16. Making pictures in your mind
   17. Using your eyes—a good way to learn
   18. Recognizing the point of view
   19. Looking for the best way to learn
   20. Listening for meaning
   21. Learning by doing

II. Managing Tasks
  A. Overview of Solving Problems
   22. Is there a problem?
   23. What strategies are you using?
   24. A process to help you solve problems
   25. Planning a way to prevent problems
   26. Breaking habits
   27. Help with our problems
  B. Specific School Problems
   28. Taking notes
   29. Getting organized
   30. Understanding questions
   31. Following directions
   32. Underlining: Finding the main idea
   33. Noticing the way things are written
   34. Choosing between mapping and outlining

(Continued)

TABLE 14.1
(*continued*)

---

35. Taking tests
36. Seeing likenesses and differences in subjects
37. Getting it done on time

III. Cooperating with Others
  A. Communication
   38. Class discussions
   39. What to say
   40. Tuning your conversation
   41. Putting yourself in another's place
   42. Solving problems in communication
  B. Fitting into School
   43. Making choices: Adapting, shaping, and selecting
   44. Understanding social networks
   45. Seeing the network: Different roles
   46. Seeing the network: Figuring out the rules
   47. Seeing the relation between now and later
   48. What does school mean to you?

The course begins with a unit on Managing Yourself. Students are introduced to the theory of multiple intelligences and to the triarchic theory of intelligence. They are given opportunities to examine their skills in each of the seven intellectual domains on both academic and practical tasks. The exercises help students become aware of different abilities in themselves and in others. Students evaluate themselves and other students on a variety of tasks (e.g., linguistic tasks: writing a book report, giving directions to someone, playing the word game Boggle; spatial tasks: identifying countries on a map, taking apart a door knob set and putting it back together again). Many of the activities, such as playing a game that requires students to use different memorization strategies, are structured so that students work in small groups and learn new strategies and ideas from each other. One gifted student shared, "Before I thought that intelligence was all one thing. . . . I didn't realize that it had different parts. It will help me recognize that someone might not be able to read but they may be really smart in being able to repair a car. . . . I used to think that other people were dumb. Now I think that they can be more intelligent than me in other categories. . . . I won't think of them as dumb anymore."

Besides increasing their awareness of different kinds of abilities, students also examine their learning and working styles. The overall goal is to get students to find out about their own strengths and weaknesses, to begin to think about the problems involved in learning, and to examine the effectiveness of strategies that they are already using.

The second unit, Managing Tasks, formally introduces a general problem-solving strategy for engaging tasks, which involves: (a) recognizing the problem,

(b) deciding what you want to do about the problem (how much time to allocate to it, what kind of solution is satisfactory), (c) gathering information, (d) thinking of strategies for solving the problem, (e) choosing one strategy to try, (f) implementing the strategy, (g) monitoring the process, and (h) evaluating the results. The problem-solving strategy is then applied to practical school problems, such as how to take notes, how to get organized, how to understand directions, and how to take tests. In addition, students apply the process both to academic problems, such as doing a grammar worksheet or solving algebra word problems, and to nonschool problems, such as how to get chores done at home or how to get along better with siblings. The teachers model the process on problems that naturally arise in the classroom and engage students in using the process when they come across a problem in the classroom. The goal is to get students to recognize problems on their own and to take responsibility for generating, attempting, and evaluating solution strategies.

EVALUATION OF THE PIFS CURRICULUM

In the spring semester of 1989, the Yale PIFS curriculum was field-tested in three seventh-grade classes in a suburban middle school in Connecticut. The students were taught in reading classes, which were formed on the basis of scheduling needs and contained a range of abilities. Three reading classes were used as the experimental group and two others as a control. The experimental group received the PIFS curriculum three periods a week for one semester. The control group followed a standard reading curriculum using a basal reader. Pretests and posttests were given to both groups. Testing consisted of three different tests: (a) the Survey of Study Habits and Attitudes (SSHA) (Brown & Holtzman, 1967), which contains four subscales: Delay Avoidance, Work Methods, Teacher Approval, and Education Acceptance; (b) the Learning and Study Skills Inventory (LASSI) (Weinstein & Palmer, 1988), which consists of 10 subscales: Attitude, Motivation, Time Management, Anxiety, Concentration, Information Processing, Selecting Main Ideas, Study Aids, Self-Testing, and Test Strategies; and (c) the Practical Intelligence section of the Sternberg Triarchic Abilities Test (STAT), which contains three subscales: Practical Inference (verbal), Practical Math (quantitative), and Practical Route Planning (figural). The STAT was included as a transfer test: None of the skills measured in the STAT was directly taught, but it was hoped that these practical-intellectual skills would improve as a result of the training.

On the SSHA, the experimental group had significantly greater gains at the final testing than did the control group on all four subscales (see Table 14.2 for a summary of the results). On the LASSI, the experimental group had significantly greater gains as compared to the control group on 8 of the 10 subscales. In particular, the PIFS group showed more improvement for the Information Pro-

TABLE 14.2
Summary Statistics

Test and Subtest	Experimental Group		Control Group	
	Pretest	Posttest	Pretest	Posttest
Survey of Study Habits and Attitudes				
Delay Avoidance	40.73	48.90	34.05	25.71
Work Methods	50.01	61.92	44.61	32.66
Teacher Approval	42.34	55.63	36.02	23.76
Education Acceptance	39.81	51.71	31.54	19.29
Learning and Studies Skills Inventory				
Attitude	50.23	56.64	50.13	34.49
Motivation	52.43	61.23	47.30	32.88
Time Management	55.52	65.25	45.75	44.90
Anxiety	58.73	68.72	52.97	43.51
Concentration	53.68	63.72	45.25	39.02
Information Processing	46.90	59.25	46.15	39.39
Selecting Main Ideas	55.72	65.08	54.25	40.15
Study Aids	42.15	62.33	33.67	42.51
Self-Testing	48.03	62.46	42.67	43.46
Test Strategies	61.47	65.70	60.07	41.02
Sternberg Triarchic Abilities Test				
Practical Inference (Verbal)	4.78	5.29	5.10	4.64
Practical Data (Quantitative)	5.21	4.29	4.58	5.49
Route Planning (Figural)	5.49	5.34	5.84	4.85

cessing, Selecting Main Ideas, Self-Testing, Concentration, and Test Strategies subscales. Each of these subscales is related to the self-monitoring and problem-solving skills that we believe are necessary for students to develop if they are going to monitor their learning. Finally, on the STAT, the experimental group showed greater gains than did the control group on the Practical Inference and Route Planning subscales, and the control group showed greater improvement on the Practical Data subscale.

In short, 14 intergroup differences significantly favored the experimental group, 1 significantly favored the control group, and 2 favored the experimental group nonsignificantly. These data indicate that the PIFS program was quite successful, even in one semester, in improving practical-intellectual skills as measured by two tests of study skills and one of practical intelligence.

The program is now being taught at two other Connecticut sites, one a middle-class suburb and the other a socioeconomically mixed urban setting. The course is taught once each week for a full year, and concepts are reinforced in content classes. Evaluations at each of these sites are currently being conducted.

CONCLUSIONS

Developing skills for identifying and solving practical problems and learning to identify the kinds of information one needs in order to understand the implicit rules that guide behavior within a given social system are important aspects of surviving and succeeding not only in school, but in life. As the students in our program begin to apply the knowledge and the skills they are acquiring in different school settings, they begin to see the relevance to life outside of school as well. But it is not easy—for students or for teachers. The most difficult part of the program is helping teachers to modify their teaching style. In essence, the teachers are asked to let go of maintaining total responsibility for learning and to let students suggest and try possible solutions—even if the solution is less than optimal. (Initially, the process of learning and solving problems takes much longer for both the students and the teachers.) Teachers are not being asked to let students brainstorm possible solutions and then to "guide" students toward the optimal solutions. Rather, teachers are being asked to let the students try out their ideas, to evaluate the results, and then to think about alternatives to try in the future.

Learning to monitor one's learning—one's understanding of any communication—is a critical part of taking responsibility for one's education. When students begin to see learning not as a passive activity that happens to them at school, but as an activity that they have some control over and as a skill that they can improve, then learning can become an important part of their everyday lives for the rest of their lives.

The PIFS curriculum is still being refined for use at the junior high level and new aspects are also being explored. Sternberg and Gardner, motivated by their long interest in creative thinking, are seeking ways in which practical knowledge can facilitate the creative process and ways in which creative thinking skills can be used to identify and solve practical problems. Okagaki and Sternberg are beginning to examine the problems faced by children who enter school with very little familiarity with mainstream American culture, for example, Southeast Asian immigrant children, and the difficulties teachers encounter given the task of teaching 30 children representing multiple cultural backgrounds. A first step in this project has been for the researchers and the teachers to ask themselves what it is about the things we do and the ways in which we do them that reflects cultural norms. That is, the researchers have to distance themselves from their own culture so that they can catch a glimmer of what an immigrant child must deal with upon entering school. It is difficult enough for adults to step back and examine their cultural identities. Teaching young children the cognitive and social skills they need to function effectively in two cultures is an enormous challenge, but a necessary one if these children are going to adjust to school and successfully meet school demands.

As educators, perhaps we have too long taken for granted that students know how to learn and more generally know how to be students. By focusing only on teaching academic content, we have neglected to teach the practical knowledge students also need to do well in school. In the present project, the findings suggest that by helping students develop their practical or tacit knowledge of school they become more active partners in the teaching-learning process. Everyone wants students to do well in school. Teaching students practical knowledge about being students can help them to do better in the school environment—it lessens the distance between what is expected of them and what they can do.

ACKNOWLEDGMENTS

Preparation of this chapter was supported by a grant from the James S. McDonnell Foundation. We are grateful to Howard Gardner and his research group at Harvard for their collaboration on the PIFS Project. We thank Alice S. Jackson and Lenora Manzella for their contributions to the development and evaluation of the PIFS curriculum and to the teachers and students who have participated in and given valuable feedback on the program.

REFERENCES

Adams, M. J. (1989). Thinking skills curricula: Their promise and progress. *Educational Psychologist, 24*(1), 25–77.

Baron, J. B., & Sternberg, R. J. (Eds.). (1987). *Teaching thinking skills: Theory and practice*. New York: Freeman.

Bransford, J., Sherwood, R., Vye, N., & Rieser, J. (1986). Teaching thinking and problem solving. *American Psychologist, 41*(10), 1078–1089.

Brown, J. S., Collins, A., & Duguid, P. (1989). Situated cognition and the culture of learning. *Educational Researcher, 18*, 32–42.

Brown, W. F., & Holtzman, W. H. (1967). *Survey of study habits and attitudes, Form H*. (SSHA). New York: The Psychological Corporation.

Carrier, C. A., & Titus, J. A. (1981). Effects of notetaking pretraining and test mode expectations on learning from lectures. *American Educational Research Journal, 18*(4), 385–397.

Gardner, H. (1983). *Frames of mind: The theory of multiple intelligences*. New York: Basic Books.

Green, J. L., & Weade, R. (1985). Reading between the words: Social cues to lesson participation. *Theory into Practice, 24*, 14–21.

Greeno, J. G. (1989). A perspective on thinking. *American Psychologist, 44*(2), 134–141.

Kiewra, K. A. (1988). Cognitive aspects of autonomous notetaking: Control processes, learning strategies, and prior knowledge. *Educational Psychologist, 23*(1), 39–56.

Moore, D. T. (1981). Discovering the pedagogy of experience. *Harvard Educational Review, 51*(2), 286–300.

Nickerson, R. S., Perkins, D. N., & Smith, E. E. (1985). *The teaching of thinking*. Hillsdale, NJ: Lawrence Erlbaum Associates.

Okagaki, L., & Sternberg, R. J. (1990). Teaching thinking skills: We're getting the context wrong. In D. Kuhn (Ed.), *Developmental perspective on teaching and learning thinking skills* (pp. 63–78). In D. Kuhn (Series Ed.), *Contributions to human development*, Vol. 21. Basel: Karger.

Perkins, D. N., & Salomon, G. (1989). Are cognitive skills context-bound? *Educational Researcher, 18*, 16–25.

Polanyi, M. (1946). *Science, faith and society.* London: Oxford University Press.

Polanyi, M. (1976). Tacit knowledge. In M. Marx & F. Goodson (Eds.), *Theories in contemporary psychology* (pp. 330–344). New York: Macmillan.

Rogoff, B. (1982). Integrating context and cognitive development. In M. E. Lamb & A. L. Brown (Eds.), *Advances in developmental psychology* (Vol. 2, pp. 125–170). Hillsdale, NJ: Lawrence Erlbaum Associates.

Rogoff, B., & Lave, J. (Eds.). (1984). *Everyday cognition.* Cambridge, MA: Harvard University Press.

Rogoff, B., & Wertsch, J. V. (Eds.). (1984). *Children's learning in the "Zone of Proximal Development," No. 23.* In W. Damon (Series Ed.), *New Directions for Child Development.* San Francisco: Jossey-Bass.

Sigel, I. E. (1982). The relationship between parental distancing strategies and the child's cognitive behavior. In L. M. Laosa & I. E. Sigel (Eds.), *Families as learning environments for children* (pp. 47–86). New York: Plenum.

Sigel, I. E. (1985). A conceptual analysis of beliefs. In I. E. Sigel (Ed.), *Parental belief systems: The psychological consequences for children* (pp. 347–371). Hillsdale, NJ: Lawrence Erlbaum Associates.

Sigel, I. E., Stinson, E., & Flaugher, J. (1991). Socialization of representational competence in the family: The distancing paradigm. In L. Okagaki & R. J. Sternberg (Eds.), *Directors of development: Influences on the development of children's thinking* (pp. 121–144). Hillsdale, NJ: Lawrence Erlbaum Associates.

Sternberg, R. J. (1985). *Beyond IQ: A triarchic theory of human intelligence.* New York: Cambridge University Press.

Sternberg, R. J., Okagaki, L., & Jackson, A. (1990). Practical intelligence for success in school. *Educational Leadership, 48,* 35–39.

Sternberg, R. J., & Wagner, R. K. (Eds.). (1986). *Practical intelligence: Nature and origins of competence in the everyday world.* New York: Cambridge University Press.

Sternberg, R. J., & Wagner, R. K. (1989). Individual differences in practical knowledge and its acquisition. In P. Ackerman, R. J. Sternberg, & R. Glaser (Eds.), *Learning and individual differences* (pp. 255–278). New York: Freeman.

Stevens, R. J. (1988). Effects of strategy training on the identification of the main idea of expository passages. *Journal of Educational Psychology, 80*(1), 21–26.

Vygotsky, L. S. (1978). *Mind in society: The development of higher psychological processes.* Cambridge, MA: Harvard University Press.

Wagner, R. K., & Sternberg, R. J. (1985). Practical intelligence in real-world pursuits: The role of tacit knowledge. *Journal of Personality and Social Psychology, 49,* 436–458.

Wagner, R. K., & Sternberg, R. J. (1986). Tacit knowledge and intelligence in the everyday world. In R. J. Sternberg & R. K. Wagner (Eds.), *Practical intelligence: Nature and origins of competence in the everyday world* (pp. 51–83). New York: Cambridge University Press.

Weinstein, C., & Palmer, D. (1988). *Learning and studies skills inventory.* Clearwater, FL: H & H Publishing.

Author Index

A

Abate, R., 174, *183*
Adamec, R. E., 83, *89*
Adams, M. J., 247, *253*
Allport, G. W., 64, *75*
Amgott-Kwan, T., 123, 127, 131, *140*
Anderson, E. R., 125, *139*
Anderson, K., 91, *107*
Anderson, L. M., 96, *107*, 147, *157*
Annesley, F., 223, *233*
Armstrong, C. M., 225, *234*
Arns, F. J., 52, *61*, 208, *218*
Asbury, C. A., 223, *233*
Atkeson, B. M., 230, *233*
Azuma, H., 9, *16*

B

Baker, N., 114, *121*
Baker, S. B., 226, *234*
Bakhtin, M. M., 12, *16*, 212, 215, *216*
Baldwin, J. M., *58*, 206, *216*
Bandura, A., 110, *120*
Baratz, J. C., 10, *16*, 31, *33*
Baron, J. B., 247, *253*

Barsalou, L. W., 189, *199*
Basov, M. I., 51, *58*
Baumrind, D., 68, *75*
Beagles-Roos, J., 162, *182*
Behr, M., *156*
Bellugi, U., 5, *16*
Berenbaum, H. L., 227, *234*
Berry, J., 9, *16*
Bjorkland, D. F., 10, *16*
Blisk, D., 125, *139*
Borstelmann, L. J., 109, *120*
Bowers, C., 180, *182*
Brannon, C., 171, 172, 173, 181, *182*
Bransford, J. D., 117, *120*, 247, *253*
Brent, S., 36, *59*
Brody, G. H., 149, *156*
Bromley, D. B., 187, *200*
Bronfenbrenner, U., 63, 64, 65, 66, 67, 68,
  69, 70, *75, 76*
Brown, A. L., 14, *16, 17,* 49, *59,* 103, *106,*
  117, *120,* 150, *156,* 207, 209, 210, *216,*
  217
Brown, J. S., 247, *253*
Brown, R., 5, *16*
Brown, W. F., 250, *253*
Bruner, J. S., 14, *16,* 49, 50, *59, 62,* 106,
  107, 126, *139,* 161, 168, 179, *182*

255

Subject Index